The Remarkable Life of

DR. ARMAND HAMMER

A *Cass Canfield* BOOK

The Remarkable Life of

DR. ARMAND HAMMER

BOB CONSIDINE

Harper & Row, Publishers
New York   Evanston   San Francisco   London

Grateful acknowledgment is hereby made to reprint the following material:

Excerpt on pages 87–88 originally appeared in The Daily News, Washington, D.C.
Excerpts on pages 132–133 and 136 reprinted by permission of Fortune.
Excerpt on pages 210–214 © 1973 by The New York Times Company. Reprinted by permission.
Excerpt on pages 264–277 reprinted by permission of The Washington Post.

Designed by Janice Stern

Library of Congress Cataloging in Publication Data

Considine, Robert Bernard, 1906–
   The remarkable life of Dr. Armand Hammer.
   (A Cass Canfield book)
   Includes index.
   1. Hammer, Armand, 1897–   I. Title.
HC102.5.H35C65   338'.092'4 [B]   74–20400
ISBN 0–06–010836–3

75 76 77 78 79 10 9 8 7 6 5 4 3 2 1

To Victor

Contents

Contents

Illustrations
(Following page 144)

Illustrations

Preface

He is a tanned, tough man who looks like a retired, undefeated middle-weight champion; one who kept his money. In the blizzard of telephone calls that enmesh him day and night, he can put a Rothschild selling Modiglianis on "hold" while he takes a call requiring a decision needed by the manager of his Nigerian oil holdings. He came out of the Lower East Side and lived to affect the economies of the Soviet Union, Libya, Peru, Venezuela . . . and California, Florida, and the coalfields of Pennsylvania, West Virginia, and Kentucky. He is nudging eighty, looks fifty, acts thirty. He was born at the end of the nineteenth century, doesn't plan to write his autobiography before 1980. One of his deals with the U.S.S.R. —a $20 billion fertilizer barter—is not scheduled to be terminated until the edge of the twenty-first century.

He bulled his way into the closely held citadels and cartels of art, cattle, whiskey, coal, network radio, and, almost as an afterthought, oil. He was a millionaire head of a multimillion-dollar pharmaceutical company while still an undergrad at Columbia University. He knew Lenin and Trotsky when he was barely out of his teens. Decades later he was on intimate terms with Khrushchev and Brezhnev. He was trained as a bacteriologist and immunologist, but never lanced a boil.

He is chairman of the nation's oldest and one of the most prestigious art galleries, Knoedler's, and all but singlehandedly arranged for the U.S. tour of Russian-owned, long-sequestered French Impressionist and Post-impressionist masterpieces in 1973. He presented a $1 million Goya to Leningrad's Hermitage and has donated or bequeathed his own $25 million collection to the Los Angeles County Museum and the National

Gallery. But there is evidence that his favorite painting is the slobbering head of an Aberdeen Black Angus bull named Prince Eric, whose prowess helped him build a breeding empire. He outlived his first two wives, a Russian baroness and a lady alcoholic from the New Jersey horse country, and now is married to an heiress who accidentally found a reference to him in a periodical neither regularly saw, *The Police Gazette*. It sparked a reunion of friendship after a twenty-year hiatus.

His father went to prison accused of performing an illegal abortion; his son was arrested on a charge of slaying a Korean war veteran. He won them their freedom. For much of his adult life he has fought in court cases that might have destroyed him had he lost. He has won all of them, the latest being a cloak-and-dagger cliff-hanger with $100 million at stake. At last count he had three Rolls-Royces, a multimillion-dollar private jet, homes in Los Angeles and New York's Greenwich Village, and apartments in Moscow and London.

But all of this is dross compared to his greatest possession—his incredible zest for, and belief in, tomorrow.

BOB CONSIDINE

The Remarkable Life of
Dr. ARMAND HAMMER

Chapter 1

Genesis of a Genius

Armand Hammer, who was romantically named for the lover in the younger Dumas's *Camille*, not for the popular U.S. baking soda, is known and often admired for his successes in a confounding variety of endeavors. His disparate lives challenge the mythical durability of (1) the cat and (2) the Bengal Lancer. His drive, as he bustles toward eighty, trailed by approximately 400,000 stockholders and employees, suggests that he over-estimated the diligence of envied rags-to-riches heroes created by Horatio Alger. Compared to Hammer, they might all have been picked up as shiftless juvenile delinquents.

The Hammer epoch emerges from the mists of czarist times. Armand's paternal great-grandfather, Vladimir, became a warship builder during the reign of Nicholas I (1796–1855) and acquired millionaire status and respect at a time when Jews were at most second-class citizens. Armand's grandfather Jacob William Hammer was wiped out literally and figuratively when an unprecedented flood of the Caspian dissolved his fortune in stored salt. He moved to America from his native city of Kherson in 1875 with his wife, Victoria, and their one-year-old son, Julius. As countless other immigrants had learned to their dismay, the streets were not paved with gold. After a year of disillusionment, Jacob moved to Paris, where he tried his hand at several enterprises including, prophetically, an art and antique shop. It and the other callings were failures, so Jacob and his family journeyed back to the United States. He settled his brood in Bradford, Connecticut, where the by then teenaged and muscular Julius found work as a foundry hand swinging a sledgehammer on piecework. He worked cruelly long hours at coolie wages to help keep the family going

1

—his parents, and two half brothers, William and Alfred, all newcomers to a generally hostile land. Two things happened to him in the course of his hard manual labor and his underprivileged life. First, he developed physically to a point where he could bend a railroad spike into a crude horseshoe or flatten, via bare fists, any challenger to his unofficial title as heavyweight champion of the foundry's bullyboys. Second, he was so moved by the poverty and exploitation of his fellow laborers that he joined and became an articulate spokesman for the Socialist Labor party.

Rugged Julius dominated the Hammer family's decision to cut loose from Bradford and the menial jobs it offered and move to New York. For him, Fortune's smile was at first fainter than that of Mona Lisa. He answered a want ad seeking a drug clerk in an Italian neighborhood in the Bowery. The owner rejected him because he couldn't speak Italian. (Neither could the owner, incidentally, although he had lived there twenty years.) But Julius refused to be turned away. He assured the owner that he could learn Italian in two weeks, if hired, and that if he failed to acquire a working knowledge of that tongue he would leave and ask for no pay.

Julius achieved that miracle, at least to the satisfaction of the druggist, and entered upon his apprenticeship behind the drug counter. In record time, as a registered pharmacist, he bought out the owner and opened two more ghetto drugstores, helped his older half brothers William and Alfred to receive their training as pharmacists, and put them in charge of the expanding little chain. Burdened by what he considered the exorbitant prices charged for standard remedies by nationally known pharmaceutical firms, he found an abandoned loft on the Upper East Side, set up his own pharmaceutical plant, and soon filled the shelves of his drugstores with much cheaper, but equally efficacious, wares.

Julius was on his way, not to be halted for a generation. He easily rejected, with thanks, an offer to become one of the pioneering movie moguls—presented to him by one of his young drug clerks, Joseph Schenck. His sights were in clear view: building up his drugstore chain, expanding his cut-rate pharmaceutical business, and marriage. He had fallen in love with a vivacious young widow with a young son.

Rose Robinson was born in Russia, was brought to America as a young girl, married, was widowed and left with a son, Harry, when she and Julius met at a Socialist outing and their remarkable family life began. It was not a bed of roses for Rose, at least at the beginning. Their first child, the delicately named Armand, was born in a cold-water flat over one of Julius's drugstores on the Lower East Side. The date was May 21, 1898, four months before Julius was admitted to Columbia College of Physicians and Surgeons at the relatively ripe age of twenty-four. Julius, a humanitarian as well as an idealist, had decided that tending to the afflicted was a more noble profession than making money in business.

Julius was a man of iron. A man of any lesser metal would have broken under the burdens he carried over the next four years. Somehow he ran his drugstores and his pharmaceutical plant and kept up with his medical education. Upon his graduation in 1902, with the encouragement of Mama Rose, as she was to be called for the remainder of her days, Julius made a command decision that changed the lives of many Hammers. He sold his drugstores and his pharmaceutical works and planted his flag as a general practitioner in a sparsely populated section of the Bronx.

Only Armand, four at the time, mourned the exodus. The boy missed shopping the Lower East Side pushcarts with his mother in happy search of hot corn on the cob, slices of iced watermelon, roasted chestnuts, ice cream, sandwiches and candied apples on sticks. But he soon came around. His father bought a horse and buggy and would take him along on sick calls. Not only that, young Dr. Julius would let the son "hold" the horse—with the help of a leaden anchor—while he tended a patient.

Fresh air, light-years removed from the ghetto, was what the young doctor wanted more than financial gain from his practice. In time, it became expansive (he was to deliver more than five thousand babies before his death at seventy-four). He was a compassionate man who never charged a patient too poor to pay. He was known to climb mountains of tenement stairways and, after treating a destitute patient, leave enough money to pay for the medicine he prescribed. He would not dun the tardiest of his affluent patients. His combination home and office became one of the most crowded places on Washington Avenue. When the walls of the waiting room bulged, and Dr. Julius's long hard day was lengthening into a long hard evening and night, Mama Rose would sometimes pass among the ailing and winnow out the hypochondriacs with a hearty proposal: "Why don't you go home and try a little bicarb?"

Shortly after locating in the Bronx, Dr. Julius and Mama Rose produced Victor, the perennial kid brother of Harry and Armand. By that time the Hammers had a veritable compound in their section of the borough. Grandfather Jacob and Grandmother Victoria moved into a ground-floor apartment in a building immediately across the street from

Dr. Julius's combination home and medical center. They were a determined pair. Jacob made some jolting alterations in his life style. He signed
up as an agent for the Equitable Life Insurance Company, joined the
Republican party, and became a member of the Unitarian Church. Later
Julius and Rose joined the same church and found it not in conflict with
their Socialist beliefs. Armand and his present wife, Frances, although she
is from a devout Catholic family, have kept up the Unitarian tradition to
this day as members of the Santa Monica, California, congregation. Jacob
Hammer had issued a strong-sounding order that only English would be
spoken in his presence. And he repeatedly lectured his successful son,
Julius, on the dangers of active membership in the Socialist Labor party.
Similarly, Harry, Armand, and Victor, as they grew up, never could accept
their father's Socialist philosophy about the traumatic complaints of mankind, but preferred, as Armand says, to "recognize the opportunities
under the free-enterprise American system for those who were resourceful
and industrious."

Grandmother Victoria, an accomplished musician, noted that Armand
alone of her three grandsons had a talent for music and hovered sternly
over his piano lessons. Armand still remembers the terror of giving a
recital, at age five, before he could reach the pedals.

As the boys grew, it was clear that Armand was the least tractable, the
most innovative. He fell in with a group of young classmates at Public
School 4 and began playing hooky. He was turned over to the custody and
mercy of his father, a man whose politics and personality rebelled at
corporal punishment. Nevertheless, Dr. Julius whipped his son with a
strap and then, filled with remorse, set about to rehabilitate this maverick
within the well-ordered family. The trouble with Armand, he decided, was
not within the boy. It was the temptations offered by evil companions,
indigenous to the streets of the Bronx. So Armand, at the age of ten, was
packed off to Meriden, Connecticut, to live with a Mr. and Mrs. George
Rose. Dr. Julius and George Rose had been laboring men together in
Bradford and fellow members of the Socialist Labor party.

Armand was placed in King Street School, near the home of the Roses,
and while there he fell in love with another teenager, Dorothy King. It
was a most platonic affair, possibly because Armand was deeply impressed
by her social standing: King Street was named for one of her forebears.
The following Christmas he invested his entire month's allowance, $1, in

a box of candy for her, practiced what he'd say at the presentation, washed out, handed the candy to the maid, and fled.*

While still exiled to Meriden, Armand made up his mind to do something about the meager allowance his parents sent him each month. He began moonlighting in the then primitive radio business, mastered the Morse Code, and built and sold rudimentary crystal sets. His dip into the business world faced disaster when Mrs. Rose would not permit him to put an aerial on her roof. It would attract lightning, she ruled. So Armand surreptitiously strung one along the attic eaves and found that it worked just as well as an outdoor apparatus.

Dr. Julius brought his prodigal son back to New York at fifteen to finish his last two years of high school at the Bronx's progressive Morris High. The sentence had worked. The lad studied hard and, characteristically, looked around for a way to make money. This time he chose model-plane building, entered his creations in contests, and was generously willing to sell duplicates of his winners—for a price. In 1915, to everyone's astonishment except perhaps his own, Armand won the gold medal in the graduation class's oratorical contest. It was early in World War I and he was determined to be topical if not prescient. His winning subject was titled "The Last War of Mankind." War, he declared manfully, had become so horrible, destructive, and wasteful that the time would soon come when nations abandoned it as a means of settling their arguments.

He had diligently continued his piano practice at Meriden, and when he returned to the Bronx his parents and grandmother were so impressed by his improvement that they arranged for him to be a pupil of the renowned teacher Eugene Bernstein. The maestro's daughter, who was to become the famous art and music publicist Constance Hope, remembers that her father had high expectations that Armand would become a fine concert pianist.

But by that time the young man was being consumed by more material-

*Many years (and millions) later Hammer asked his friend Senator Styles Bridges, the New Hampshire Republican, to recommend a lawyer to represent him in a tax litigation. Bridges proposed former Senator John Danaher, Connecticut Republican, and introduced him to Hammer over the telephone.

"Hammer?" Danaher repeated. "Is your first name Armand? Yes? That's interesting. I'm married to Dorothy King. She's never forgotten you. She's saved a snapshot she took of you in your short pants and button shoes."

Danaher won the case for Armand.

istic ambitions. His life as an extraordinary entrepreneur was taking shape. An example:

When he was sixteen and still at Morris High he saw the car of his dreams—a secondhand Hupmobile roadster—beckoning to him from the show window of a used-car dealer. The price tag on its windshield was a breathtaking $185. He knew it would be senseless to ask his parents to buy it for him. They would say that he was too young to drive and that there were a lot of poor people who needed $185 much more than Armand needed the fire-belching roadster. So Armand took his case to his half brother Harry, who was then (1914) working as a drug clerk in a Liggett's chain store. Harry wavered.

"How do you hope to pay me back if I lend you the money?" Harry wanted to know.

"I'll get a job," the kid said with resolution.

Harry laughed. "You, a job?" But he liked the boy, who later made him a millionaire, and advanced him the money—with the understanding that he himself could use the car whenever he wanted to.

Armand knew where the job was before he made the deal. He had detected a small ad in a newspaper as the Christmas season approached. A popular candy maker of that era, Page and Shaw, was ready to deliver its Christmas specials to thousands of outlets in the New York area. The advertisement offered twenty dollars per day to car owners who would serve as the delivery force.

On the appointed morning the hiring began at the candy plant. Armand chugged up in his tiny Hupmobile and was dismayed to find that even at 8 A.M. he had to join a long queue of cars. Worse, all the cars were bigger, their drivers much older. When the man in charge of selecting the candy couriers reached Armand's place in line he looked over the tiny vehicle and said, "But where are you going to put the candy?"

"I'm going to take the seats out and sit on a box," Armand heard himself immediately answering. "And if I don't make as many deliveries as the big cars, you don't have to pay me anything." At the end of two weeks he paid off Harry, owned the car outright, and there was money jingling in his pockets.

"My first big business deal," says a man whose oil and allied interests grossed over $55 billion in 1974 and whose barter deals with the Russians will amount to more than three times that sum eventually.

For as long as he could remember, Armand Hammer knew—and was quietly proud to know—that when he was old enough he would one day approach the desk of the registrar of Columbia's prestigious medical school and present his application. That day came in 1917 after he had completed his two-year pre-med course. Before he directed his attention to the application blank, the elderly registrar ran his eyes over the young man's face and muscular build.

"You're Julius Hammer's son, aren't you?" he said rather than asked. "Welcome. I processed your father's application . . . a long time ago."

It was a proud moment for the young man, tempered by the knowledge that his father was in deep financial trouble. Not long before that the father had come to see his son at the Phi Sigma Delta fraternity house on the Columbia campus. He brought bad news. He had run into problems with his investment of a lifetime savings in a new pharmaceutical company—called Good Laboratories, oddly enough—and was facing bankruptcy. His problem was that it was next to impossible to continue his exhausting practice and keep an eye on the drug company at the same time. Matters were further complicated by Dr. Julius's suspicion that the partner he had taken in when the new company was formed was robbing the company in what appeared to be an effort to break it, so that he could force Julius out and rehabilitate it in his own name.

Dr. Julius pulled no punches in his talk with his son. He told him he wanted him to take his place at the pharmaceutical plant but not drop out of school.

"I did it, son, and you can do it, too," Julius said. Armand needed no further orders. Together they trooped to a friendly bank, borrowed $20,000, and bought out the suspected partner—and Armand, eighteen, became what amounted to titular head of the Hammers. Harry at the time was in France, having enlisted as a pharmacist in the U.S. forces in World War I.

But there remained the problem of how Armand was going to stay in school and keep abreast of his difficult courses while spending hours at the little drug plant on upper Third Avenue, trying to pump new life into it.

He solved both problems quite neatly.

First, he took in as a boarder at a furnished flat he had rented just off Central Park West an impoverished classmate. In exchange for free room, board, and creature comforts, the latter attended school every day, took

7

voluminous notes, and brought them home at night to Armand. Armand, a total recaller, submitted the notes to his memory tank and used them to prepare his papers.

He had to charm his teachers at Columbia into believing that he attended classes regularly enough to avoid being expelled. This he did with the excellence of written work—thanks to the small mountain of material turned over to him by his boarder. But some of his classmates were always startled when they saw him. "I thought you had dropped out," they'd say.

Turning Good Laboratories around was a case of supersalesmanship bordering on the suicidal. It was customary at that time for the nationally known pharmaceutical houses to distribute small samples of their products to doctors everywhere within normal reach. The thought was that they would use the products, approve of the samples, and prescribe to their patients full-sized bottles, cans, and packages.

Armand decided that most doctors accepted the little samples and either threw them away or put them in the remotest corner of the medicine closet. So he worked his staff overtime to build up the supply of Good products, including prescriptions that had been born in Dr. Julius's mixing bowl. And he decided to distribute full-sized "samples," too big for any doctor to throw away or hide.

He disdained the use of the mails. Good would show its face to the doctor. Hammer bought a map of New York, divided its boroughs into smaller districts, and began hiring what he called "missionaries" to go into those areas visiting doctors and nearby drugstores armed with his large economy-size give-away and stacks of laudatory literature and pamphlets that he himself had written.

His original missionaries, twenty-five carefully selected men and women, began taking actual orders for Good's goods, and in a relatively short time there were three hundred of them fanning around the city, spreading out to other New York cities and the cities of New Jersey and Connecticut.

The industrious moonlighter moved his plant to much larger quarters on the Harlem River. The work force exploded from a dozen to 1,500. Good went national, changed its name to the high-sounding Allied Chemical and Drug Corporation, and challenged the industry's heavyweights.

His first war with the giants was waged against the background of the Volstead Act—Prohibition. He wanted his share of the tincture-of-ginger market. Some unsung Southern chemist, bootlegger, or bathtub mixer had discovered that alcohol-laden tincture of ginger mixed well with ginger ale and, enough of it consumed in highballs, could make a person as drunk as he ever was when liquor was legal.

The big companies had earlier taken notice of the heavy upturn in demands for tincture of ginger in the South. Armand went on a tour of Southern cities and was impressed. He also discovered that ginger prices were soaring. So he sent his buyers into the handful of countries that exported ginger to the United States—India, the Fiji Islands, and Nigeria. They bought so much of it, for immediate delivery or futures, that he virtually cornered the market. The big firms had to buy from that little firm run by a kid.

The federal government eventually got around to putting its foot down. It required that the formula for the "jump-steady" be changed under pain of criminal action and that alcohol contained therein be made as unpalatable as that in Sterno cans.

The bottom fell out of tincture of ginger, but Armand landed on his feet like an able-bodied cat. His experience with ginger led him into the business of importing crude drugs of every kind. Then he made a most prophetic guess. Unlike most of his competitors, he guessed that the ending of World War I would not necessarily mean that there would be a dizzying drop in the pharmaceutical trade because of canceled U.S. military and government contracts. So, while others retrenched and laid off chemists and pharmacists, Hammer built up his staff and his stores. He had correctly divined that drug prices would rise instead of fall as a public that had been rationed gave vent to a buying spree.

He became the only instant self-made millionaire in Columbia's College of Physicians and Surgeons and probably the only undergrad tycoon in the land. He moved into an old carriage house in Greenwich Village and furnished it around a Steinway baby grand (still the hideaway's *pièce de résistance* more than half a century later).

The pharmaceutical business boomed, but Dr. Julius found himself in extraordinary new trouble—political trouble, growing out of his dedication to the principles laid down by the Socialist Labor party.

In effect, Julius Hammer had the moral courage to fight City Hall. He spoke out against corruption in places high and low, and, inevitably, most of his targets were Tammany politicians. He not only would not join in the standard vilification of the Bolsheviks, who had taken over from the postwar Kerensky government in Russia, but he managed to induce Armand to ship them a small treasure in medical supplies from his Good laboratory, with which he sent no immediate bill. Julius, on call virtually around the clock, still had time to spearhead left-wing causes that swept the Socialist Labor party in the Bronx. His political foes waited for him to make a slip.

Which he did, or so it was judged.

During the Spanish influenza epidemic at the end of World War I (it killed ten million persons in 1918 alone) Dr. Julius was visited by a pregnant Russian woman who had a history of heart attacks. Her husband had been a minor diplomat attached to the Russian embassy in Washington during the czarist period. Dr. Julius and his associate, Dr. Benjamin Diamond, duly noted from her record that two other physicians had aborted her in previous pregnancies because of her heart condition. Dr. Julius reached the conclusion that the only way to save the life of the patient, by then in the throes of a miscarriage, was to perform an immediate abortion in the operating room of his office-residence.

In due course, the woman was sent home in care of a nurse, in her chauffeured limousine.

The woman died. Dr. Julius Hammer was arrested. A headline read "MILLIONAIRE DOCTOR ACCUSED OF CRIMINAL ABORTION."

He was prosecuted by a Tammany district attorney before a Tammany-controlled judge and a Bronx jury that had come to the conclusion that, whatever his good works, he was a radical . . . virtually a bomb-throwing Bolshevik.

The good man's defense was pathetic.

His first lawyers, recommended to him by a lawyer friend who was in jail for showing an alleged bankrupt client how to hide his assets, were caricatures of proper advocates. One had the insensitivity to arrive each morning at the grubby Bronx courthouse in a chauffeured Rolls-Royce and to affect a monocle and the hauteur that goes with it while talking to the Tammany judge and the carefully selected antagonist jury. The other lawyer was a drunk.

The verdict was guilty, the sentence was a minimum of three years in Sing Sing, and Armand was enraged. He didn't have a lick of legal experience, but as some of his latter-day platoons of attorneys have attested, he might have switched from medicine to law and become another Brandeis.

Naturally, he had never heard of Brandeis when, as a young undergrad in the College of Physicians and Surgeons, he made up his mind to help reverse the verdict against his father when it came before the Appellate Court. He felt strongly that his father would have been cleared in the first place if the man with the monocle and the man who drank too much had made a proper point—in view of influenza remedies found in that unfortunate lady's home—that the patient had died of influenza, not the abortion. He was also aroused to the point that he wished to throttle the dead woman's husband, who withheld testimony that could have cleared Dr. Julius because he, the czarist husband, had become a rabid anti-Bolshevik.

Armand, the precocious head of the family by now, paid off the man with the monocle and the man with the bottle and, in addition to his other duties, took over his father's appeal.

He sought out and found Maurice Wormser, described to him (accurately) as one of the most respected lawyers in the land. In addition to his regular law practice, Wormser was editor of the *New York Law Journal*, author of the book that was required reading on corporation law, and one of the few Jews ever to be appointed to the faculty of the Jesuit Fordham Law School.

After more than half a century, Armand Hammer still speaks of Wormser with deep respect and shades of humor:

"I think he might have made the Supreme Court, but he had one failing," Hammer says today. "He was as deaf as a post and adamantly refused to wear a hearing aid. He used his handicap astutely. If a judge or a prosecutor tried to cut him off or shut him up, he just kept on making his point. They couldn't do much about it. Actually, he could read lips all the way across a courtroom, but never let anybody know he could.

"He wrote a masterful brief for my father's appeal, but told me that if I wanted the best man to deliver it, argue it in court, I should try to get the services of a former member of the Appellate Division of the State Supreme Court, Judge Francis M. Scott."

The young medical student more or less invaded Scott's offices, was turned down by Scott, who explained that he had never been associated with a criminal case, but masterfully overcame the old gentleman's protests; sold him on the proposition that he, Scott, had it in his hands to right a terrible miscarriage of justice, the conviction of Dr. Julius in the lower court. To provide Scott with additional ammunition, industrious young Armand lined up two hundred New York doctors who signed a petition that stated, in effect, that if confronted with the case that had faced Dr. Julius, they would have reacted in the same way.

Former Judge Scott, in the opinion of his relatively juvenile client, performed brilliantly before the Appeals Court. He lost by one vote. "There just weren't enough errors of law to win the appeal," Armand later philosophized. But he never let up in his crusade to clear his father's name. (See Appendix B.)

Armand breezed through the homestretch at Columbia without the services of his roommate who had previously been cast out of the Central Park West pad for overdoing the "creature comforts" clause in his contract. Armand came home unexpectedly one afternoon and found him in bed with Armand's best girl friend, a pretty nurse he had some thoughts of marrying.

But at Columbia, nobody questioned his prowess. He made Alpha Omega Alpha, the Phi Beta Kappa of medical schools. Internationally renowned bacteriologist Hans Zinsser hailed him as a brilliant student. Two of the most distinguished members of the faculty, Dr. Van Horne Norrie and his assistant, Dr. Morris Dinnerstein, selected him as the graduating class's "most promising." He was awarded one of the two prized internships offered by Bellevue Hospital, an ultimate source of human experimentation, care, and research.

It was June 1921. His internship would not begin until January 1922. He would fill the interim by doing something useful, he decided. What he considered useful flabbergasted the Hammer family. He contracted to sell Allied Drug to his employees for $2 million, making all the Hammers affluent people. And he decided to go to Russia until his internship was ready to be served. He had read about and—though by now a firm disciple of the capitalist system—deeply sympathized with the plight of the typhus- and famine-stricken Russians.

Nobody was going to ostracized Bolshevik Russia at that time, but Armand Hammer arranged passage and arranged to bring gifts. He bought a World War I surplus field hospital for $100,000, stocked it with about $60,000 worth of supplies, instruments, and the like, bought an ambulance for $15,000—and launched himself and his gifts in the direction of a country then as separated from most Western minds as the prospect of an exploration of the moon.

It made sense to Armand in more ways than one. It would mean that he could acquire a wealth of experience that would serve him well when he began his internship. It would be a humanitarian journey that would please his father.

Besides, it might be an opportunity to collect the money that the government still owed him from his earlier shipment of drugs.

And so Armand Hammer, twenty-three, embarked on a course that would change his life radically and deeply affect the lives of millions of others.

Chapter 2

Russia, Bolshevik Style

Walter Duranty of the *New York Times*, for a number of years virtually the only conduit between bleak and blocked-off Bolshevik Russia and the United States, wrote this in his foreword to Armand Hammer's 1932 book, *The Quest of the Romanoff Treasure:*

> His book is like a motion picture of ten thrilling years in the life of an amazing country. He came to Moscow at what was perhaps the most critical period in Soviet history, when exhaustion, caused by civil war and foreign intervention and blockade, was about to culminate in the Great Famine of 1921, and Lenin himself was compelled to make a profound, if temporary, sacrifice of socialist theory and return to a system of private enterprise. . . .
>
> Lenin had a long struggle to convince his followers that the change was necessary. One of his arguments was that it would facilitate economic relations with the outer world, an inflow of foreign capital in the form of concession agreements. . . .
>
> I don't think anyone has had a better opportunity of gauging the Why and How of Soviet development [than Hammer]. He has proved himself a competent observer. Like a film indeed, his narrative runs smoothly from picture to picture, each illustrating a stage in the vastest and boldest experiment Humanity has known. . . .

That was an assessment made more than a decade after Hammer's arrival in Moscow and two years after he had departed from Russia with his Russian wife, their son, and a considerable fortune amassed from a bewildering variety of commercial and artistic ventures. Laurence Stallings, reviewing Hammer's book in the New York *Sun*, wrote, "Dr. Hammer is a gentleman commercial adventist, who in 1921 had more sense than a whole boardroom filled with Titans of Industry."

But in the early summer of 1921 the main drive of the young graduate was to join the crusade battling a plague that had knocked a huge land mass to its knees. Getting to Moscow in those days proved somewhat more difficult than today in his jet. At Southampton, he was held incommunicado by Scotland Yard for several days because it considered any mission to Moscow at that time, however humane, undesirable. (Unless it was a British trade mission, which was reported in the press while Hammer was in London.) In Berlin he reserved a train compartment to Riga for the following day, then called at the headquarters of the local Soviet delegation to pick up the earlier-arranged-for visa that would clear him through Latvia and onward into the Soviet Union. A slovenly attendant and later a bored official told him his visa might come through in perhaps two or three weeks. Hammer shot off a protest to the Foreign Office in Moscow, then took off on a mountain-climbing trip to Garmisch-Partenkirchen in the Bavarian Alps. On his tenth day there he received a message from Moscow, relayed to him by the Adlon Hotel in Berlin. It read, "Your visa granted. Litvinov." (Maxim Maximovich Litvinov was an old Bolshevik and Deputy Foreign Minister who would help obtain U.S. recognition of the Soviet Union in 1933.)

Hammer reached Riga after a stormy three-day sea voyage from Stettin, Germany, and there underwent an unnerving stopover. At his hotel the distinguished-looking headwaiter with a goatee engaged him at dinner in a whispered exchange:

"You are going to Russia?"

"Yes. What about it?"

"Why court death? Because it *is* death."

Hammer did not sleep well that night. The next morning he went shopping for the provisions he would need on his last lap into Russia. He bought a small packing case of cheese, butter, jam, sardines, bread, and biscuits and whiled away the day until it was time to go to the railroad station in a carriage for the scheduled 11:45 P.M. departure. No one was able to tell him how long the trip to the Russian frontier station would take. A day or two, he was told with shrugs.

He arrived at the blacked-out station where a darkened train was berthed in plenty of time, accompanied by a well-wisher, a man named Boris Mishel, the European agent for the Hammer company's pharmaceuticals and uncle of Hammer's old roommate. Mishel checked over the two carriages of baggage and victuals Hammer had brought to the station, then said, "Good heavens! I forgot to tell you about candles!" He sped off in the darkness. At 11:45 a bell rang, reducing the young doctor to a mild panic as he stood on the platform next to a large mound of impedimenta and an equally large Lett porter who could understand no word Hammer uttered. At midnight, with the train and its mute and huddled passengers still standing in the dark, Mishel raced back breathlessly with four candles.

"There are no lights on the train," he explained.

It was time to leave. The porter loaded all of Hammer's baggage into a pitch-black compartment with bare wooden benches in need of a scrubbing. A candle was lighted and erected on the pad of its own melted wax.

"You're lucky," Mishel said, looking around the dismal accommodation. "The 'soft' cars are full of vermin and typhus germs." He had another comforting word as the train began to move. He jumped off and from the platform he shouted, "Good luck. I'll cable your folks at once . . . if anything happens to you."

Armand was to write in his book with a buoyant skill generally discouraged in the lackluster prose of his chosen profession:

> Not even the moment when the detective tapped me on the arm at Southampton, gave me such a thrill [sic] as when our train halted just beyond the actual frontier between Latvia and Soviet Russia, beside a tiny hut over which floated a red flag, and a patrol of Red Army soldiers clambered by.
>
> Here, at last, was the Red Army, of which I had heard so much, with the strange peaked caps, resuscitated, I had been told, by Trotsky, the Bolshevik warlord, from the ancient history of Russia; the headgear of those Scythian archers who more than two thousand years ago had driven back the hosts of Darius, the Persian King of Kings. Their commander, a good-looking young fellow, neat and clean-shaven, passed through the train collecting our passports. He spoke only Russian, but I understood the word "pass."
>
> Husky porters with white aprons lifted out the baggage for customs examination. The dreaded Bolshevik customs proved quite simple. An official who spoke excellent English seemed to know all about me, and the purpose of my journey. He hardly allowed me to open my trunks.
>
> "That's quite all right, citizen," he said. This was the first time that I'd

heard "citizen" in this sense. It had but recently replaced the term "tovarish" or "comrade," which latter was more often used by members of the Communist party. "I will tell the porters to put your things on the Moscow train."

"When does it leave?" I asked.

He waved his hand and replied vaguely, "Soon."

I was later to learn that "soon" (Seichas, literally "this hour") corresponds pretty exactly to the Spanish "mañana."

"Have I time to get something to eat?" I asked.

"Oh, yes, citizen, you have time."

I had, indeed, because the train didn't leave until seven hours later.

It was a repetition of the journey from Riga. Unlighted compartments save for my candle. Wooden benches and an atmosphere that was not clean. After each station there was a little hut marked "Kipyatok," hot water, where everyone ran with kettles to get water for their tea.

"There is much cholera and typhoid," said one of my companions, "so we have boiled water at every station. It is good, nicht wahr?"

Finally—I'd lost count of time; it probably wasn't more than eighty hours after leaving Riga—the same man caught my arm and pointed eastwards. Far off in the distance an enormous golden dome glittered in the morning sun's rays. "Moscow!" he cried. "The great Cathedral, built to commemorate Napoleon's defeat. Moscow, our Red Moscow!"

Was he more proud of Red Moscow, or the victory over Europe's conqueror? This was my first meeting with the contrast between national and revolutionary pride, which is such a paradox of modern Russia. But I did not think of it then. I had reached Moscow at last!

It was a depressingly dilapidated capital on which most of the world had turned its back. Hammer found himself a kind of captive of a rosy-cheeked little man named Wolff, from the Anglo-American desk of the Foreign Office. Wolff helped the porters pile the American's belongings into a wobbly truck, climbed to the peak of the top-heavy mound, and cheerfully invited Hammer to join him. It was from that dismal peak that Hammer first surveyed the central city of his forebears, the city in which he was destined to preside over a handsome pre-Revolutionary brownstone mansion stuffed with millions of dollars' worth of the mementos of the Romanoffs and the branches of that imperial family's tree.

The trip to the paint-peeled Metropole Hotel was a journey through a battered and deserted metropolis. Great holes yawned in the streets. Store fronts were broken and blind, or boarded. Houses looked ready to collapse as if made of playing cards. Hardly any edifice was without its bullet scars. Stores were empty, the streets mostly deserted. From nearly every window protruded the end of a tin stovepipe, gushing ugly black smoke.

"The people seem clad in rags," the visitor wrote. "Hardly any wore stockings or shoes but had wrappings of dirty cloth around their feet and legs; others wore felt boots. The children were all barefooted. No one seemed to smile, everyone looked dirty and dejected. Here and there, one saw a neater figure in the black leather coat and breeches and high boots worn by Communist officials, or a military uniform. But they, too, seemed pale and careworn. I wondered if Wolff was the only man in Moscow who looked cheerful and had pink cheeks."

The officials the earnest young American wanted to see on his first day in Moscow were not available. He learned to his consternation, having been an early riser all of his life, that they slept through most of the day and received such rare visitors as he between midnight and four A.M. Wolff, helping him to kill time, took him to the Government Treasury Department, where he exchanged his dollars for sheets of coupons, unperforated. He found scissors and was thus in business, including the purchase of a shoeshine. There was a shoeshine boy/man at virtually every corner near the Metropole. They used spit instead of polish. Hammer snipped coupons to pay them.

His hotel, he learned, was not to be the Metropole, mostly used at that time by the Narkomindel, a contraction of the Russian words for the People's Commissariat of Foreign Affairs. The hotel selected for him by the Russians, though certain of them had been alerted that he was generously volunteering to help their forlorn cause, was the Savoy. Wolff deposited him and his baggage in a room and left. That meant he was the sole occupant of quarters in what had to be the worst Savoy in the annals of inns of that proud name. There was a bed and mattress but no sheets or blankets, a grease-stained table with a cloth top, two rickety chairs, and a cupboard. The floor was uncarpeted, the wallpaper hung like abandoned hammocks. Rats and mice gamboled underfoot. Hammer inquired if there was a dining room. *Nyet.* Eventually, someone said, he would be given a *payok*, or ticket, by the Foreign Office, which would entitle him to draw meat, vegetables, and bread from the state food depots, if available.

"I rang the bell and after a long interval a slatternly girl appeared," he wrote in retrospect. "I made signs to her to clean up the room, especially the horrible-looking mattress, and put on the sheets and blankets I had brought with me. She stared at me. I offered her a row of my coupons, but she shook her head. I was at my wits' end, but suddenly she caught sight of some cakes of soap in my open bag and burst into a flood of Russian. I gathered that soap was better currency than Soviet paper, and made signs that she would receive a cake if she fixed the room as I wanted her to."

Over the next few days at the Savoy, and some expenditure of soap, Hammer got the room cleaned and more rough furniture moved in. The rats retreated to his bathroom, where there was no running water. The bedbugs stayed in residence, under and above his expensive sheets.

The uncomplaining young New York millionaire did not blow his stack. There was no one in Moscow to impress with either his wealth or his precocious reason for being in the Soviet Union in the hope of lending a hand in its monumental despair. He shared the bleak life of other Savoy inmates. He duly sympathized with an old tenant who bitterly complained, "I threw away my old mattress and sprayed all the ironworks of the bed with kerosene, put my own bedding on it, moved it away from the wall, and put each of the feet of the four legs in saucers of kerosene. I thought it was safe. But the bedbugs are too smart for me. The little devils climb up to the ceiling and bomb me from the air, never missing!"

The young American became ill on his diet of Riga groceries (mostly cheese and sardines) while trying to memorize and use one hundred words of Russian each day. After three days in Purgatory, representatives of the Foreign Office barged into his room as he lay awaiting death at age twenty-three and brought him milk, vegetables, and fresh meat. Moreover, they fulfilled their promise and presented him with a coveted *payok*. He would never have to stand in line again to buy anything, they told him proudly.

He tried it out at the nearest market as soon as he was strong enough. About a hundred shoppers were queued up. *Payok* in hand, Hammer went to the front of the line, past women with children in their arms and ragged men who stared enviously at his good suit and shoes.

"I decided then and there that I would rather starve than deprive a single one of those people of their food," Hammer wrote a decade later. "I hid my payok and walked back to the Savoy."

Hammer solved the matter of his rapidly approaching condition of malnutrition by means of some rudimentary detective work. He noticed that one of the men in the Foreign Office, one Gayov, was unusually fat and contented. Gayov, he further noted, never ate his lunch with the other comrades, all of them as hard up for food as the people in the streets. Instead, Gayov would slip off by himself and when he returned an hour later could be heard giving vent to contented burps.

One day Armand followed him at a safe distance. The unsuspecting Gayov led him to what appeared to be a small private apartment on the second floor of a tattered building. Gayov entered when the door opened to his knock. The door then closed and the American, hiding in the stairwell, heard it bolted. But during the brief period while it was open there drifted from the place an intoxicating aroma of good food. The slightly starving young man drooled for an hour, waiting for Gayov to emerge and depart for the Foreign Office. Then he went up to the mysterious door and pounded on it. A stout German woman, obviously the owner, came to the door of what turned out to be a food speakeasy. After a brief exchange of words and money, he became a member—surely the happiest of them all.

Three days of hot soup, flaky biscuits stuffed with meat *(piroshki)*, roast duck, stewed apples, bread and butter—at about twenty American cents per meal—made a new man of the young visitor. His luck continued: Gregory Weinstein of the Foreign Office would see him and, when he did, introduced him to Dr. Nikolai Aleksandrovich Semashko, the Commissar of Public Health. Semashko expressed gratitude over the American doctor's offer to serve as a volunteer until such time as he must return to New York and begin his internship. The Russian painted a dismal picture of conditions: a critical need of medical supplies caused by a blockade of the country by most European powers; operations being performed without anesthetics; discharged hospital patients required to leave their bandages behind, to be sterilized and used for others.

Hammer was eager to go to work then and there. But the international section of Public Health was not. The official who had the power to assign him a specific area was not available when the eager young American called.

"When will he return?" Hammer hammered.

A subordinate shrugged. "A month or so," he answered.

Hammer had had it. He began making plans to leave his field hospital and quit this chaotic country. But Weinstein changed his mind and, in effect, his life. The commissar invited him to join a mixed group of observers being sent to the Urals as guests of the government to inspect and report on conditions in industrial areas. This trip would last perhaps a month, Weinstein said, after which the official Hammer had tried to see might well be back at his desk. Hammer accepted the invitation and was given the special train's timetable.

For three consecutive nights he made the trip to the train station with his bags and food locker, only to be told that the train's departure would be the next night. On the fourth day of the vigil he was told that the train would definitely depart at 5 P.M. Hammer arrived at 4:30, three and a half hours before the train backed into place. He located an upholstered bunk in the car reserved for members of the party, and to his surprise the train began to move at 11 P.M. He lighted a candle. It flickeringly illuminated his compartment but could shed no light on the impending events that would alter his life's course.

He wrote about it in his book nearly half a century ago:

The chief of our expedition was Ludwig Martens, formerly Soviet Representative at New York, [later] in charge of the Soviet metallurgic industry. He had taken along with him several of his assistants, for the most part engineers. Besides myself, there were two other Americans in our party, A. A. Heller, a Socialist writer who sympathized with the new Russian regime, and Miss Lucy Branum, a plucky little social worker and former Suffragette.

For three days and nights the train rumbled slowly eastward until, as we neared the Volga, we came into a region of parched fields and sunburnt crops. As far as the eye could reach, one saw grain fields which should now have been ripening golden, standing four feet high and ready to harvest. Instead, there was nothing but dry, stringy grasses, or so they looked, only eight or ten inches tall above the cracked dry earth.

There was a sobering stopover in Ekaterinburg, where several years earlier the Bolsheviks, fearing that the advancing White Army (financed partly by the United States) would capture the city, liberate the imprisoned imperial family, and put it back in power, carried out the execution of Czar Nicholas II, his consort, their children, his brother and hoped-for successor, Grand Duke Michael, and other members of a dynasty that had begun in 1613.

If Moscow had been depressing, Ekaterinburg was infinitely worse. The city (now called Sverdlovsk and best known in modern times as the site of the May 1, 1960, shoot-down of C.I.A. spy pilot Francis Gary Powers) was swollen with refugees from the baked outlands, come to the urban area in search of food. One passage-free trainload of them arrived the day Hammer and the Moscow observers pulled in. It was a nightmarish scene that moved him to write in his book:

> Cholera, typhus and all the epidemics of childhood were rife among them. I had imagined that my professional training as a physician had steeled me against human suffering, but the first vision of that refugee train struck me cold with horror. There had been, I learned, a thousand persons aboard the train when it left Samara in the Volga region. When it pulled into Ekaterinburg, after several days' travel, not more than two hundred of the strongest were living. Some had died of hunger, but disease had claimed most of the victims. This was but one heart-breaking case out of many.

He was soon to have his knowledge of famine expanded. Children by the hundreds, with shriveled limbs and protruding but empty bellies, knocked on the sides of the train from Moscow, begging for food. Stretcher bearers carried the dead from the refugee train to a common grave in a ceaseless file. The mission from Moscow heard stories of cannibalism. Wild dogs circled the horrid scene, carrion birds wheeled overhead.

The inspection train and its deeply concerned passengers pulled out of Ekaterinburg after twenty-four hours and chuffed into the nearby complex of mills, factories, and mines. To his amazement, Hammer was shown stocks of platinum, Ural emeralds, semiprecious stones, and mineral products, as he had been shown mounds of furs in Ekaterinburg.

"Why don't your people export these things and buy grain in exchange?" he asked a Russian. Then another. Then another. They had the same answer generally:

"It is impossible. The European blockade against us has just been lifted. It would take us too long to organize the sale of these goods and the purchase of food in return." "The American" was told that at least a million bushels of wheat were needed to save the population of that area of the Urals until the next harvest. There had been a bumper grain crop in the United States and the price had fallen to a dollar a bushel. Farmers preferred to burn it than take it to the market at this price. "I have a million dollars—I can arrange it," Hammer said, as if he had been in that trade all his life. "Is there anyone here with authority to make a contract?"

A meeting of the local soviet was hastily convened. He cabled his brother Harry to buy the million bushels and ship it by the next available boats to Petrograd, where it would be picked up and distributed by the Ekaterinburg officials. In his cable Hammer stated that the ships would return with $1 million worth of furs, hides, and certain other goods, and that there would be a "small commission of 5 percent" on both sides of the transaction. Actually, he wrote later, the profit motive was far from his mind. All he could remember was the cordwood dead waiting to be rolled into their trenchlike grave and the pleading faces of thousands of children at the windows of the special train.

Word of what the young man had done spread ahead of the train as it meandered through the Urals. At one stop the local soviet greeted him as a potential savior and asked him to make a speech. It was the first real opportunity Hammer had had to vent his painfully acquired new language. In ten days he had learned one hundred words a day or a total of about a thousand commonly used Russian words. When he finished, the applause was more or less deafening, which pleased him mightily. Turning to an English-speaking Russian official, Hammer said, "I'm grateful to your countrymen for not laughing at my incorrect pronunciations and mistakes. They seemed to understand that I'm trying to help them."

The man laughed. "They didn't understand anything. They thought you were speaking English," he said. "That noise you hear is from people asking for a Russian translation of your remarks." Martens provided it, and there was even more applause for the strange young man from the other side of the world who had come to save them from starvation.

A day or two later there was a most significant stop at a large asbestos deposit near Alapayevsk, where lesser members of the imperial family and court notables had been executed three years before and their bodies thrown into a quarry. Hammer wrote in his book:

> One of my friends on the train, a Russian mining engineer who had worked in the neighborhood, explained to me how valuable this asbestos property might become with proper development. The whole outfit, buildings and plant, was as it had been left after the revolution. Not a soul was working. It was ghostly. I must admit his facts and figures interested me considerably. But I was still thinking about doing famine relief work, and simply earmarked his information as of possible interest to business people in America.
>
> We continued our trip through the Urals at the same slow speed, amid the same scenes of suffering and desolation. One day the train stopped for

23

several hours at a small wayside station. Glad of the opportunity to stretch our legs, several of us took a walk along the dirty road leading to a village two or three miles away. Halfway between the station and the village we found a little lonely hut and in the yard an old man with a gray beard, a prototype of the Russian peasant, laboriously sawing pine wood into planks.

"What are you doing, little uncle?" asked one of my friends.

"Sawing wood," the ancient replied laconically.

"But why make planks?" one asked. "One saws wood for the stove but not like this."

The old man looked at him, a strange dumb look like a hurt animal. "For my coffin," he said simply. "I am all alone. I have food for three more weeks only, then I must die. But before that I will have made my coffin, and will lie in it to await death so that I shall not be buried like a dog in the bare ground."

It was a terrible paradox to Hammer that locked in the Urals were some of the greatest treasures of the world, almost every known mineral, yet the people were unable to utilize them even to provide themselves with the barest necessities of life.

It was on that somber day, at the next telegraph stop, that Martens was summoned to the telegraph key and told that there would soon follow an exchange with Lenin himself, communicating from the Kremlin.

After a tense period, the thin line that stretched from Moscow to the Urals sputtered the beginning of a question to Martens that all but stupefied Hammer. The words fell slowly into place:

WHAT IS THIS WE HEAR FROM THE EKATERINBURG ROSTA [telegraph agency] ABOUT A YOUNG AMERICAN CHARTERING GRAIN SHIPS FOR THE RELIEF OF FAMINE IN THE URALS? LENIN.

Martens dictated to the operator:

IT IS CORRECT. DOCTOR ARMAND HAMMER HAS INSTRUCTED HIS ASSOCIATES IN NEW YORK TO SEND GRAIN IMMEDIATELY TO PETROGRAD ON THE UNDER-STANDING, WHICH HAS BEEN APPROVED BY THE EKATERINBURG SOVIET, THAT A RETURN CARGO OF FURS WOULD BE TAKEN BACK TO COVER THE COST OF THE GRAIN SHIPMENT.

A pause, then Lenin came back on the wire:

DO YOU PERSONALLY APPROVE THIS?

Martens smiled, looked at Hammer, and dictated:

YES. I HIGHLY RECOMMEND IT.

A longer pause. Hammer does not remember breathing during it. Then:

VERY GOOD. I SHALL INSTRUCT THE FOREIGN TRADE MONOPOLY DEPARTMENT
TO CONFIRM THE TRANSACTION. PLEASE RETURN TO MOSCOW IMMEDIATELY.

Chapter 3 ═══════════════════════════════════════

Lenin—The Ice Breaker

═══

Hammer was called to Lenin's office the morning after the train reached Moscow. He hardly had time to notice that Moscow had undergone a progressive change from the day he had last seen it, a month before. Lenin had introduced his New Economic Policy in the meantime. Once-abandoned shops had been repaired and filled with foods, even French wines and choice Havana cigars. NEP—and Lenin's enormous power—had sprung these goods from hiding places and activated the spirits of the people. Hammer's excitement over the prospect of meeting one of the world's leading figures face to face filtered into a memoir he later penned in his book:

> Accompanied by one of the men attached to the Foreign Office, I walked to the Troitski Gate of the Kremlin, a curious little round white tower connected with the main body of the fortress by a bridge over gardens where, doubtless, in the past was a moat or other work of defense. At the gate, they verified my passport and took it away from me. I was a little disquieted, but they told me they would give it back to me when I returned. Meanwhile, they gave me a pink ticket, a pass, on which was written my name.
>
> Passing under the big archway, I found myself in a large square courtyard flanked by cannons captured from Napoleon. I called the Kremlin a fortress, but in reality it is more than that. It is a sort of central town within a town, the citadel of Moscow guarded by enormous walls and towers. There are churches in it of great antiquity and beauty, and palaces and barracks and streets of buildings formerly occupied by members of the Czar's Court, now used by Communist officials. Lenin's office was on the

second floor of a large building on the central square.

Afterwards I was told that this building was formerly the High Court of Moscow, where the Czar signed decrees of national importance. Little did Nicholas II think when some twenty years before he affixed his signature to the "Act of Repressive Measures," which permitted the hanging of a young student named Alexander Ilyitch Ulianof for alleged revolutionary activity, that one day Ulianof's younger brother Vladimir, who changed his name to Lenin, would sign in the same building another decree to punish "Enemies of the People's Revolution" which gave to the Ekaterinburg Soviet the legal authority to pass sentence of death upon the Czar and his family.

I passed a sentry before I entered the building and there was another sentry at the door of the corner rooms which the Soviet leader occupied. Since that August day in 1918 when the Social Revolutionary Fanny Kaplan shot Lenin as he was leaving a workers' meeting in Moscow (though not fatal, the bullet undoubtedly shortened his life), he had been guarded from assassination by every possible precaution.

I passed through a large room, full of people working busily at roll-topped desks, like the outer office of any big American businessman, and was conducted to the double door of Lenin's private office by his secretary, Glasser, a little hunchbacked girl. She shared the innermost secrets of the Red Dictator, possessed his full confidence, and never on any occasion used her position for her own advantage or that of her friends.

Lenin rose from his desk and came to meet me at the door. He was smaller than I had expected—a stocky little man about five feet three, with a large dome-shaped head, wearing a dark gray sack-suit, white soft collar shirt and black tie. His eyes twinkled with friendly warmth as he shook hands and led me to a seat beside his big desk. The room was full of books, magazines and newspapers in half a dozen languages. They were everywhere, on shelves, on chairs, piled up in heaps on the desk itself, save for a clear space occupied by a battery of telephones. There was a piece of gold-bearing quartz used as a paperweight, and ivory and bronze statuettes sent to Lenin by peasants' and workers' organizations.

He spoke eagerly and emphatically, in English, without many gestures except for a quick cutting movement of the hand to drive home his point, one of his characteristics in public speaking. Occasionally he paused for a word, but for the most part his English was easy and fluent.

He drew his chair up close to mine and gave me a quick glance sideways, as if to probe me with his sharp brown eyes, in which there seemed a trace of laughter. I told him I was trying to learn a hundred Russian words a day. Lenin gave me a smile of great sweetness and charm. "I used the same method myself when I was in London," he said. "Then I used to visit a library and read books to see how much I could remember. At first it is not so bad, but the more you learn, the more difficult it is to retain."

The United States and Russia, as Lenin explained it, were complementary. Russia was a backward land with enormous treasures in the form of undeveloped resources. The United States could find here raw materials and a market for machines, and later for manufactured goods. Above all, he said, Russia needed American techniques and methods, American engineers and instructors. He picked up a copy of the *Scientific American*.

"Look here," he said, running rapidly through the pages, "this is what your people have done. This is what progress means; building, inventions, machines, development of mechanical aids to human hands. Russia today is like your country was during the pioneer stage. We need the knowledge and spirit that has made America what she is today."

Several times during our conversation there were interruptions by secretaries with documents. Lenin waved them aside.

"You have traveled in Russia?" he asked, or stated. I told him I had just spent a month in the famine region of the Urals. His face changed, the eager interest faded from his eyes and his expression grew infinitely sad. In that moment I realized what a weight lay upon the shoulders of this man.

"Yes, the famine," he said slowly. He spaced his thoughts. "I heard you wanted to do medical relief work. . . . Yes. . . . It is good and greatly needed, but . . . we have plenty of doctors. What we want here is American businessmen who can do things as you are doing. Your sending us ships with grain means saving the lives of men, women and little children who would otherwise helplessly perish this winter. To the gratitude of these agonized people I add my humble thanks on behalf of my government." He appeared on the point of tears. Then his voice firmed up and he said, "What we really need is American capital and technical aid to get our wheels turning once more. Is it not so?"

I said that from what I had seen in the Urals there was plenty of available material and manpower; that many factories were in much better shape than I had expected.

Lenin nodded. "Yes," he said, "that's it. The civil war slowed everything down and now we must start afresh. The New Economic Policy demands a fresh development of our economic possibilities. We hope to accelerate the process by a system of industrial and commercial concessions to foreigners. It will give great opportunities to the United States. Have you thought of that at all?"

I said that one of the friends on the train had wished to interest me in an asbestos proposition which seemed to have a most hopeful future. I added a few words about my own affairs being insignificant, by comparison.

Lenin checked me. "Not at all," he said, "that is not the point. Someone must break the ice. Why don't you take an asbestos concession yourself?"

I was rather surprised. From what I had seen of Russian methods, such a deal might take months. I said something to that effect.

Lenin caught my meaning like a flash. "Bureaucracy," he said, "this is one of our curses! I am telling them so all the time. Now here is what I'll do. I'll appoint a special committee of two men, one of whom will be connected with the Peasant and Workers' Inspection Commissariat, and the other with the All-Russian Extraordinary Commission—Cheka—to deal with this matter and give you all the help they can. You may rest assured that they will act promptly. It shall be done at once!"

Thus in my presence was created the embryo of what later was to grow into the Concessions Committee of the Soviet Union.

"You will make your arrangements with them," Lenin continued rapidly. "When you have reached some tentative agreement, you will let me know. We understand that we must insure conditions that will allow concessionaires to make money in Russia. Businessmen are not philanthropists and unless they are sure of making money they would be fools to invest their capital in Russia."

I told Lenin there was a doubt in my mind as to the possibility of working without friction with Russian labor, especially since it had become accustomed to look upon a capitalist as an enemy. I asked him if he could assure me that I would have no labor troubles.

Lenin answered promptly. "Our workers will be happy to get employment and good wages," he said. "It would be foolish for them to cut away the limb of the tree on which they are sitting. While our Government cannot give orders to the Trade Unions, still, as a workers' Government, we have sufficient influence to insure that the Unions will carry out fully the terms of their collective contracts with you. Above all, it is essential that you become thoroughly familiar with our labor laws. If you obey these laws you will have the full protection of our Government. . . . Don't worry too much about details. I'll see that you receive fair treatment. If there is anything you want, write and tell me.

"To repeat, when you have made a provisional contract we shall approve it in the Council of Commissars without delay. What we decide goes, you understand," and again he made that decisive cutting gesture with his right hand. "In fact, if necessary, I won't even wait for the Council to meet. A matter like that can easily be arranged by telephone."

Lenin was as good as his word. In short order, Hammer became the first foreign concessionaire, pledged to reconstruct an industry he knew nothing about.

Many years later (1967), the Marx-Lenin Institute of the Central Committee of the Communist Party of the Soviet Union published the private papers and letters of Lenin. In Volume 45, covering the years of Hammer's friendship with the Soviet leader, there are no less than fourteen page references to Armand Hammer. (See Appendix A for references in Volume 45, as well as other volumes.) The first document, written after Lenin's first meeting with Hammer, is a handwritten note dated October 14, 1921, to the Members of the Central Committee of the Russian Communist Party, advising them of a report on Hammer which Lenin had received the day before from Boris Reinstein. Reinstein and Julius Hammer had been fellow members of the American Socialist Labor party. Reinstein was by now a highly placed Communist residing in Moscow, and Lenin rested great confidence in him. In this note to the Central Committee, Lenin relates the terms of Hammer's contract to supply the Ural workers with a million poods of bread and accept in return Ural goods to be sold on commission to the United States "on very favorable terms (5 percent)."

Reinstein had informed Lenin that the Hammers were American millionaires and that Armand's father, Julius Hammer, was in prison, "accused of illegally performing an abortion, but actually because of Communism." Lenin told the members of the Central Committee of Hammer's gift of medical equipment to the Minister of Health, Semashko, and of his decision to take an asbestos concession, which would help in the reconstruction of the Urals industry.

Reinstein had mistakenly informed Lenin that Julius Hammer was a partner of his son (probably because of Armand's youth). The reverse was the case; when Julius Hammer was indicted, he turned over his shares to his son, so that it was all Armand's now.

On October 15 Lenin wrote a note to Ludwig Martens to see if he could interest Armand Hammer in financing a plan for the rebuilding and the electrification of the Urals and "to supply electrical equipment (on the basis of a loan, of course)."

Then there are a series of handwritten notes from Lenin to Martens, Chicherin (the Minister of Foreign Affairs) and Bogdanov (Minister of

National Economy) showing that Lenin was following up every step of the negotiations involved in the implementation of the concession agreements with Hammer. In a note to Martens dated October 19, Lenin emphasized that the agreements be put in the legal form of concessions, even if they were not true concessions. He stated it was important to show the outside world that Americans were taking concessions (under the New Economic Policy instituted by Lenin to grant concessions to foreigners). In a memorandum to Martens dated October 27, 1921, Lenin writes:

> I received both contracts. I am returning them. Why weren't the additional points put in which were shown to me (in draft form) by Reinstein and Hammer? We must re-edit them and put them in the agreement. We must give careful attention that we punctiliously and factually carry out our word. Do not rely on giving orders! Unless we verify everything personally and supervise same, nothing will be done well.

In a handwritten note to I. I. Radchenko, Minister of Foreign Trade, dated the same day, Lenin wrote:

> It appears to me that this agreement has tremendous significance as the beginning of trade. It is absolutely necessary that you pay strict attention to the factual carrying out of our obligations. I am sure that without intensive pressure and attention not a thing will be done. Take steps to carefully check and verify the execution of this agreement. Keep me informed who you are appointing to be responsible for carrying this out. . . .

Lenin evidently feared government bureaucracy and other delays due to red tape which still plague the Soviet system and he wanted to receive reports two to three times a month so he could follow up matters.

On November 3, on the eve of Hammer's departure from Moscow, Lenin wrote him a warm note ending with the words "This beginning is extremely important. I hope it will be the beginning of great significance." Lenin apologized in a P.S. for his extremely bad English, although the letter was written in fairly good English.

On December 17, 1921, as Lenin was preparing his address to the 9th All Russian Congress of Soviets, he asked Bogdanov to supply him with the latest information on the progress of the Hammer concessions to include in his report to the members of the Congress.

Hammer has had decades to assess and reassess those first impressions of a man who altered the course of history. He has told fellow American tycoons and a new crop of Soviet leaders who envy him his old association with their finite god:

> Before entering Lenin's office that day I had been greatly impressed by the terrific veneration which he had aroused. I somehow expected to meet a superman, a strange and terrible figure, aloof and distant from mankind. Instead, it was just the opposite. To talk with Lenin was like talking with a friend one knew and trusted, a friend who understood. His infectious smile and use of colloquial expressions, even slang, his sincerity and natural ways, put me completely at my ease. He has been called ruthless and fanatical, cruel and cold. I refused to believe it. It was his intense human sympathy, his warm personal magnetism and utter lack of self-assertion or self-interest that made him great and enabled him successfully to hold together and produce the best from the strong and conflicting wills of his associates.

Hammer's office in Occidental Petroleum headquarters in Los Angeles today features a framed photograph of his late great friend. The eyes are almost hypnotic. The inscription reads, "To comrade Armand Hammer, from Vl. Iulanoff (Lenin) 10. XI, 1921."

In Lenin's Kremlin office, now a national museum and untouched since his death in 1924, tourist guides call attention to an ornament on the desk, a small bronze monkey contemplating a human skull. The monkey is seated on a stack of sculptured books, featuring *Origin of Species* by Charles Darwin. It was a gift from Armand Hammer, boy capitalist. He had purchased it in London, when Scotland Yard was looking the other way, and presented it to the Russian leader on a subsequent visit when he saw Lenin briefly in September 1922. Hammer gave Lenin a progress report of his asbestos concession and other activities in developing trade between the Soviet Union and the United States. Lenin was taken with the symbolism of the bronze statuette and Hammer recalls his remark that with the weapons of war becoming more and more destructive, civilization could be destroyed if mankind didn't learn to live in peace. The time might come, he said, when a monkey would pick up a human skull and wonder where it came from. Lenin gave orders that the bronze was not to be removed from his desk.

Chapter 4

Trade and Trotsky

Hammer emerged from his first meeting with Lenin walking about one foot above the cobbled expanse of Red Square. His new-found prestige had preceded him. After a dire night with his rats at the Savoy he complained the next morning when he visited the Foreign Office. Gregory Weinstein expressed shocked surprise.

"My dear Dr. Hammer!" he exclaimed. "Why didn't you tell us sooner? I shall make different arrangements at once!"

Thirty minutes later, Hammer was sitting with all his luggage in a World War I limousine on the way to the Government Guest House, across the Moscow River from the golden-tipped Kremlin. He was headed for what Muscovites called the Sugar King's Palace, formerly the property of a long-gone banished or purged Ukrainian named Haritonenko, a crude man who amassed an estimated fortune of a quarter of a billion dollars in sugar beets before the Revolution's roof fell in on him. Hammer's interest at the moment was moving into a place that offered him some modest protection against typhus and/or bubonic plague. Although he was some years removed from becoming interested in objects of art or antiquity, he noticed that in the confusion of acquiring a massive amount of heavy junk for his "palace" the Sugar King had picked up a lovely Corot and some very good lesser masters to lace the debris of his suits of armor and grotesque Japanese bronze statuary and incomparably bad furniture. It was better than the Savoy. Anything was. He wrote in his book:

Suddenly, I found myself in a palatial suite with bathroom attached—and actually hot and cold water on tap—clean as a new pin, and, wonder of wonders, a large, comfortable bed with real sheets and blankets. There were well-trained servants, an excellent cuisine, and, if need be, a bottle of old French wine from the well-stocked cellar. It had been retained by the Government as a place to entertain foreign visitors. I could hardly believe it was real, after the Savoy. Such was the magic of Lenin's name and of my new status as a potential concessionaire.

It was a spooky Grand Hotel, Russian style. Hammer won the apartment once occupied by the English financier Leslie Urquhart, whose Russo-Asiatic corporation had been the greatest foreign enterprise in czarist Russia: limitless oil rights over the richest section of westernmost Siberia, endless timberland, countless mines. Urquhart could never get to first base with Lenin, however. The next apartment had been used by Clare Sheridan, the American pro-Bolshevik writer. Across the corridor was a suite once dominated by Washington Vanderlip, who almost won an awesome concession to develop the Kamchatka oil reserves because the commissars thought he was one of the National City Bank Vanderlips. Down the hallway was the suite recently vacated by Enver Pasha, a hero of the "Young Turks" revolution and enemy of Kemal Pasha. Enver Pasha was to be killed by the Red Army later in a skirmish on the Afghan frontier.

But these had gone; others came. Hammer needed his European manager, Boris Mishel, who had returned to Berlin from Riga after promising to let the Hammer family know if anything lethal happened to the young adventurer. The Foreign Office supernumeraries leaped to their feet and promised to arrange for Mishel's visa immediately, if not sooner. Hammer wired him to come, pronto, by train. But then Hammer remembered—it seemed an unlikely thing to forget, considering his tender age and interest in cars—that he had ordered a Mercedes Benz during his relatively brief stay in Berlin for future delivery. So he sent a second wire to Mishel asking him to drive the car to Moscow as quickly as possible. After sending it, he received word that Lenin had been helping him, as promised, and the asbestos concession was about to come through. So he sent a third cable: "Arrange come direct by airplane."

As often happened in those days, the cables were delayed. Mishel received the second cable first. He concluded that Hammer must be out of his mind to assume he, Mishel, could burst across the border in a fancy car without any credentials. The third message was the second to reach him, and it, too, made no sense to him. Then he received the first message,

ERRATUM

Page 6, line 36: *For* $55 billion *read* $5.5 billion

the order to come by train and saying that the visa had been granted. That made sense. But Mishel still concluded that Hammer must be mad, probably from starvation.

He weighed whether to inform the Hammer family or first try to track down the madman and nurse him back to health. He chose the latter. He filled most of a train compartment with food and set off for Moscow. Armand met him at the terminal in a big freshly imported limousine supplied by the Foreign Office. With the baggage and food loaded, the flabbergasted man turned to Hammer and said, looking around the limousine and its chauffeur, "Good God, is this yours?"

Hammer just smiled and said, "Why don't you give some of this food of yours to the people around the station? Look, the sausages are popping out of their packages."

It seemed to confirm Mishel's worst fears about his precocious employer.

"But we'll need this food, won't we?"

"Not with me you won't," Hammer said, as if he headed the Chamber of Commerce. "Now roll down the windows and we'll start giving this food to people who need it." At the Sugar King's Palace he further shook his associate. "Perhaps you'd like a hot bath before dinner," he said airily. "And now about the wine. Would you prefer Johannesburg or Burgundy?"

"So *this* is Moscow," the man muttered amidst his shattered preconceptions.

Mishel recovered rapidly. As a man of business acumen he was not impressed by Hammer's assurance that Lenin would take care of any problem that might present itself at the asbestos concession.

"We don't need anything more than that," Hammer said.

"The hell we don't!" Mishel said, rolling a sheet of paper into his Corona. Between the two of them, the following amendments to be granted were spelled out:

1. We are entitled to receive from the Government, offices, warehouses, etc., wherever we consider it necessary. The Soviet Government undertakes whenever needed to supply us with soldiers to protect our property.

2. The Government grants the right to our employees to travel freely about Russia and to enter and leave the country at will. This, of course, pertains only to American citizens.

35

3. The Government radio and telegraph stations are placed at our disposal for the prompt transmission of our telegrams.

4. The Government renders us every possible assistance in the prompt movement of our freight cars and also places at our disposal private cars to transport our employees throughout Russia.

5. To avoid all red tape, delays and hindrances, the Government undertakes to appoint a committee of two persons, one from the Workers' and Peasants' Organization and one from the Cheka, to whom in case of misunderstanding we can refer as competent authority to settle all disputes without loss of time.

Ten minutes after a phone call to Lenin's office a courier arrived by bicycle to pick up the list of audacious demands. When the concession agreement was signed not long later, the five amendments were attached to it, countersigned by Lenin and the secretaries of the president of the Council of Commissars. Not a word had been changed. (See Appendix A.) The formal signing ceremony at the Foreign Office, Hammer recalls, was presided over by Vice-Commissar of Foreign Affairs Maxim Maximovich Litvinov, himself. Hammer, whose eyes might possibly have been bugged by the swift turn of events, still thinks of the document's red seal as the size of a saucer.

The first headquarters offered to him was a four-story marble building in the center of Moscow, a noble edifice that had been an important bank in czarist times. The rent suggested by the Moscow Housing Department was interesting: $30 a month. Hammer opted for smaller quarters on the first floor of another centrally located building on Kuznetski Most, 4, which had been Moscow headquarters for Fabergé, the court jeweler. This location would now command several thousand dollars' rental per month. Lenin's young friend got it for $12.

He was worried about that clause in the approved-of amendments that bound the Russians to provide troops to secure his holdings. It seemed to him a bit too much to expect, with nothing more than a clause in a contract to fall back on, so he took his doubts to the Foreign Office. The Foreign Office tacitly agreed and suggested that for positive verification he call upon the second most important leader in the revolutionary government, Commissar of War Leon Trotsky.*

It is better to utilize Hammer's impressions of that visit with the

---

*Still known variously at that time as Lev Davydovich Trotski and Leon Bronstein.

towering soldier-statesman-politician who was fated to be murdered, by a man accused of being one of Stalin's supporters, at his exile home in the Coyoacán suburb of Mexico City nearly two decades later as related in his book:

The War Office was situated in a large building with white columns outside the Kremlin. The moment I entered it, I was struck by its great difference from all the other Soviet administrations I had visited. The place was scrupulously clean and tidy. There were no chatting groups of comrades in the corridors, no cigaret stubs on the floors, no tea glasses in saucers on the desks. Instead, the same order and precision as in a business office in New York.

The sentry at the door examined my credentials and directed me to an ante-room upstairs. At three minutes to 4 P.M. in came a snappy young aide in khaki uniform with a Sam Browne belt and a heavy revolver at his hip. "Comrade Trotsky is waiting for you," he said curtly. "Please come with me."

He led me through rooms filled with diligent workers. The place was a hive of industry, everywhere neat and trim. We passed other sentries, and it struck me that the Red Warlord was guarded more closely than Lenin himself. Of course, the latter lived in the Kremlin, a fortress in itself, which made a difference, but the Bolsheviks had learned from the attack upon Lenin and the campaign of assassination undertaken by the Social Revolutionaries in the summer of 1918 to leave no stone unturned to protect their leaders.

Not that anyone ever questioned Trotsky's personal courage. Indeed, on one occasion he showed the rarest kind of bravery in facing a mob howling for his blood. It occurred in Petrograd—the erstwhile St. Petersburg—in the early days of the Revolution. There was, it appeared, a scandal in high Communist circles. One Dybenko, the idol of the Red Fleet, a handsome young officer who had brought the cruiser *Aurora* up the river from Kronstadt to shell the Winter Palace and drive Alexander Kerensky's short-lived government out in panic, had eloped to the Crimea with a married woman, a Bolshevik heroine named Kollontai. Trotsky was quoted as stating that both should be found and shot as deserters.

This statement became known to the sailors of the Red Fleet. One fine morning a body of them, several hundred strong, appeared in the courtyard of the building where Trotsky worked, shouting threats of vengeance. A terrified secretary ran into Trotsky's office.

"The sailors have come to kill you, Comrade," he cried. "Save yourself immediately by the back staircase while there is yet time. They have defied

37

the guards and swear they will hang you on the lamppost in the courtyard."

Trotsky leapt to his feet, ran down the front staircase, and out into the courtyard. "You want Trotsky, here I am!" he shouted. Then he launched into a speech excoriating Dybenko. Such was the magic of personality and oratorical power that within ten minutes the sailors were carrying him around the courtyard on their shoulders.

Lenin disposed of the Dybenko-Kollontai affair in a characteristic way. At a meeting of the Central Committee of the Communist Party to decide finally what punishment should be inflicted, Lenin waited until the rest had finished speaking, then said quietly, "Comrades, you are right. Their offense is most serious, and the penalty should be exemplary. Personally, I think shooting is far too good for them. I propose, therefore, a fate more terrible still. Let it be resolved that our erring comrades be condemned to mutual fidelity for the space of five years."

. . . Heavy curtains shrouded the door of Trotsky's office. The big room was in semi-darkness as I came into it, although it was afternoon of an early autumn day. The shades were drawn over the windows, shutting out all daylight. Trotsky sat at a desk on the far side of the room under an electric light, the only illumination in the place, like a spotlight in a theater. He had always a strong sense of dramatic values. I learned afterwards that a steel netting protected the windows outside from a possible grenade or bomb. This netting had been installed in the summer of 1919, when a couple of anarchists killed some 20 members of the Moscow Communist Committee by hurling a heavy bomb into the room where they were holding a meeting.

The Red Warlord wore khaki breeches and a plain tunic buttoned up to the neck. He greeted me quite cordially, but his glance was cold and piercing, very different from Lenin's human and friendly attitude. We talked in German, which he spoke perfectly. He knew all about our concession, and the contract I had made before to supply grain to the Urals in exchange for goods. He spoke of the unlimited possibilities of that region. Its mineral resources, he said, had hardly been scratched. He had just returned from an inspection trip through that area and was convinced, he added, that it offered great possibilities to American capital.

He asked what I, hardly half his age, thought about it. Did the "financial circles" of the United States regard Russia as a desirable field for investment? I told him the truth. I told him that I didn't know for sure. It was too early. . . .

Trotsky came back with a curious argument. He said that inasmuch as Russia had had its revolution, capital was safer there than anywhere else because Russia, no longer in ferment, would adhere to any agreements it might make.

"When our Revolution comes to America," he said, as if it were just around the corner, "the people's properties will thus be nationalized. Those who have invested money in Russia will find that our agreements hold good, and thus they will be in a more favorable position than the rest of their fellow capitalists."

. . . Trotsky readily agreed to supply the guards we required. I left him after an interview of about half an hour with the feeling that this was a man of remarkable, but imperious, character, with great ability and unflinching will, but a degree of fanaticism of which Lenin had given me no sign.

Chapter 5

Fords in His Future

The first shipload of Hammer's promised wheat ordered in October 1921 did not arrive in the Soviet Union until December of that year. There were extenuating circumstances, a frozen port at Petrograd, and rerouting to Reval (Tallinn), an old czarist naval port that had a rail connection from Estonia to Petrograd. The timing of the barter deal was not bad, however. The Ekaterinburg soviet's furs and hides had not been delivered to specified warehouses in Moscow until November. Examining them, Hammer asked the official in charge of their eventual shipment to America, "Why don't you also send some caviar? We haven't had any in my country for a long time. It should sell like hotcakes." The Russian was a little confused by "hotcakes," but he shrugged and agreed. As a fillip to the deal, he threw in a *ton* of prime caviar in fifty-pound kegs, each containing ten five-pound tins.

Unloading the chartered ship of its grain and reloading it with hides, furs, and caviar required Hammer to display all of his nimble-footedness and repeated showings of his credentials and his extraordinary agreement with Lenin. Reval was a crossroads of trade conspirators, smugglers, and gold dealers. Hammer's biggest obstacle turned out to be the Soviet Foreign Trade Office located there in the vortex. It had arranged for the purchase of a million pairs of surplus American Army boots. Their soles, supposedly capable of enduring Russian winters, had turned out to be made of compressed paper, not leather. The responsible officials, furious with Americans in general, gave young Hammer and his strange cargo clearance most grudgingly. But after its safe arrival in New York, the sales of the furs, hides, and caviar amply covered the cost of the first shipment of grain, plus the 5 percent commission on both ends of the trade.

If it was to be that simple, Hammer decided, he should return to the United States and arrange for additional deals with the manufacturers of machines and other products he knew the Russians needed, to be paid for by the export of commodities from the Soviet Union (the birth of today's U.S.-Soviet barter deals). Envious subsequent competitors in a dozen fields have groused that Hammer has a knack of expanding a one-inch opening into a replica of Mammoth Cave. He'd be the last person to find that an uncomplimentary assessment.

In the field of catalysis he set an enviable record on his previous trip to his homeland in November 1921, shortly after the signing of the asbestos concession, some twelve years before the United States diplomatic recognition of the Soviet Union and fifty years before the Nixon-Brezhnev Moscow summit. In essence, he brought together the Bolsheviks and one of their most emphatic foes, Henry Ford I. The one-inch opening in that case was an uncle, Alexander (Sasha) Gomberg, a former Russian millionaire then living in exile in Berlin. Sasha had owned a Ford agency in southern Russia before the Revolution—improbably enough. Though it seemed to the uncle highly unlikely that Ford would be interested in trading with a sworn enemy, he nevertheless wrote to the cantankerous billionaire and asked him to receive Armand. Ford replied that he would be most happy to do so. He even sent his famous production chief, Charles E. Sorensen, to the railroad station in Detroit to meet Hammer and drive him to Dearborn. He was taken to the office of W. J. Cameron, arch-conservative editor of Ford's fiery *Dearborn Independent* and fountainhead of Ford's crusade against Jewish bankers and Communists. Ford soon entered and came immediately to the point. He said he agreed that the Russian market would prove lucrative for his products but that he wouldn't send a nut or a bolt there until there was a change of government more to his ideological liking.

Ford's crisp manner did not invite responses, but the visitor who could have been his grandson spoke up and said, "Well, Mr. Ford, if you're waiting for a change of regime in Russia you won't do any business there for a long time."

Ford gave him a wintry look. "Why do you say that?" He was not accustomed to being contradicted or crossed.

Hammer told him of what he had seen of the Russian people, their zeal to make a go of their lives, their reverence for Lenin, who had given the workers ownership of the factories and the peasants the land they had hungered after for centuries and their stoic patience in the face of disaster. To his surprise, Ford became interested and invited him to remain for lunch. He even provided a revealing anecdote:

Seems that he had read about the bomb-throwing anarchists loose in the streets of Russia near the end of the czar's reign. One day he received a round package in the mail, littered with Russian stamps. Mrs. Ford and Edsel urged him to call the police immediately; it might be an "infernal machine." He did so, and with the Ford family standing at a safe distance the package was gingerly inspected by an expert from the Bomb Squad. He muttered that he didn't like the shape of it, but after pressing an ear to it for a time he reported that it was not ticking. However, he added, maybe it was the kind that didn't tick. He then asked Ford, "Have you a concrete cellar with strong walls?" Ford pointed the way downstairs at the Dearborn mansion and waited for the expert and the estate house to go up with a roar. The man came back upstairs with a sheepish grin. "It's all right, Mr. Ford. It's only a cake." It was a traditional *koolich*, the Easter cake. It had been sent to him by Uncle Sasha, the Ford dealer.

"And a mighty good cake it was," Ford concluded on the day of the nephew's visit. "I wouldn't share it with anyone. I used to take a big hunk with me to work every morning until it was finished."

At lunch, Ford frowned when his guest said that Russians were more interested in tractors than in automobiles.

"Tractors are all right," he said, "and I shall never rest until I have proved to the world that animal traction on a farm is out of date. But the automobile is progress. If Russia is to develop, it must have mechanical traction and, above all, cars."

"But the Russian roads are impossible."

"That's one of the great mistakes backward countries make," Ford said tartly. "Cars must come before roads. If you get the cars, the roads will follow automatically. That's been true in America. It must apply to Russia, also. What you must tell your Russian friends is that automobiles are not a luxury, but a means of service required by modern conditions."

Something was happening inside the host's inventive brain, Hammer sensed in an ensuing silence.

"How many tractors do they want?" Ford abruptly asked.

"Millions of them," Hammer enthused, then added more soberly, "if they can afford to pay for them."

42

"Ah, that's the trouble, Dr. Hammer," Ford said. "You know, we're losing money on every tractor we produce. When the plans for our tractor output were being made, my financial department told me that I'd lose money on every tractor until I was selling a thousand of them a day. We haven't reached that production yet, but we will, I reckon. In the meantime, well, I can afford to lose," one of the richest men in history mused.

After lunch, Ford took Hammer on a tour of his model mechanized farm. "This is what they ought to have in Russia," he said, scanning the farm with satisfaction. "If the Soviet state is as stable and powerful as you say it is, why can't they do it? You tell me they are trying to jump from the Middle Ages to the twentieth century in one leap. Well, there's no reason why they shouldn't, as far as I can see, if they are as good as you say they are."

This gave Hammer an opening he had been waiting for, phrasing it in his lively mind:

"Mr. Ford, you may not believe this, but in Russia they think you're one of the most wonderful people in America—you and Edison. Putting all questions of communism and capitalism aside, they know that you and Edison have done something here they want desperately to do in their country, and they're eager to learn how."

Hammer saw that he was on the right track.

"Would you be willing, if I could arrange it, to let some young Russians come here and learn your methods, and all about tractors and autos, so they can teach people when they return home?"

"I don't see why not," Ford said, as if he were author of the proposition.

Before he left Dearborn that day, Hammer had the old man's blessing as sole agent for Ford products in the Soviet Union. With Ford in the bag, other U.S. companies clamored to get aboard the Hammer bandwagon. In relatively short order, he was the exclusive agent in Russia for U.S. Rubber, Allis-Chalmers, the National Supply Company (oil-well equipment), Ingersoll-Rand, American Tool Works, U.S. Machinery, Underwood Typewriter, Parker Pen, and others of similar stature.

Hammer put his impressions of Ford on paper at an early opportunity as stated in his book:

It was most interesting to me to meet this simple-minded giant of American industry, after my conversations with Lenin and Trotsky. Henry Ford had more in common with the former than with the latter. Like Lenin, he

43

cared nothing for outward appearance or dress; like Lenin, he was human and friendly and shrewd; like Lenin, he had the prestige of success, and his wealth gave him power, as Lenin had power. What is more, and of this I am convinced, both men were honestly trying, according to their lights, to accomplish something which would benefit large numbers of their fellow-men. Fundamentally, both were interested in achievement. Both of them, Ford in his first little workshop and Lenin in Switzerland, were mocked as dreamers. Both had the strength of character to burn through to their goal. . . . As I talked with Ford, I could not but feel that compared to Lenin and Trotsky, he was no match for them in international affairs. They combined acute political statecraft with knowledge of history and peoples, and a profound insight into the principles of international policy. But there rang through every word Ford said something of the same quality of genuineness which had so impressed me in my talk with Lenin. Here, too, in much different circumstances, was a man who believed in humanity and progress.

Hammer did eminently well with Ford, as we shall see. But as early as the spring of 1923 he had enough prescience to realize that, out of pride and economic necessity, the Russians would want to build at home instead of importing from abroad.

With that in the back of his mind, young Armand retained a remarkable middleman between himself and the Dearborn billionaire—his father, Dr. Julius Hammer, who had been recently freed after serving his minimum sentence. Even Albany, no bedrock of socialism, agreed that Julius Hammer had been railroaded. Governor Al Smith of New York pardoned him with a written statement that he was convinced, after a thorough investigation, of the doctor's innocence. Twenty years later, Smith, along with former U.S. Ambassador to Germany James Gerard, took an active role in having Dr. Julius's medical license restored and his good name cleared by the New York Medical Board of Regents. (See Appendix B.)

With the help once more of Uncle Sasha, Hammer arranged for his father to meet Ford and suggest that the automotive titan start thinking about building a plant in Russia, to be manned by Russian workers and supervised by Ford foremen and other experts.

Ford listened attentively to the elder Hammer's proposal and promised to give the matter some thought, even some thought about shipping an entire plant to Russia. Some months later Armand's diligent employee, his father, visited Moscow at the son's invitation for the first time since he left Russia as an infant. Armand urged him to joggle Ford's memory. The following letter soon was mailed from the Moscow office of Armand's company, the Allied American Corporation, Kuznetski Most 4:

Mr. Henry Ford
Dearborn
Michigan (USA)

Dear Sir:

I arrived in Moscow on the 1st of May. As I intended to visit Rostov-on-Don I did not wish to write to you before.

I arrived yesterday from Rostov-on-Don. I am attaching importance to Rostov-on-Don for two reasons:

1) Because our best customer in Russia is the Governmental Institution for Foreign Trade of the Southeastern part of Russia, to whom the recent shipment of three hundred (300) tractors and accessories were sent, as well as a considerable number of touring cars;

2) Because it is the most suitable region, in my estimate, for establishing manufacturing plants for your products, as I mentioned to you, if you will kindly recall.

The head of that governmental institution and many others are firmly convinced of the superiority of the automobiles and tractors of your manufacture for Russian conditions and needs. Difficulties for large purchases of your products, however, are due to larger economic considerations. Under the present circumstances when reconstruction is making large forward strides, the demand on capital resources of the Nation exceed their ability to meet it. As a result, a policy was adopted and is strictly adhered to, namely, to diminish imports of machinery and to cultivate their construction in Russia.

Although there was an embargo placed on the import of automobiles and trucks, the production of these models by you on Russian territory, employing Russian materials and labor, would be highly welcomed. On the Fordson tractors no embargo was placed, private combines such as cooperative associations or individuals may continue buying them but the import of such by Governmental institutions with Government funds is discouraged as they wish to patronize and place a demand for their local productions of tractors cf Russian manufacture, for which purpose an appropriation was made of ten million gold roubles.

It is realised here by many that the supply of tractors as a result of such an appropriation would be inadequate, long in coming and may be very

45

expensive if at all practicable. However, the exigencies of the present situation are believed to dictate such a course.

I have spoken to some of the responsible members of the Government with reference to the subject of the manufacture of tractors in Russia or their import. The unanimous opinion was expressed that your construction of tractor building factories in Russia would be a great boon to the Nation and every assistance and opportunity would be granted to you to facilitate the profitable operation of same.

I was authorised to invite you to send a mission of your experts to look over suitable grounds and to work out desirable conditions for the consummation of this plan. Assurance was given to me by Citizens Piatakov, the Chairman of the Chief Concession Committee, Smolianinov, Director of the Council of Labor and Defence, and Frumkin, Acting Chief of the Government Foreign Trade Monopoly. The general outlook makes the success of such an enterprise definitely assured. The need for large numbers of tractors is most urgent; many tens of thousands would be required to take the place of the perished draught-animals.

Mr. Belinky, the Chief of the Trade Monopoly of the Southeast of Russia, assures me that to replace the draught-animals lost in that region alone would number conservatively between twenty and thirty thousand tractors and these are urgently needed at once. No efforts are being made to replace these lost animals. The land must wait untilled for the coming of the tractors. Besides, there are hundreds of thousands of acres of steppes with soil highly suitable for cultivation by tractors, which land has never been touched by human hand. A large sized factory would have its entire output absorbed for many years to come.

While a profitable enterprise, at the same time its benefits would be so vast because it would hasten greatly the reconstruction, not of Russia alone but of the whole of Europe and would help to replace the atmosphere and danger of strife and warfare by the peaceful pursuits of agriculture and industry. I fervently hope that you will see your way clear of fulfilling your intention to build a factory in Russia as you expressed to me in your interview. The plan that you mentioned, a complete unit of a plant, would be admirably suitable to Russian conditions. The Don Basin seems to abound in all the factors requisite for the efficient operation of such a plant.

With the clearing of the political horizon, with the future looming up more promising for Russia than ever, your undertaking now would be highly successful.

I will close this long letter for which I ask your kind forgiveness, reiterating the hope that you will send on your group of experts. I will be glad to be of every possible kind of service in this connection, such as procuring of visas, of comfortable quarters and travelling, and of expert assistance.

Yours very truly,
JULIUS HAMMER

JH:HR

P.S. The accompanying clipping from the "Economic Life" of June 1st, 1923, with its translation from the Russian, shows that the embargo is against the import of *all* automobiles.

J.H.

Ford's response was deliberate, to say the least. Armand was wrapping up his near decade in Russia when the motor mogul of Dearborn finally got around to signing an agreement to cooperate with the Russians in the building of a car- and truck-building complex on the Volga at Nizhniy-Novgorod, now Gorky. The date was May 31, 1929. Another three years passed before the Gaz-A (Model A) and Gaz-AA (standard two-and-a-half-ton Ford truck) began coming off the production lines. The actual deal was signed with Amtorg, which had taken over Armand Hammer's lucrative operations to a great degree. Ford received an order for $30 million worth of cars and spare parts for delivery over the next few years in compensation for his technical assistance, patents, and know-how. In addition, the Russians paid cash for the necessary machinery and equipment. The Russians carried out their part of the contract punctiliously.

Ford, in turn, guaranteed that the plant would produce at least 70,000 cars a year. Eventually, production reached 100,000 units a year, and old Henry, who had mistrusted bolshevism like pizen, was pleased with the deal. Incredibly, he had become a kind of godfather to the Soviet Union's industrial revolution.

Chapter 6

Death of a Friend

Hammer returned to Moscow early in 1922, took up residence in his palatial digs at the Sugar King's place, looked across the river at the Kremlin, and said to himself as uncounted generations of youthful conquerors before him had said, "I've got it made."

He was wrong. Russia had stumbled in the course of its attempt to skip all the way to the twentieth century. He assumed that the Russians he had ordered hired to work his asbestos concession at Alapayevsk were happy with the grain and other foods he had dispatched to them from America. He found out differently when frustrating things began to occur at his Lenin-approved asbestos bonanza. The workers were in a mood to shoot him and everybody else in charge.

"We promised them food," his anguished Russian manager told him as Hammer reached the bleak meeting place, one hundred miles north of Ekaterinburg, by troika. "The food has not come. They are hungry. They say we have tricked them. The position is dangerous. Threats have been made against me. A mob of hungry workingmen surrounded my house and I had to draw my revolver before they would leave. I've cabled a dozen times for explanations. There are no replies. Unless the food comes soon, some will die of starvation. I cannot answer for the consequences."

Appalled, Hammer sped to Ekaterinburg, where at least there were communication facilities. He learned there that the shipment of grain had arrived at Ekaterinburg some time before that in sealed cars from Petrograd, guarded by Trotsky's troops, and then had moved northward. Hammer and his manager, now accompanied by an official of the railroad administration, headed back toward Alapayevsk. About fifty miles later they found twenty-five cars, the first shipment, standing on a siding. The seals were unbroken and the guards reported that no person, however desperate with hunger, had tried to break in. It developed quickly that the station manager was the bottleneck. He told Hammer and the Russian railroad man that there was a bridge just ahead that could not stand the weight of a twenty-five-car freight.

"Why didn't you send them across it in small lots?" he was asked. He shrugged, but presently took Hammer's Russian manager aside and whispered, "You are a businessman. Give me five hundred poods of grain [about half a carload] and your cars will move." The manager relayed the message to Hammer. Hammer returned to Ekaterinburg and dispatched a wire to Lenin's office, and two things happened in quick succession: (1) the food train rolled into Alapayevsk, and (2) after a brief inquiry the stationmaster was shot.

With his asbestos concession under control, Hammer turned his attention toward his Ford interest. He made a swing through Kharkov and the Ukraine, Rostov and the potentially rich North Caucasian grain region, Baku with its burgeoning oil, and Tiflis, the old capital of Georgia. He returned to Moscow with his pockets filled with orders, mostly for tractors —hundreds of them. When the first shipment of fifty Fordsons was about to arrive in the spring of 1922 at Novorossiysk, Hammer went there with fifty young and old Russians who had been instructed in how to drive the exotic machines by a group of Ford mechanics on loan from Dearborn. Hammer and the Ford hands supervised the uncrating on the dock and the gassing and oiling. Then Hammer climbed aboard the first tractor and led the noisy parade into the city.

The apparition caused a panic. The people thought the tractors were U.S. or British tanks. Bells clamored, the Communist Guard was called out, the local soviet quickly convened to draw plans to meet the invaders. Then magically a great change. The word spread that these were friendly machines, soon to be owned by Russians. They would increase food production many times over. Fears gave way to tears. The governor of Novorossiysk emerged with a hastily constructed speech of welcome. After acknowledging it, Hammer signaled the column to move onward toward Rostov-on-the-Don, a bumpy hundred miles away. It stopped at every populated place along the road to demonstrate to marveling crowds the versatility of the tractors. Fields never broken except by man and beast were carved swiftly with long furrows. The tractors also obediently pumped water, sawed wood, pulled and lifted heavy loads, sent electricity surging into light bulbs.

In Rostov, where a demonstration area had been set aside in a midtown park, Hammer met and was impressed by the energetic young head of the local soviet, an intense Armenian named Anastas Mikoyan, destined to survive decades of purges and palace revolts and to become second only to Khrushchev in power before age dimmed his star. He and Hammer would meet again, a veritable lifetime later.

In the midst of these triumphs, Hammer was alerted that his chief benefactor, Lenin, was dying. Hammer followed the physical decline of his extraordinary patron through Lenin's chief physician, German brain specialist Professor Otfried Foerster, a fellow guest at the Sugar King's Palace. He recalls especially one report from the doctor: "He often says, 'I have so much to do, and the time is so short.'"

Lenin rallied remarkably in the late summer of 1922 and was able to resume work in the autumn. Professor Foerster's well-published departure from Moscow for a holiday in Germany was proof enough to most Russians that their leader was cured of his arteriosclerosis. He bolstered the folk belief by making several public speeches. It was during this period that Hammer had a second brief meeting with Lenin in his office in the Kremlin, described in Chapter 3.

But a grave stroke hit him at Christmastime, 1922. His right side was paralyzed. He was moved to Gorky, a dacha thirty miles from Moscow, once the estate of the multimillionaire textile tycoon and art patron Savva Morosov. It seemed a dismal choice. Morosov had committed suicide there in the belief that he was going mad. With a determination that spellbound Foerster and a succession of specialists brought in from several medical centers of the world, Lenin learned to speak again, conquering his aphasia like a learning child, with the patient tutelage of his wife, Krupskaya, and his sister, Maria Ulianova. His right hand was dead; so he learned to write with his left.

Through Foerster, he sent a message to Hammer that moved the American almost to tears. Lenin had said to the German, "Tell young Hammer I have not forgotten him and wish him well. If he has difficulties, tell him to be sure and let me know."

Incredibly, his condition improved so much during 1923 that in early December he attended a hunting party, sitting propped with cushions on a sleigh. At Christmastime he gave a large party for the children of the estate's employees and people from the nearby village, images of jolly old Father Frost, a gaily decorated tree, and toys enough to go around. He died on January 16, 1924. Professor Foerster, spent and stricken, awakened Hammer in the middle of the night to break the news.

Hammer wrote about Lenin's funeral in his book with the flair of a top journalist:

> A group of his nearest associates met the train bringing his coffin at a station on the outskirts of Moscow and carried it for five and a half miles through the streets on their shoulders, changing relays every half mile. An artillery gun carriage had been provided with six superb black horses. Lenin's friends waved it aside—they and they only should bear their leader's body.
>
> He was laid in state in the many-columned hall of the former Nobles' Club of Moscow, now the headquarters of the Union of Labor Federations. Here, as if sleeping, Lenin lay for seventy-two hours, with four motionless watchers standing at the corners of his couch. They were changed every quarter of an hour, so many and eager were those who wished to share that death watch. Meanwhile, in endless procession, day and night alike, the people of Moscow filed through the hall to pay their final tribute. Three-quarters of a million men, women and children formed that silent river, flowing through without a break.
>
> It was a period of intense cold, between thirty and forty below, Fahrenheit. The average time of waiting outside before one could enter the hall was five hours. The long lines extended for miles, moving forward at slow intervals. There were great wood fires burning every hundred metres and at night it was a weird and striking spectacle, the dark masses of people, whose breath rose up like a fog, the lurid flames and the drifting clouds of smoke. From villages fifty miles away came peasants afoot, to pay homage to the man who had given them the land for which their forebears had hungered for centuries. From the distant cities of Russia those in authority sped headlong in special trains, cursing each delay in fear they might not arrive in time. No King or Emperor or Pope ever received such a final homage.
>
> . . . The Mausoleum in Red Square, at the foot of the great red-brown walls of the Kremlin, was built in two and a half days, with constant shifts of workmen toiling day and night. On the morning of the funeral, Lenin's body, which was later embalmed by an elaborate process, was placed in the Mausoleum. On the top of this strange building, part Egyptian pyramid, part dream of Cubist architecture, there was a small gallery where Soviet leaders took their places as if on a rostrum. After Lenin's body had been borne to its last resting place by his dearest friends, the garrison of Moscow

and organized masses of workers marched through the Square in serried lines. I saw Trotsky, unquestioned head of the Red Army, standing in the little group atop the Mausoleum. As his legions roared salute, I saw his face light up with fierce pride. Here was a man who had given of his best to defend the Revolution, who had done more than any other to make the Red Army a victorious fighting force. Although devoid of the least trace of personal greed, Trotsky was a man consumed by ambition. He wanted always to play a big role, be a shining figure. But he lacked Lenin's selfless absorption in the Cause.

Lenin needs no praise from me. History will give him his place among the great of the world. I'm proud that I was able to talk with him, and that he took my hand in friendship.

. . . There was another man standing there. He made no speeches, received no salutes. He was quiet and unobtrusive, but his eyes were keen and watchful. His name was Joseph Djugashvili. He had taken the Bolshevik pseudonym of Stalin. . . .

Chapter 7

Invincible Victor Hammer

Mama Rose Hammer had something to do with the invasion of Bolshevik Russia by Victor Hammer, destined to become a world-famous art dealer. Mama Rose had a protective interest in the youngest of her three sons. She did not particularly admire the company the gregarious Princetonian was keeping. Nobody in Victor's effervescent circle, in which an impoverished Morton Downey was one of the leaders, looked to her very much like a promising pharmacist, doctor, Ford representative, or friend of Lenin and Trotsky. It was an arts-oriented set, and Victor was one of its young lions. On Armand's third business trip to the United States, in the summer of 1922, Mama Rose suggested that he take Victor back with him. Armand, by now the man of the house, agreed. Victor assented.

It turned out to be a boon for Hammers in general.

"I had wanted to be an actor," says connoisseur-raconteur Victor today. "I've always been a ham about performing. I started when I was five years old. I used to do an imitation of 'Mary Had a Little Lamb' in several dialects, with quick changes. I wasn't a good student during my year at Colgate or the year at Princeton, really. It meant more to me when I took an examination and won a scholarship to the American Academy of Dramatic Arts. That was in July 1922. I decided not to go back to Princeton, but Armand had an influence on me after our mother had had a talk with him. Armand said, 'We know you've got talent. We've been watching you since you were a little boy. But let's face facts. The chances of your becoming a success in the theater must be one in a thousand. You may have the dedication, talent, self-sacrifice, discipline, and so forth. But luck is the most important.' "

Armand successfully urged Victor to forget the Academy scholarship by dangling before him the prospect of attending a semester or two at the Moscow Art Theater. But it was a come-on.

"I'm not returning to Russia until October, but in the meantime you can be of some help to me," Armand said. "There's a school here in New York called the Miller School of Shorthand and Typewriting. In one month, if you work eight hours a day, they can teach you all you need to know. Then I'll make you my assistant." Victor went for it and in the fall of the year accompanied his brother to Moscow. He was all for rushing to the Moscow Art Theater, but Armand counseled patience. He must first learn the language, and toward that end Armand hired a Russian language teacher for him.

"A little fellow with a goatee," Victor still laughs. "He would show up every morning for two hours, give me the words and the pronunciations, and for the next two hours I'd study by myself. Then I'd leave the Sugar King's Palace and go sightseeing around town, using English or the little French and German I knew. The only headway I was making in Russian was with my seven-string guitar and the gypsy songs I memorized.

"Then I got a nice break. I had become friendly with a Russian businessman who was a brother of a friend of my mother. This fellow was a big success, which, in those days, meant he had to be doing something illegal. Sure enough, one day he confided to me that he was planning to leave the country. He was bribing his way out, he told me, and he almost had it made.

"So I made him a fair proposition. I said, 'Grisha, I have one request, and if you don't grant it I'm going to squeal on you. I want to meet a Russian girl, some girl who doesn't know a word of anything but Russian. I've got to learn this damned language, and soon.' He said fine, and off we went in his sleigh. We went to several addresses. Not one of the girls was home! I said, 'Grisha, you must have one more. If you don't lead me to her, you're not going to leave Russia.' He gave a big sigh and took me to the place of his current girl friend, to whom he was saying farewell that night.

"She was called the Black Panther of Moscow," Victor reminisces contentedly. "Georgian. Her name really was Hope—in Russian, Nadyezhda—and she was one of the most excitingly beautiful women I ever met. I made such fast progress with her, I mean in learning the language,

of course, that the poor little professor started referring to me as his prize
student.

"I was with her for maybe a year and a half before Armand found out.
'No kid brother of mine is going to marry a vampire,' he said and sent
me to London to work with Harry in our import-export business. . . . She
sure was a knockout."

Victor's enthusiasm for Armand, and his boundless sense of loyalty,
dates back to a time when he was eight or nine and Armand was a mature
twelve or thirteen, building flying machines that actually flew and radio
sets that miraculously crackled music and talk into earphones. No wish
of Armand was too much for Victor to attempt to fulfill, including giving
up his dream of acting. Victor even became an asbestos miner for a time.
There is a picture of him still extant which makes him look more like a
Russian peasant than a product of those two sophisticated New World
societies, Princeton and Colgate. He had been pressed into service in that
lunar-like crater on the earth's surface near Alapayevsk by Armand's
suggestion that he should know a little more about the first concession
ever extended by the Revolutionary government to a foreigner: Armand.
Victor was somewhat comforted during the latter stages of his first trip
to the mine, made aboard a sleigh pulled through what seemed to him
a forest alive with howling wolves, to find that his older brother could doze
off as if he were at home in his favorite bed. But he was not comforted
for very long. Suddenly, the horse veered to avoid a tree and spilled
Armand out into the snow. It was a tense minute or two before the driver
could control the animal and return to the scene of Armand's jettison.
Armand lay like a dead man awaiting interment in his furs. Victor rushed
tearfully to his side. Armand awakened and stretched and asked what the
commotion was all about. His nap had not been disturbed by his catapult.

And so Victor went to work on the least likely job of his life. His
Broadway friends had predicted many things that might happen to him,
but working in an asbestos mine in Alapayevsk was not one of them.
Victor's unflappable good nature somehow prevailed. Things could have
been worse: Armand might have gained his concession from a czar. Indeed, between the time Armand took over and his modern mining machinery arrived, there was little to distinguish the operation of the American brothers from the grim past. The doctor wrote in retrospect in his
book:

Never had I seen anything so primitive as the way this property was worked. The workers picked away at the ore with cumbersome hand drills, usually taking two or three days to bore a hole deep enough for a dynamite charge. After a blast, the fragments of ore were carried up the slopes in baskets on the men's backs to a terrace where they would then sit in rows with little hammers, chipping away the stone from the ore. When the ore was clean it was transported by peasant carts to the nearest railroad station, ten miles away. If the weather was bad enough to make the wagon trails impassable, the ore just piled up at the mine.

It was bad enough when we got there, but it had been much worse before the Revolution. Under the last czar, the workers were herded in filthy barracks like animals. They worked a twelve-hour day, six days a week, for an average wage of seven dollars a week. The foremen sometimes used whips to drive those human cattle to greater exertions. Cases of violent assault and even murder were not uncommon. On Sundays, everybody got drunk. That was the only relaxation.

The machinery that Armand had ordered months earlier began to trickle in. Mechanical crushers took over from the termite practices of old. The fusillade of platoons of compressed air drills, followed by dynamite detonations multiplied a hundredfold, could be heard for miles around. A narrow-gauge railroad was stretched along the ten miles over which men and women had struggled not unlike the builders of the pyramids. But the innovation that produced the most awe and respect was the bank of four-bladed automatic saws that reduced whole trees to planks in a couple of minutes. "Like a knife cuts butter," the Russians marveled. Some of the planks went into comfortable houses and barracks, a hospital, and several schools. Morale jumped, and so—by chance—did the value of the concession. In razing some of the old buildings it was discovered that they sat on top of some of the richest veins in the area. The mystery of this disappeared after a short investigation: In prewar days the mine had been a government property and under the tax conditions then in force should have been most profitable. But the operators of a privately owned mine in the same area arranged by bribery to forestall the exploitation of the government's best ore. Buildings were erected over one rich deposit after another. Other deposits were used as dump sites for waste stone, and thus hidden under tons of debris.

When it moved into high gear, the Hammer operation must have been startling to behold. Armand once wrote:

56

In addition to food and shelter, we provided clothing for our people—World War I American military surplus clothing. It was comical, really. There in the heart of Soviet Russia a visitor might find a driller in a U.S. Marine Corps full dress uniform. Another might be wearing a snappy American officer's tunic above his baggy peasant breeches and felt boots. Mothers cut up Doughboy uniforms and made them into clothes for the children. Most of the material wouldn't have been considered first quality in the U.S., but it made a tremendous impression in Alapayevsk. Everybody came to the conclusion that the Americans must have the only army in the world made up exclusively of millionaires.

There is no proof that Victor wound up in General Pershing's pants. He was content, as always, to be of some service to Armand.

Chapter 8

The Pencil — Mightier Than the Sword

With Lenin in his mausoleum, apparently preserved for posterity, and Stalin consolidating the naked power that Lenin never thought he warranted, Armand Hammer continued to prosper in the land his impecunious grandfather had left. He had bathed in the glow of his friendship with Lenin. Stalin was much less accessible. But Hammer's Allied American Corporation, as his company was now called, continued to flourish. It was the pipeline connecting over three dozen American companies confidently doing business with a sprawled and still undeveloped land that would not gain diplomatic recognition from Washington for a decade to come. Hammer's asbestos concession was finally making money, after its product was hampered by a world surplus. By now he was involved in the fur business, and his fur-gathering stations dotted the remotest reaches of the Soviet Union. His export-import business ballooned to such an extent that he opened branches in London and Berlin, with a head office in New York. He even bought a bank in Reval, Estonia, and put Uncle Sasha in charge. Bales of rubles piled up in his Moscow bank accounts. (He was the proud holder of a bankbook that testified to the fact that he was the first depositor in the Soviet State Bank.) Government law placed only two restraints on his burgeoning wealth: (1) he was not permitted to purchase Soviet real estate, and (2) the law forbade him to convert his rubles into dollars except once a year, when, after verification of his balance sheet, he could export his profits.

But these things were of small concern. Everything he touched turned to gold. Every doorknob turned. When it appeared that he would be forbidden to exhibit his Ford line at the Agricultural Exposition of 1923, because of a new and virulent anti-Bolshevik and anti-Semitic attack by the *Dearborn Independent,* Hammer had the guts to go to the top Bolshevik Jew, Leon Trotsky. Trotsky ordered the embargoed Fords released and put on display. Still the top military man in the country, Trotsky issued what amounted to a communiqué stating that regardless of Henry Ford's attitudes, no true Marxist would allow sentiment to interfere with business.

Hammer's business and social obligations increased with his wealth and prestige as a master salesman. To accommodate his escalating list of clients and guests, he moved out of the Sugar King's Palace and, dipping into his store of rubles, took a lease on an empty twenty-four room Moscow townhouse at Sadovaya-Samotechnaya 14. It had been built by a wealthy textile man in the long ago of czarist power. Its last previous occupant before Hammer rented it and began to evict its dirt and ghosts had been Colonel John Haskell, of Herbert Hoover's American Relief Administration, which had greatly supplemented Armand's earlier grain shipment to Russia and saved ten million Russian lives.

In time, with the notable help of the artistic Victor, the Brown House, as the Americans called it, became an unofficial U.S. embassy. The Hammers, soon increased by the arrivals of family members from New York, played hosts to the likes of Mary Pickford, Douglas Fairbanks, Averell Harriman—many years later the U.S. ambassador to the Soviet Union—junketing members of Congress, and visitors as distinguished and varied as Will Rogers and John Dewey. Dewey, like the others, was struck by the boardinghouse informality of the increasingly ornate pleasure dome. One morning he appeared in the dining room for an early breakfast to find he had been beaten there by Mama Rose Hammer, whose idea of the Breakfast of Champions differed from his. Mama Rose was spooning herself some of the caviar Armand always kept in view and washing it down with delicate glass thimbles of what looked like water.

"May I ask what you are drinking?" the father of U.S. progressive education asked in his courtly manner.

"Vodka," Mama Rose said, surprised that he should ask.

"Vodka? For breakfast?"

"Sure," she said pleasantly. "It's made from cereals, isn't it?"

A cloud that spread over the rousingly successful Hammer enterprises gathered all but imperceptibly.

First, a series of minor complaints from a state trading department named Gostorg. The doctor characteristically went to see its director, one Kagan. Kagan kept him waiting in an anteroom for an hour, in contrast to the courtesies that Lenin, Trotsky, and many others had shown him in the past. When Hammer finally entered, accompanied by the business manager whose job it was to handle complaints such as had been lodged, Kagan went into a long monologue on how difficult it was to obtain needed articles from abroad.

"My father-in-law is a doctor," he said, "but he can't get rubber gloves for operating. Can you have a few pairs brought in?"

"Of course," Hammer said. "We'll be happy to oblige you."

Then Kagan said quite boldly that perhaps Hammer would have no more trouble with Gostorg if he showed himself to be "a little more accommodating." It smelled like graft. Hammer had the presence of mind to pretend that he did not know what Kagan was insinuating. It was just as well he did. Shortly thereafter, the GPU (secret police) arrested Kagan. It found 100,000 British pounds hidden in his apartment. He had had the power to charter freight cars for the transport of goods. He had run a regular business of moving goods for private speculators at a time when transporation was urgently needed to bring food supplies to the people. He had made plans to "visit" Germany as a purchasing agent for Gostorg, and there he would have defected and lived happily ever after. He was tried for treason, under the article of the Soviet penal code which concerns abuse of position for personal profit by state officials, and condemned to be shot. He missed the firing squad because his wife was permitted to see him in prison. She (like Frau Goering years later) slipped him a poison capsule.

There seemed to be other attempts that smacked of luring Hammer into a position that Soviet authorities could declare culpable. One was an attractive-sounding plan by an English-speaking young Russian to join him in a group bent on building new housing and restoring old dwellings —a chance to use up some of his fortune in rubles. Hammer backed off by instinct, and the promoters went to prison.

There was no mistaking the message Hammer received in 1924 from Leonid Krassin, chief of the Foreign Trade Monopoly Department. He remembers it letter-perfect:

"Perhaps of all the Bolshevik leaders Krassin looked least like a revolutionary. He had the pale, rather stern face and assured manner of a big business executive abroad. Prior to the war he had, in fact, held an important position in the German electric firm of Siemens-Schukert, who paid him what was an enormous salary for prewar Europe. Despite ridiculous stories abroad about Krassin's personal wealth, he died penniless and his wife was given a pension by the state. For years before the Revolution he contributed all of his salary, save bare living expenses, to the Bolshevik party, of which he was an old and trusted member."

Then the crusher.

"He explained to me, cordially but quite firmly, that the development of Soviet trade abroad through their own organizations, such as Arcos and the newly formed Amtorg, made it henceforth undesirable to do business through foreigners. That did not mean, however, he added, that the Soviet authorities were blind to the great service we had been able to render in building up Russian-American trade during the difficult period of organization, and he expressed the hope that we could find other, but no less profitable, fields of enterprise in Russia."

It did not seem possible to Hammer.

"But there are so many things pending," he said. "For example, we've been approached by an English shipbuilding corporation with a view to the sale of shipping to the Soviets."

Krassin was momentarily attracted. Then he shook his head and frowned.

"No," he said. "We hope to build our own ships at home. The yards are being reorganized and we expect to produce what we need more cheaply than the English will sell. Don't you see, Dr. Hammer, that what is needed in this country is industrial production? Why don't you interest yourselves in industry? There are many articles which we have to import from abroad that ought to be produced here."

There went thirty-eight productive contracts—Ford, Allis-Chalmers, Underwood, etc., etc., etc.—up in smoke.

Hammer might have closed his operations then and there and returned home without ever dipping into the realm of Romanoff art if it had not been for a purely accidental stroke of luck. While he was pondering whether he could or wanted to stay in Russia and buck the backwardness and bureaucracy, he dropped by a stationery store to buy a pencil. The salesman showed him a German-made pencil whose counterpart in the United States cost two or three cents. The price was fifty kopeks, twenty-six cents.

"Sorry, I want an indelible pencil," Hammer said.

That didn't sit well with the salesman. But he relented. "As you are a foreigner, I'll let you have one," he said. "But our stock is so limited that as a rule we sell them only to regular customers who buy paper and copybooks as well."

Hammer bought the indelible for two rubles—one dollar.

He parlayed it into millions of dollars. He did not buy a pad that day, but the pencil turned out to be the pad that launched him to assorted new and rewarding careers.

He went back to Krassin.

"Is it true that your government has set itself the goal that every Soviet citizen must learn to read and write?" he asked the commissar.

"Of course. We consider it one of our basic tasks."

"In that case," Hammer said, "I'd like to obtain a license for the production of pencils."

It was done, but in the maddeningly lethargic manner he had come to recognize as routine. There was the question of what to do about the state pencil factory, which, though launched with high hopes and heady speeches, had produced nothing that could write like the pencils the Russians had been importing from Germany's great Faber plant for generations. Someone had said of the Russian-made pencil that it was good only for writing on rocks. It ripped holes as it moved across a page. There was also the little matter of putting up $50,000 in cash as a guarantee that Hammer would begin production within twelve months after signing the contract and deliver $1 million worth of pencils in the first operating year. Beyond that, there were attacks on "foreign capitalists who try to exploit Russia's wealth," concocted by officials of the state pencil plant. But in October, Maxim Litvinov signed the agreement for the Commissariat of Foreign Affairs.

That did it, except for one thing: Armand Hammer did not know how to make a pencil. His strength, as always, was that he knew where the people who did know lived.

He took the first train to Nuremberg.

Chapter 9

Early Raids on Nuremberg and Birmingham

Armand Hammer was about as welcome as a plague when he popped into Nuremberg, soon to become a mecca of Hitler's sinister dream of a thousand-year reich. In Hammer's case, ideology and ethnic background had nothing to do with the inhospitality. He was there, quite frankly, to proselytize a cadre of professional pencil masters. He had gone to the right place for that. The Faber pencil company was founded by Kaspar Faber in 1761, some fifteen years before the single-minded visitor's country was born. The founder's great-grandson, Johann Lothar von Faber (1817–1896), made the firm world-famous by spreading outlets to New York, Paris, London, Berlin, and elsewhere. Another of his coups was a contract with the Russian imperial family for control of all graphite wrung from the czars' Siberian labor-camp mines. A renegade great-grandson, risking the close-knit family's anathema, went to the United States and opened the Eberhard Faber plant there during the first administration of Abraham Lincoln.

Suffice it to say that the parent company, A. W. Faber, had a virtual monopoly on the world's pencil business when Hammer checked into town with the intention of breaking up the cartel. The family literally owned the picturesque town of Fürth and dominated the affairs of nearby Nuremberg. Its commands easily superseded those issued by any elected official, the police, those in charge of public utilities, and others ostensibly official. The Faber hierarchy had ruled years before that there must be no rail connection between Nuremberg and Fürth, not even a trolley car, because it might bring in "undesirables" who possibly might alert the laborers and foremen of the house of Faber that certain social reforms had made things better in the outside world. The suspicion of strangers in town was equaled only by the suspicion of actual Faber employees. As was to be the case in the creation of the American atomic bomb many years later, only the most trusted members of the ruling family and the top Faber executives were privy to knowledge of the entire process of making one of the most familiar utensils on earth, the lead pencil. It was like trying to pirate the secret recipe for Coca-Cola or Angostura Bitters.

Hammer got a break after a week or two of isolation. Through a letter of introduction to a local bank, and some private investigating, he met a disgruntled Faber pencil master named George Baier. Seems that Baier, when younger and adventurous, had announced he planned to accept an attractive offer to build a pencil factory in Russia. He left Fürth, treated as if he were a carrier of the plague, took up residence in Russia, and was caught there in the grip of World War I. The Russians interned him for a time as a German alien, then released him and told him he was free to return to his native Fürth.

But such was the power of Faber, even in the midst of war, that he was not permitted to return to Germany. So he married a Russian girl and, at the end of hostilities, was allowed to return home. He was blackballed in Fürth for a time but finally was grudgingly allowed to return to his old job. Promotions thereafter were few and far between. He had committed the crime of letting Faber down.

Baier told Hammer of a Faber foreman with twenty-five years of service who accepted an offer to work in a newly opened South American pencil factory but was actually forbidden to leave Germany by the Nuremberg police. He was confined to Nuremberg at the company's demand for ten years, unable to find work in the only trade he knew.

Hammer persuaded Baier to spirit him into the pencil fortress. The American found the morale very low. He knew he had his needed manpower. He hired Baier at a salary of $10,000 a year—Faber was paying the man $200 a month.* Through him Hammer arranged to acquire machinery, raw materials, and a select cadre of other masters willing to make the great break and move to Moscow. Higher wages and generous bonuses swung the deal for them as well.

That much attended to, Hammer moved on to Birmingham, England, to set up a similar nucleus of a steel pen-point division of the future

*Hammer agreed to pay him an additional bonus of a few cents on each gross of pencils, which amounted to several times his salary.

Moscow pencil plant. It seemed an unnecessary imposition on him, but the Russians had insisted that this be part of the concession. He found in Birmingham almost the same tyranny imposed by Faber. It was a closed industry, with most of its workers trained from childhood under semifeudal conditions. But Hammer uncovered another rebellious master who, in turn, rounded up for him a group of young men who had returned from World War I to find only the disheartening old grind of their fathers and grandfathers before them.

Hammer returned to Moscow to choose a factory site and was immediately reminded of how greatly things had changed since his golden years of patronage under Lenin. Two or three years earlier he could have had his choice of locations and for what amounted to token rent. Now the progress of the New Economic Policy and the stabilization of the ruble on a gold basis had eliminated such opportunities and bargains. After a lengthy search, he concluded that the only solution to his problem was to locate his plant elsewhere in Russia. Then, in the nick of time, he heard of an abandoned soap factory on the outskirts of the city on the banks of the Moscow River. The plant had been skeletonized, but what was left of it sat on a square mile of land—space enough for the cottages, schools, churches, clinics, gardens, and recreational facilities he proposed to build for the immigrant specialists and their families. There was also room to expand the future plant, once the original structures had been repaired. That latter became a massive endeavor involving a thousand men, building new walls, reroofing, plastering, painting, and the installation of a modern steam-heating plant to replace the heating system of old.

The pencil masters and their families were sprung from their cloistered life in Nuremberg and Fürth on the pretense that they were taking vacations in Finland. Hammer had Russian visas waiting for them in Helsinki. The machinery left Germany almost as surreptitiously. At Baier's suggestion and Hammer's insistence, it was sent to Berlin from its point of manufacture with the understanding, by the manufacturers, that a new pencil factory would be built there. Suspicions about its eventual destination were not aroused, even though Hammer requested that all of it be delivered to Berlin disassembled and that the companies concerned with making the machinery assign an expert to the task of reassembling the myriad parts. Once arrived in Berlin, each bit was numbered, then shipped to Moscow. The experts went along to see to it that every part was fitted and bolted in its proper place. Hammer had seen countless millions of dollars' worth of fine foreign machinery ruined by improperly trained or indifferent Russian workers.

Pencil and pen production began months ahead of the allotted date in the contract, to the amazement of the concessions committee and the still struggling state-owned plant.

In an interim report on what was to become one of the world's largest pencil factories, Dr. Hammer wrote in his book:

> A manufacturer's problem in Soviet Russia is not, as in America, principally one of sales, but almost wholly one of production. Production in Russia, on the other hand, is more difficult. It is not always easy to obtain raw materials, especially if, as was the case with us when we began work in Moscow, most materials had to be brought in from outside of Russia. Efficient labor, too, is scarce and its discipline apt to be slack. From the outset, therefore, I found myself up against the problem of producing more and more pencils to meet the demand. Beginning with one shift I soon found it necessary to employ two, and in some departments, three. It was a time of great stress and effort but we steadily forced production upwards. During the first year, instead of $1,000,000 worth of pencils we were pledged by our concession agreement to produce, we managed to turn out $2,500,000 worth. In the second year we increased this to $4,000,000. In the first year we cut the retail price of first quality pencils from 50 cents to five. Imported pencils were henceforth forbidden, which gave us a further stimulus. We were enjoying a virtual monopoly. The greater part of our output was taken by State organizations and co-operatives but we were not precluded from doing business with private dealers.

Hammer increased production by introducing piecework, American style, a startling innovation in the Soviet Union at that time. It was at first difficult for the slow and listless workers—who were driving their German and British overseers to distraction—to comprehend this alien creed that stated, in effect, "More output, more income." Hammer asked Victor to go on the production lines and establish the best rate of production for each operation in order to set a price for piecework. Victor still winces about it:

"They accused me of never taking a coffee or tea break," he says indignantly. "They said I never even went to the bathroom. It was terrible, but they got the idea."

Eventually, wages at the Hammer plant edged past those in Fürth and Birmingham and the word inevitably spread through Moscow and, indeed, the Soviet Union. The company was besieged with tens of thousands of job applications. At least one Communist con man waxed rich selling phony certificates for "jobs" at Hammer's, until the police closed in on him. Obviously, everybody in Russia wanted to write, and there was only one place to obtain the wherewithal, Hammer's. By 1926, production was reaching near the 100-million-pencils-a-year mark; steel pens jumped from 10 million in 1925 to 95 million one year later. Hammer's could not not only take care of Russia's voracious needs, but export about 20 percent of its production to England, Turkey, China, Persia, and a dozen other countries.

The remarkable success of the operation produced various reactions. One young woman who needed Hammer's superior wages to support herself and her children carried her case for employment all the way to Mikhail Ivanovich Kalinin, first president of the Supreme Council of the Soviet Union, and Hammer was happy to give her a place. Many trade-union delegations visited the plant to marvel at its efficiency and to congratulate Hammer on how well his company treated the workers. But there were occasional blasts in the local press against Hammer the capitalist and the New Economic Policy (NEP).

Hammer knew that, slowly but surely, he was being forced out of his happy hunting grounds. He was comforted to know he still had an ace in the hole. A diamond-studded ace.

Chapter 10

El Dorado, Russian Style

One bone-chilling Sunday in the winter of 1922–1923, Armand and Victor visited the Moscow Flea Market, an exotic junkyard where Muscovites browsed for bargains and for sociability's sake. It was, if anything, a seedier version of the ragamuffin flea and thieves' markets of Paris, London, and Madrid. But here and there among the piles of cast-off belongings of poorly clad and shivering vendors might be found some valuable relic of a gentler age, an age that would never return.

An exquisite procelain plate caught the Hammers' eyes. A few rubles made it their property.

"That was the spark," Victor will say, his merry eyes looking back over half a century of collecting, buying and selling countless millions of dollars' worth of objects of art. The plate was of royal lineage. It had been wrought in some dead czar's private porcelain works, a plant commissioned by Elizabeth, the daughter of Peter the Great, and greatly expanded by Catherine the Great in 1744. Intrigued by the fragile dish that had somehow survived wars and want, Victor began to haunt state museums and libraries and sit at the feet of dispossessed art dealers and old buffs. He took a crash course in the wonders of czarist art.

He learned that before Catherine the Great, the imperial family had for many years bought their porcelains mainly from the royal works of Germany's Meissen and, later, France's Sèvres. More than national pride was involved in Catherine's determination to expand and improve Elizabeth's dream. Catherine sometimes entertained as many as three thousand guests for dinner. Her crown and monogram were on every piece of china and glassware used in her castles, as were the insignia of the czars who followed.

Victor, the busy young businessman, became a modest and increasingly knowledgeable collector with the help of his brother's interest, indulgence, and bankroll.

"I moved on from china and porcelain figurines to ikons," he likes to recall of those adventurous days when the Soviet Union was stirring like a great bear taking leave of hibernation. "Armand encouraged me, to say the least. I was never the moneymaker. I was the money spender. Hunting antique ikons was something like exploring. A Russian regarded his ikon as a religious object, not a work of art. Let's say your name was Michael and you inherited your grandfather's ikon honoring St. John. So you'd take it down the street to the village painter and he'd paint over St. John and change the figure to St. Michael. Same with oil paintings. I had a friend, a composer, who knew these tricks far better than I did. He taught me how to clean old ikons and paintings and find out what was on the bottom of the layers that had been added through the decades or centuries. I found some wonderful works of art hidden beneath commonplace exteriors. I found fifteenth- and sixteenth-century ikons, beautiful things, buried under a nineteenth-century alteration. It became more than a hobby with me; it developed into a passion. I thought of us as being dropped in the center of countless treasures, an untouched gold field. Believe me, it was most exciting. Armand was a great help. He had signed a contract with the Parker Pen people to sell their pens in Russia, and deliveries were just beginning to reach us. Remember those big, fat orange-red pens with the black top? Well, any Russian who could afford one wore it in his outside coat pocket, like a Legion of Honor. The pens opened doors for me. There were a number of Moscow art dealers who had been forced to shut down their galleries and find work in government offices. I gave them free Parkers, and they treated me like a king. They taught me what to buy, how to buy it, and how to clean it."

Bit by bit, piece by piece, the Brown House began to take on a luster it had not known since before the Revolution. It was transfigured into a lived-in museum, frequently open to passing art lovers, a place where the Hammers could and did entertain visitors from abroad and a broad spectrum of Communist officials and well-known figures in the Russian theater and ballet. And relatives and a stream of friends of relatives.

In due course, it housed a flabbergasting variety of treasures, some of them acquired by sheer and happy accident. For example, one day the brothers were lunching at a small hotel in Petrograd when Victor, noticing the translucent glow of a plate that had been set before him, turned it over and started with surprise. It had been fashioned by the imperial porcelain factory a full century before! It bore the crest of Nicholas I and the date 1825. The brothers asked the manager how he had come by dishes such as that. The manager shrugged and said that all he knew about it was that it—and others like it—had come from "the palace," and he didn't like such ware. "The dishwashers complain they break too easy," he said, not knowing he was committing a sacrilege.

The Hammers made him a proposition: they would take all that breakable czarist china off his hands and replace it with thick, modern tableware that could stand up under the ministrations of the dishwashers.

The manager was delighted.

On another occasion, while rummaging through the basements of the Winter Palace in Leningrad, Victor came upon a remarkable scene of desecration. A group of workers was ripping apart a huge mound of richly brocaded priestly capes and chasubles, stripping them of their gold and silver threading and throwing away the remainder of the superbly woven and decorated vestments. Victor alerted Armand in Moscow, and Armand came up with an idea: Victor should offer whoever was in charge to buy the lot for a sum equal to the amount of gold and silver that might be "mined" from the hallowed robes. The shredding stopped while the offer was bucked up to Antiquariat, the Soviet clearinghouse for treasures considered expendable. Armand took over at that point and bought the lot for the equivalent of $60,000. The closets and storage rooms of the Brown House assumed the glitter of a czar's private chapel.

There was added to the growing collection a few hundred glasses from a wine service with the royal emblem, twin-headed eagles in gold and enamel between two delicate layers of glass, an art that had died with its creator at the end of the nineteenth century. The brothers mourned their inability to buy more of this glassware. But it had been largely destroyed by time and temperament. Russians of the noble class had for generations considered it proper, if not obligatory, to smash their glasses after offering a toast. The legend was that there was a better chance of a toast's coming true if no one else could drink from the glass with which it was proposed. In the more excessive occasions the vandalism extended to the demolishment of dishes, wall mirrors, and precious chandeliers. The brothers sighed particularly over being able to acquire only a fraction of the fabled Bird Set of Nicholas II, originally 6,000 pieces of china each bearing three different hand-painted bird motifs, the creation of some of the country's finest artists over a twelve-year period.

The brothers had to be satisfied with a service for eighteen, all that survived the wanton destruction of old.* But hardly a day passed that did not see the arrival at the Brown House of some Romanoff rarity, as Victor scrounged and Armand paid. A dusty imperial tapestry cumbersome enough to need four men to carry it might be followed by the arrival, in Victor's coat pocket, of Nicholas II's jade snuffbox set in diamonds.

But this was only the beginning. . . .

*Sold years later by the Hammer Galleries to the renowned connoisseur Chester Beatty for a czar's ransom.

•

Chapter 11

Moscow and Paris
to Gimbels

The Hammers' horizons in the world of art were largely limited originally to furnishing the Brown House with whatever they and their agile Russian agents could rake from the rubble of the Romanoffs. They wanted to make their Moscow residence a showplace for their business associates and Russian friends. They did not consciously anticipate a day when there would be Hammer Galleries. Armand, especially, entertained no such ambition. He was interested in more tangible methods of turning a profit, and he had amply proved that he could do so in a broad spectrum of ways. His exports to the United States and Europe would attest to that. He shipped out sable, mink, beaver, and squirrel pelts; goatskins, pigskins, and calfskins; barrels of caviar and tens of thousands of long tons of lumber. And, to an American sausage-making firm named Berth-Levi, he uncoiled literally miles of Russian sheep intestines—a sausage skin long since replaced, for better or worse, by delicious nonfattening plastic. So who needed to make a ruble or a buck out of a dead empress's diamond-studded Easter eggs?*

If there was a time and place when the doctor's indifference to art underwent an abrupt reappraisal, and he began his long journey toward the summit of the art world, it could have been the night a frustrated American antique dealer named E. Sakho came to dinner at the Brown House. They had met that afternoon at Hammer's office. The visitor had a letter of introduction from a mutual friend and a long sad story: He could make no deals with the stubborn Russians. He had been in Moscow

*Thirteen of these fabulous Easter eggs were later sold by the Hammer Galleries to collectors such as Marjorie Merriweather Post, Mrs. John L. Pratt, and others, for from $50,000 to $100,000 each.

and elsewhere for three long weeks, rebuffed by bureaucrats and exorbitant price tags on objects that piqued his interest. Dr. Hammer clucked sympathetically and extended the dinner invitation.

The moment Sakho stepped inside the Brown House his eyes appeared to be on the verge of popping out.

"My God!" he cried, looking around the mansion. In fact, that was about all he said for the first hour of his stay, except "What did you pay for this? And what did that cost you?" Victor had all the answers. After each of them, the visitor would sigh or cry, "My God!" He returned to the finite later that night.

"If you can ship these things out of the country, I'll make you full partners in my business," he said.

"I haven't given it much thought," the doctor said, picking up the spoor of new income. "I'll take it up with the government." He did just that the next morning and got his usual fast answer: The Hammers could ship all their booty to America after payment of a 15 percent export tax, with the exception of such items as the Soviet art commissar wished to repurchase and retain in the U.S.S.R. for their museums. The doctor accepted Sakho's offer of a full partnership in his business and put Victor in charge of the Hammer interests.

The commissar and his men were regular callers at the Brown House after that. "Taking inventory," they explained. The brothers gathered the impression that they were going to be robbed, somehow, of all the rare bargains they had amassed. Under Stalin, the attitude of the government was undergoing sharp change in respect to the value of the baubles left behind by a demolished dynasty. Moscow commission stores in certain cases would not accept rubles any longer in payment for antiques and other works of art. In the case of the Hammers they demanded American dollars. The Hammers had plenty of them and their collecting continued without a pause. Their biggest competitors were the more affluent embassies, not the few representatives of foreign galleries who were able to thread their ways through the wilderness of bureaucracy. The two most determined collectors among the diplomats in residence were the ambassadors extraordinary and ministers plenipotentiary of Germany and France. But they were no match for the Hammers, who had cagily put together a team of scouts that would know within minutes if something interesting had been delivered to a commission store for sale. Victor would then drop whatever he was doing and dash off to the store at the fastest speed permissible and pay for it in cash. Count Brockdorf von Rantzau, the German ambassador, was so enraged that he made a formal protest to the Kremlin, complaining that nearly every time he or his aides tried to buy Russian art objects they found that "a certain Mr. Hammer" had been there earlier and the pieces were labeled "Sold."

There were other complaints against the Hammers, particularly the doctor, about his exploitation of the workers at the Alapayevsk asbestos works and the large profits of the A. Hammer pencil plants. But old friends tried to reassure him that nothing really had changed since the days of his fine rapport with Lenin. One night during a dinner at the Brown House given in honor of Minister of Culture A.V. Lunacharsky, the minister whispered to his host, "I have been following the attacks on you in the newspapers. Don't pay any attention to them. You know, some of the comrades have to let off steam periodically, and since they haven't any local capitalists to train their guns on, you have to be the goat. Haven't you seen the way the newspapers have been attacking *me?* Even we Bolshevik ministers get plenty of abuse in our press."

The doctor diagnosed this as a hint. He dropped the price of his pencils and other products of his five factories: pens, metal and celluloid products, and allied products. And, as a shrewd businessman, he began preparing for his retreat from Moscow. He did better than Napoleon, who had been there for a much briefer period.

The doctor had a friend at court, the remarkable Lev Borisovich Kamenev, whose sorry fate it was to be shot by Stalin's GPU in the bloody purges of 1936. But at the end of 1929, when Hammer was working out the logistics and economics of leaving Russia, Kamenev was president of the Main Concession Committee. No mean interpreter of handwriting on walls, Hammer approached the commissar with a view to obtaining the best possible sale of his pencil and other properties. He had great trust in Kamenev as well as admiration for what this son of a Jewish engineer had stoically endured through the turbulent years under the czar and the Bolshevik leaders who followed.

Kamenev had the authority to strip Hammer of just about everything the American had, without risk of hue or cry. Diplomatic relations between Russia and the United States were still more than three years away. Instead, in the name of his government, he bought out Hammer's pencil plants and certain other holdings for what was called a "fair price" of several million dollars. Each party compromised. Hammer accepted part cash and the balance in foreign trade bank notes to be paid over a period of thirty-six months. Kamenev's Concession Committee gave Hammer permission to leave Russia with "all household effects." That meant the unshipped treasures of the Brown House, which by then had overflowed into several warehouses because of bureaucratic delays in obtaining export approval from the museum officials and the Foreign Trade Department.

There were other "household effects" to take with him when he left: his young Russian wife, their infant son, the child's Russian nanny, and the expensive furnishings of a second residence he had ordered built— behind a high fence—not far from the Brown House.

The first Mrs. Hammer—there have been two more in the intervening years—must have been the doctor's major acquisition at the beginning of his art-collecting career in the middle 1920s. He has described her as a tanned beauty "with sparkling light blue eyes." She had been the Baroness Olga von Root, daughter of a czarist general whose forebears were prose-lyted from Germany by Peter the Great to add style and spine to the Russian military. (On her mother's side Olga was a descendant of the famous Polish General Kosciusko, who had come to the aid of George Washington in 1776.) As befitted most young titled children and young ladies of her time, she studied voice at Petrograd's Smolny Institute, never dreaming that a day would come when war and revolution would blow her world apart, and her throaty gypsy songs would save her life and the lives of her family.

The future Mrs. Hammer had a life that could have served as a film scenario for Garbo or Dietrich. The Bolshevik Revolution split the family. The baron, loyal to the dethroned czar, commanded White Russian units in the scattered civil war that followed. While in the field he moved his family out of Moscow to Kiev. Kiev was an unlikely city for von Root to have left his family for safekeeping. Control of it changed hands many times in the bloody swirl of revolution, and its people were sorely dis-tressed. Olga sang her gypsy laments in smoky cabarets and dumps to eke out enough to support her mother and a young sister and brother. One grim day she was rounded up with other suspected White Russian sympa-thizers, jailed, and peremptorily ordered to be executed by a Bolshevik firing squad. She was actually in line and in earshot of the murders of other suspects when she was pulled out of her position of doom by a Red colonel who had heard her sing.

The colonel took her back to the battered house where she and her family were living, only to find the place in utter pandemonium. A squad of Bolshevik soldiers had pounced on the premises scarcely minutes before to search it and question its occupants. Olga's mother had made a calamitous mistake. She had assumed, the times being what they were, that the raid on the household meant that Kiev had undergone another change of hands; that these surly searchers were from the ranks of the White Russian forces. So she had dug out and proudly displayed a studio photograph of the proud baron in his full dress uniform glittering with czarist decorations! The Red troops arrested them on the spot and were in the process of hauling them tearfully off to prison, and probably worse, when Olga appeared with her special savior. The colonel barked an order and dismissed the search party, in all probability saving the lives of the rest of the von Roots.

Through him, Olga was able to send an important bit of information to her father on the other side of the loose lines: He would be granted amnesty if he defected and joined the Communist side. He must have been a nimble man because he made it from the White to the Red lines without being shot by either and settled easily into a post as an instructor in the Soviet Military Academy.

Olga's star rose as Communist control of the country expanded. Under the name of Olga Vadina she became one of the top stars of post-Revolutionary Russia's concert theater. She was appearing in Yalta in the summer of 1925 when mutual friends introduced her to the young American millionaire who had become something of a Soviet institution himself because of his earlier association with Lenin and subsequent business successes.

Both were bowled over, as Hammer recounts it:

"By that time, Olga was married to her manager. Fortunately, he had been left behind in Moscow. By the end of the week, our first week together, we decided that we couldn't live without each other. We took a train to Moscow and Olga obtained a divorce. It was easy in those days. We were married in a civil ceremony and had a wonderful reception at the Brown House for our families and friends." Their only child, Julian, was born in Moscow in 1928.

In 1930, when the Hammers took leave of Moscow, all was serene. All the *dosvidanias* had been said to Russian relatives and friends, all the *auf Wiedersehens* to the old Faber hands at the pencil works, all the till-we-meet-agains to the pen-point masters from Birmingham.

Hammer bought an exquisite little chateau at Garches, overlooking Paris, and entertained the thought of an entirely new career. He would become a private banker based in Paris. He was accidentally prodded into this by a chance meeting with an American manufacturer who had sold machinery to the Soviets but had received only 50 percent of his money in cash, the rest in the same kind of promissory notes Hammer had willingly accepted for his own properties. The distressed man asked Hammer if he would be willing to buy the notes at half their face value. Hammer readily agreed, and the manufacturer spread the word to others who were being held in the same state of suspense by Russia that he had dug up a combination succor-sucker who would buy up their notes and assume the risk of future payment. Hammer was swamped. He bought whatever was offered. Several of Averell Harriman's partners in a manganese concession which they sold back to the Soviets were so eager to unload what they considered little more than pieces of paper that they turned over their three-year notes to Hammer at a whopping 72 percent discount.

The Soviets paid off every penny of their debts, which amounted to millions to Hammer alone. Meanwhile the Hammers' art partner, Sakho, had invested heavily in the stock market and was wiped out by the 1929 crash. The doctor had fortunately kept out of the stock market, so he was able to buy out Sakho when the latter offered to sell the Hammers his share of the business.

The doctor's future took on a clearer focus. He would build a large international bank, perhaps someday giving the Rothschilds real competition. But his brothers Victor and Harry changed his mind with a cablegram that said, more or less, "Help!" It was 1931, nadir of the Great Depression in America. The economic disaster had staggered many business endeavors, among them the hoped-for sales of the tons of Romanoff and other Russian art Armand had arranged to ship to New York.

The doctor returned to a New York that had been described to him as a scene of "stockbrokers jumping out of windows, if they weren't selling apples on the corner." He found his brothers in a lesser but just as real panic. Nobody wanted a forgotten czarina's ruby-studded swizzle stick.

"Nonsense," Armand ruled. "Not everybody could have gone broke in the Crash. It's just a question of proper merchandising, and I think I have an idea."

He had, indeed, and it would be the talk of the art world for years to come.

Hammer's vision was to sell the dazzling lode in department stores rather than through the traditionally small, obscure, and not very democratic galleries. Hammer had gotten the idea by studying the success of a friend, S. L. Hoffman, a dress manufacturer with a national reputation for volume sales. He called for a list of the chief executives of the leading emporiums in the United States and with the help of Hoffman wrote each of them a personalized letter.

All the letters carried a central theme: a brief account of why he went to Russia in the first place, what he had achieved there as a businessman, and why he became interested in Russian art. He became interested, he wrote, "because of the failing ruble and my desire to convert my rubles into something tangible. We were not art dealers, as such. But we were (and are) interested in disposing of this art."

He promised to consign the treasures to stores at a 40 percent discount from the listed retail selling price. In expectation of an ecstatic response, Armand directed Victor to make a complete inventory of the items—some marooned in a warehouse and others still reposing in Customs. The next step was to hire a printer to make up a batch of price tags embossed with the double-headed eagle crest of the imperial family, below which was typewritten the history of the object. They looked as authentic as if they had come directly from the Winter Palace.

Only two stores responded to Hammer's first pitch. One wrote guardedly asking for more details. But Joseph Laurie, head of St. Louis's Scruggs–Vandervoort and Barney, sent Hammer a telegram accepting the proposition and asking for an immediate shipment. Some instinct sent Armand and Victor to Sixth Avenue in search of secondhand theatrical trunks. There they found a mound of them that were relics of a musical comedy company that had failed on Broadway after a tour on the road. They bought cheaply, trucked the trunks to the warehouse, filled them to the brim with precious objects the original owners never dreamed would wind up in a place named Scruggs–Vandervoort and Barney, and headed for Penn Station. Their planets must have been in amicable positions: The railroad even permitted them to check the array of trunks on their tickets!

While Victor set up the exhibition, Armand had photographs made of all the more historical pieces and persuaded Laurie to introduce him to the editors of the St. Louis *Post-Dispatch* and the *Globe-Democrat.* Laurie was reluctant. It was against the policies of both papers to give free publicity to department stores or any other commercial undertaking, he explained. But Hammer painted a rosy prospect of increased profits, got his interviews, spread his photographs and captions before the editors, and related the fascinating stories of their histories and acquisition, and made both front pages.

When the store opened on the morning of the unique sale, about five thousand shoppers were waiting in line. After a few days the empty theatrical trunks were sent back to New York, where Harry was instructed to reload them and rush them back to St. Louis. Marshall Field, which had not answered Hammer's letter, rushed a vice-president from Chicago to St. Louis to study and assess the phenomenon. His raves caused the renowned Chicago store to book the Hammer collection after three unprecedented weeks of merchandising in St. Louis. The Chicago sales were even more successful, prompting Armand to leave Victor there in charge of a posh bazaar that extended for months beyond the scheduled three weeks while he, Armand, took side shows to Bullock's Wilshire in Los Angeles, Halle's in Cleveland, J. L. Hudson in Detroit, The Emporium in San Francisco, Kaufman's in Pittsburgh, Hutzler's in Baltimore, Woodward & Lothrop's in Washington, and other choice marts. The original rates prevailed: 40 percent discount for the stores, and the stores paid for all advertising and salesmen's commissions. Even the Orthodox vestments Victor had saved from destruction in Leningrad began to "move," some to serve as lush evening capes and grand piano throws, others to be cut up and reincarnated as richly brocaded and illuminated scarves, pillows, and evening handbags.

The grand tour was climaxed with a three-year joint venture with Lord & Taylor, New York. That partnership ended when the Hammers, annoyed by an officious Lord & Taylor executive who professed to know more about czarist art than they, opened their own Hammer Galleries on Fifth Avenue at 54th Street as a tenant of John D. Rockefeller, Jr. They were off the road at long last and collectively several million dollars richer.

"I *told* you not everybody went broke," the doctor chided his respectful brothers.

Dr. Hammer felt that he was finished forever with selling exotic art over bustling department store counters like bolts of dry goods or Grand Rapids furniture. But the fates and William Randolph Hearst, Sr., ruled otherwise.

Spectacularly.

Hearst, the most unflagging collector in the nation's history, had fallen out of favor with two supporters of old, (1) Franklin Delano Roosevelt, a man he helped put in the White House, and (2) the banks. Both their doors closed on him in the mid-thirties. For the first time in his life he needed money, large sums of it. Several stockholders' groups carried their complaints to court, demanding a receivership. What may have been the publishing giant's gloomiest hour came when he learned that his principal rival in California journalism, Harry Chandler, owner of the Los Angeles *Times* and grandfather of Otis Chandler, the present publisher, was the actual holder of the mortgage on his beloved San Simeon.

Chandler generously extended the loan, but other creditors were not so kind. It took supersalesmanship on the part of Hearst executive Richard E. Berlin to circumvent a Canadian newsprint cartel's determination to shut down Hearst's newspapers and magazines. Berlin also blocked Joseph P. Kennedy's self-serving offer to "help the old man" by taking all his magazines off his hands for $8 million, a fraction of their present worth. But, in the main, it was a shambles. When former Undersecretary of the Treasury John W. Hanes was called in by Hearst directors to save the sinking ship, one of the first things he learned was that there were ninety-four separate Hearst corporations, many of which owed each other money. Hanes was also asked by one indignant stockholders' group to explain why American Newspapers, owned by Hearst, sold the Hearst Baltimore, Atlanta, and San Antonio papers to Hearst Consolidated for $8 million in 1935 when those three papers were losing $550,000 a year.

But there was a flickering candle at the end of the long dark tunnel: the Hearst art collection. W. A. Swanberg in his *Citizen Hearst*, published by Charles Scribner's Sons, states that Hearst collected art in 504 categories during a half-century of patient browsing and sometimes reckless bidding. In his estate homes, three in California, St. Donat's, his castle in Wales, the ranchhouses on his Mexican properties, and in special suites at his New York hotels—the Ritz Towers, Warwick, Lombardy, and Devon—and in warehouses in New York and Los Angeles, this astounding magpie had collected *objets d'art* at a cost of about $50 million, ranging from sculpture chiseled 2,500 years before Christ to a knocked-down and boxed Cistercian monastery built in 1141 in Sacramenia, Segovia, Spain, by Alfonso VII of Castile, to $2 doorknockers, to Van Dyck's portrait of Queen Henrietta, queen consort of Charles I, youngest daughter of Henry IV of France and Marie de Médicis. For this he paid that masterful art hustler, Sir Joseph Duveen, $375,000.

It was most difficult for the members of the Hearst board to persuade him that he had reached a point financially where his only liquid assets were his collection. He needed at least $11 million and swiftly if he was to save the publishing kingdom he had built up over the decades. At the end of the 1930s he consented reluctantly to dispose of about half of his homeric harvest. But he wished to avoid any impression that it was an emergency clearance sale.

"I am not disposing of all my art collection, only about half of it," he wrote cordially to Jack Alexander of the *Saturday Evening Post,* who was preparing an article on the subject.

> The remainder I propose giving to museums. You know I am not merely an art collector but a dealer in art and antique objects.
>
> I shall reserve some things for my children, things which they can use advantageously. But the children naturally would prefer for the most part inheritances which would bring them an income.
>
> Taxes have a restraining influence on bequests, of course, but I make donations to public institutions with some frequency.

Hearst insisted that his treasures be disposed of with decorum, and so instructed his agents, the International Studio Art Corporation. Accordingly, the agents offered articles to the better known galleries of the United States, Britian, France, and other European countries, whose dealers had marveled over his spending sprees of old when it was not unusual for him to buy $1 million worth year in and year out. But little interest was aroused. So, with great misgivings, Hearst consented to let his treasure-trove be placed on sale at some of the same department stores where the Hammer art had done so well. Curiously, no sparks flew, no queues formed. Less than $200,000 was raised over a trial period which saw more than that sum spent on advertising, salaries, and other expenses. "It would have been cheaper to give the art away," grumbled the chairman of the Hearst trustees, Judge Clarence Shearn. The trustees next tried the auction route, but important dealers banded together so as not to bid against one another.

Enter Armand Hammer. With tongs.

He and Victor had become friends some years earlier with Charles B. McCabe, a United Press editor then stationed in Chicago. In the interim, McCabe had been hired by Hearst to be publisher of the New York *Mirror* and made a trustee. Like his peers, McCabe was disappointed by the indifference shown to the Hearst collection.

"There's only one man who can unload this art, and that's Dr. Armand Hammer," McCabe told fellow trustee Martin Huberth, who had the double duty of heading Hearst's real estate division and disposing of enough of the art to placate the angry creditors. Huberth called Hammer to his office, briefed him on the murky situation, and asked if he would lend a hand. Hammer said yes, with a proviso: He must be given 10 percent off the top on all sales and a free hand to set his own prices until he had raised $11 million. The contract was signed forthwith.

Hammer thought big. He called his friend Beardsley Ruml, chairman of Macy's, who was also an adviser to Presidents, author of the innovative "pay as you go" income tax plan, and chairman of the Federal Reserve Bank of New York. Through Ruml, Hammer had become friends with Nelson Rockefeller, and the three had on occasion flown to Washington in Hammer's Executive Beechcraft to give counsel to Franklin D. Roosevelt, a friend of all three.

"This could be the greatest project in the history of merchandising," Hammer enthused into the telephone. "Just think—fifty million dollars' worth of art passing over Macy's counters! It will make department store history!"

"Come on down," Ruml said quietly.

There followed several tense months of negotiation and lint-picking, with Hammer operating without counsel against successive waves of Macy's inside and outside legal staffs. It was a nerve-snapping experience for an entrepreneur accustomed to acting on the spur of the moment, if not sooner. But one day when Hammer had a delusion that he could hear the whole Hearst empire collapsing offstage, Macy's came forth with an agreement.

"It was three inches thick," the doctor recalls with residue heat. "They had put in a clause which gave them the right to pass on all prices to be asked for the art. I protested that they just weren't competent, and they soon proved it. I arranged with the Hearst warehouse in the Bronx—it stood six stories and covered a city block—to pull out some china, lamps, and furniture. I wanted to test the Macy experts on those items. So off we went to the Bronx, with Victor along, of course.

"Having Victor with me made me well armed. During those months of dickering over the contract, Victor had set a record that probably will never be topped. He examined a hundred and fifty-two Hearst-compiled catalogs, rummaged through thousands of photos that in some cases Hearst himself had never seen, and compiled price tags and descriptions for more than twenty thousand items.

"Well, Victor and I sat there and listened to the Macy buyers as they looked over the sample items. We didn't know whether to laugh or throw them out of the warehouse. Their lamp specialist judged that a pair of lamps whose bases where Chinese Hawthorne vases from the seventeenth century should be offered for twenty-nine-ninety-five. Hearst had paid twenty thousand for the pair!"

Victor blurted the original price to the man, but the fellow was not impressed.

"Maybe that's true," he said, "but twenty-nine-ninety-five is all our kind of customers would pay for them." At the end of the disheartening day, Armand called Martin Huberth and it was agreed that Macy's was not the proper stage for the supersale.

That left Gimbels.

A tentative deal giving Hammer complete control was quickly made by Hammer with Frederic (Fred) and Bernard (Bernie) Gimbel, subject to the approval of Huberth. It provided that the entire fifth floor of the huge middle-calss store would be stripped of its racks of boys' clothing, infant wear, and what not, to make way for the treasures of San Simeon and the Bronx.

But there was no immediate rush on the part of the Hearst group. The hangup there was the legendary publisher himself. He had been deeply hurt when first told that Dr. Hammer had selected Macy's as the market-place for his treasures. It must have been a towering humiliation for a man who had devoted so much time, talent, and money to learn that his accumulation would be picked over by shoppers more accustomed to buying pots and pans, electric fans, and winter underwear. He had jour-neyed countless miles to find and acquire a collection he hoped would one day be housed in a great public museum in California for millions to marvel over long after his death. Now to have his precious things piled up in Macy's must have been all but too much for him to bear. Moreover,

83

he questioned the selection of the place of sale: "Who would go to Macy's to buy a monastery?" he asked those who urged this drastic action on him.

The monastery he had in mind (actually, he had bought a spare at some point in his majestic browsings) was the Cistercian cloister that had pleased his eye during his 1928 tour of Spain. He paid $500,000 for it as it stood—barely stood—and to make the deal more palatable to the monks (and presumably the Vatican) he built the brothers a new and much more comfortable monastery for a larger sum than he had paid for the original. Then he engaged a team of American architects and engineers to dismantle the twelveth-century retreat, number every stone, and pack each separately. Some 10,700 cases were needed. A three-mile narrow-gauge railway was constructed to move the heavy boxes to a standard railway spur.

But Hearst's troubles with his hallowed purchase had hardly begun. When the cargo arrived in New York it was seized by agents of the Department of Agriculture. Government inspectors suspected that the straw padding wrapped around the stones to protect them from chipping while en route to the New World might contain bacteria capable of spreading hoof and mouth disease. Therefore, they ruled that every one of the 10,700 packing cases must be opened and the insulating straw examined. The uncrating and recrating (no bugs were found) cost Hearst $53,500. There is no estimate of the cost of then trucking the monastery to the Bronx, spreading it over two entire floors of the warehouse, labor, rent, and so on.

But if Hearst was distressed to learn that Macy's was to be the dispenser of his treasures, for a miserable commodity named money, he was shocked to hear that the sales arena might now be Gimbels. He said, with an understandable trace of indignation, that he had not gone to all that labor and love to see them dispensed "in Gimbels' basement."

Out of love and respect for what Hearst had meant to all of them, none of his trustees and other advisers was in any mood (or authority for that matter) to press Gimbels upon him in any heavy way.

"Martin Huberth told me that he had had a change of heart and would not agree to the selection of Gimbels," Hammer recalls. "I knew what he was trying to tell me, so I looked for a way to soften the blow for Mr. Hearst. I went to Bernie Gimbel and said, 'Look, you own Saks Fifth Avenue, too. A class store. Why don't you let me put some of the Hearst pieces in there, with the bulk of the collection going into Gimbels? I believe it might reassure Mr. Hearst and get Martin Huberth off the hook.' Bernie said he was sorry. There was no space available in Saks Fifth Avenue. I asked him why not make space available and after a bit he told me. Bernie said, 'We don't want people to know that there's any connection between the two stores. If rich Saks Fifth Avenue customers learned that Gimbels owns Saks, well, they might drift away to some other quality store.' "

Hammer was not easy to shake off. He took his unusual case to Fred Gimbel, who arranged for him to talk it over with his cousin Adam Gimbel, youngest of the merchant princes and the one chiefly responsible for the prestigious position of Saks Fifth Avenue. Adam agreed to set aside a small second-floor area facing the elevators. The battle for face was more or less won; the matter of selling $11 million worth of largely mystic merchandise was still not resolved. Hearst was more or less contented by the Saks Fifth Avenue showing, Huberth was relieved, Hammer was happy, but Bernie Gimbel had misgivings. With the help of Fred Gimbel, Hammer dissolved Bernie's doubts. Hammer successfully urged Bernie to forget the social differences between the two family-owned stores. Gimbels in general, he argued, would not only make a fortune out of the Hearst sales but also probably encourage the clientele of Saks Fifth Avenue (who would be discreetly informed that even greater Hearst collection bargains lay on the fifth floor at a West Side store named Gimbels) to venture there and perhaps join the several hundreds of thousands who were already on Gimbels' easy-payment plan. Also, Hammer troweled, the very presence of Saks Fifth Avenue patrons inside Gimbels would upgrade the store. That did it for Bernie.

Now a clear track lay ahead for Hammer. He phrased and sent out to Saks Fifth Avenue's charge-account list 100,000 expensive-looking invitations to a three-night black-tie and formal-gown preview and simultaneous sale at both stores. Victor, in the meantime, had selected a sales staff with great care. He astoundingly found sales people who ranged in their approach all the way from Gimbels' hard sell to the cultured diffidence of a disciple of Duveen. Some spoke pure Brooklynese, others were in command of the languages of much of the world. Some were finding their first rewarding employment since becoming refugees from Hitler's rages. Others had left museums and galleries to help whittle away Hearst's magic mountain.

"How will we publicize the sale in addition to paid advertisements?" the board of Gimbels asked Dr. Hammer. One of the directors wanted to spend $100,000 for the best public-relations firm in the country. Someone suggested Ivy Lee, who had been employed by John D. Rockefeller, Sr., to give him a new public image. "If Mr. Bernard Gimbel will take me around to meet the publishers of the New York papers, we won't need to hire anybody," Hammer said. The board was dubious, but Robert Lehman of the banking house of Lehman Brothers and Gimbels board member was impressed by young Hammer's enthusiasm and convictions. Sure enough, Hammer and Bernie visited Mr. Arthur Sulzberger of the *Times*, Mrs. Ogden Reid of the *Herald Tribune*, Roy Howard of the *World-Telegram*, and Dorothy Schiff of the *Post*. Hammer pulled out his photos of Hearst's greatest treasures before each editor and related the story behind each object. The result was something that never happened before—front-page stories and pictures of a department-store sale.

Police had to be called to control the crowds of guests and innocent bystanders on each of the three preview nights. On the first night alone, sales reached $500,000 at the two stores. Somewhat surprisingly, Gimbels rather than Saks Fifth Avenue was to arouse the keener buying sprees, prodding Swanberg to write:

> People from Hell's Kitchen as well as Park Avenue came to gape at the array of wonders. Even the Spanish Cloister was on sale there at Gimbels, through the medium of pictures, the stones themselves still being up in the Bronx. A titled guide with a distinctive foreign accent was on hand to impress the mink trade. Gimbels had advertised "Bargains in Del Sartos and Broadlooms." The ads stressed the chic of wearing a Hearst necklace, and invited one and all to use the Easy-Payment-Plan. People who bought a scarab, a canvas, or a set of fireplace tongs were probably not aware that they were doing their bit to save the Hearst Organization from bankruptcy.

A housewife named Klotz wrote a penny postcard to Gimbels which read, "Dear Sirs: Please send me a Benvenuto Cellini bowl, as advertised." (She had seen a photograph in a newspaper of John D. Rockefeller, Jr., standing with Bernie Gimbel examining the historic bowl.) "Kindly choose a good color to go with a blue dining room." There was only one of the bowls, alas. Gimbels replied to Mrs. Klotz that Victor Hammer had placed a $25,000 tag on it.

While New York art galleries cried "Foul!" the great sale picked up more and more momentum. The items assigned to Saks Fifth Avenue were moved across Manhattan to Gimbels without incident or a sales recession. Jack Alexander's article in the November 1, 1941, issue of the *Saturday Evening Post*, which coincided with the passing of the $5 million plateau in Hearst sales, was an interim report on the Miracle on 32nd Street:

"Around 50,000 persons responded in the first days of the regular sale. Edward Alden Jewell, the art critic of the *New York Times*, who, of all persons, might have been expected to stay calm, wrote, 'Only an experience-toughened specialist wearing blinders could, we cannot but decide, fail to be staggered by the sheer inclusive heterogeneity of this vast congeries of art objects of all periods and from all parts of the world. The impact is amazing." (Dr. Hammer had brought in a group of Hollywood set designers and lighting experts to illuminate the drama of the items and their countries of origin.)

Seldom a day went by without a feature story in the newspapers or an event or incident on the fifth floor. There were frequent visitations from a lunatic who would step off an elevator just long enough to curse Hearst, then jump back on before the doors guillotined him. Hammer, in one of his frequent talks with reporters and radio people, quoted a fifth-floor visitor as saying, "It was like walking through the Metropolitan and the Louvre and finding a price tag on every object." The pilgrim from the Washington (D.C.) *News* wrote:

When the collection was thrown open to the subway trade, the lure of acquiring something that belonged to Mr. Hearst proved a potent one. The crush was savage. Gimbels estimated that 100,000 persons came in during the first week. In a triumphant newspaper advertisement, it contrasted this figure with the 30,000 persons who, it was said, were attracted in a week's time to the three largest museums in New York.

The casual way in which average people bought fairly expensive items was startling, even to Gimbels. A woman from St. Louis, who was visiting in New York with her son, a lad of about 11, boarded the escalator on the street floor, intending to get off at the sixth and buy him a suit. In changing at the fifth, the pair fell victim to a natural curiosity and began wandering through the Hearst display. In the Americana section the boy went into a kind of trance before a case which contained a score or more of Abraham Lincoln autographs. The one the boy fancied was scrawled on a rough slip of paper at the end of a message to a Union general requesting the release of a Confederate prisoner. The note was written on the day Lincoln was assassinated and was quite possibly the last thing he wrote that is still extant. Some of the autographs were priced as low as $40, but the boy wanted this particular one, and his mother bought it for him for $304.

A dark, chesty fellow from Brooklyn, who seemed to be in a hurry, asked to see some paintings; any paintings at all, he said. A clerk showed him one marked at $800. "Not enough," said the man, hardly looking at the canvas. He was shown one at $1,200. He frowned, saying reprovingly, "I can go higher than that, pal." The clerk led him to a painting for which $1,500 was asked. "Sold!" said the customer, paying in cash. "Send it to this address, and leave the price tag on. I want to show some of my smart neighbors I can pay a higher price for Hearst stuff than they can."

Victor's price tags, sometimes subject to change with little notice, remain marvels of high and low finance. He was a reverse alchemist, transmuting Hearst gold into Gimbels pewter.

To this day, no man knows—perhaps not even Victor—how and why he concluded that two suits of sixteenth-century Maximilian armor bought by Hearst for $4,000 should be knocked down and successfully sold at Gimbels for $1,995. For $17.50 an American navy officer bought a powder horn that had been used on Nelson's *Victory*. A woman from Philadelphia rather predictably bought a high-case clock that had belonged to Benjamin Franklin for $1,895 (Hearst had paid $4,675), but missed out on two pairs of Franklin's spectacles, purchased by a Madison Avenue physician for $500 per focal. George Washington's hot-water urn fell into the hands of a New York building contractor for exactly the price Victor had set, either by instinct or ESP, $2,185.

Seventy paneled rooms were sold, including Myles Standish's from the ancestral estate in Lancashire. Victor had divined that the old haunt of the defender of the Mayflower Pilgrims, and runner-up for the hand of Priscilla Mullens, was worth exactly $5,985. A New York lawyer dropped by Gimbels one day and picked up three thirteenth-century stained-glass windows and sent them off to a simple frame church in remotest Wyoming, where his father had been an itinerant preacher. A California oilman breezed onto the fifth floor and decided that a council chamber of a sixteenth-century Venetian doge, with wall frescoes by Bernardo Parentino depicting the life of Scipio Africanus, was "pretty." He bought it for Victor's inscrutably Venetian price, $9,495. Before the day ended, the oilman had spent $100,000 without a coffee break.

The Hammers followed the ebb and flow of the Hearst sale with professional acumen. If an item or a series of related art moved sluggishly, down dipped the price. Victor never ran out of price tags, ink, or his special relationship with the spirits that whispered price to him alone. Who but Victor would know that the bedroom of Lady Hamilton must cost its new tenant $2,995; that François Boucher's *Venus Disarming Love* should cost $26,983; that four fifteenth-century Gothic tapestries, ten by thirty feet, must bring precisely $199,894; or that the pair of seventeenth-century Italian bronze busts originally priced at $198 each, which was mystery enough, should be reduced to $122.50?

When buyers grew shy about the $375,000 Queen Henrietta by Van Dyck, Victor slashed that busty consort all the way to $124,998, and a purchaser sprang out of Gimbels' elevator.*

John Walker, former director of the National Gallery of Art in Washington, in his book *Self-Portrait with Donors* (Little, Brown) mentions that *Queen Henrietta Maria with Her Dwarf* was later purchased by the Kress Foundation and is now in the National Gallery of Art. Its present value would probably be once more what Mr. Hearst paid for it.

To give tone to the sale, Armand Hammer published an elegant monthly art magazine entitled *The Compleat Collector*, whose contents featured articles on sale at Gimbels. Hammer wrote most of these articles himself under various pseudonyms. The editor of the publication was Braset Marteau, which translated from the French is "arm and hammer."

In less than a year the Hammers reached the $11 million mark and the end of an entrancing contract. Hearst was saved. It was a time for jubilation.

"I was given a big dinner," the doctor said a long time later.

"By Hearst?" a reporter asked him.

"No," Hammer said cheerfully. "By his banks."

---

*Victor Hammer noted recently that some of those who made the pilgrimage to Gimbels during the sale took home what later became astonishing bargains.

"There was a tondo [circular picture] of the Madonna and child with the infant John the Baptist and two angels by Raffaelino del Garbo which sold for twelve thousand, nine hundred and ninety-eight dollars," he told the author. "In today's market it would bring close to half a million dollars.

"A Flemish painting by David Teniers the Younger of a village dancing scene was sold for nine hundred ninety-eight dollars and today would bring at least seventy thousand. Both of these works of art were from England's great Holford collection. They had to be some of the greatest bargains Gimbels has ever offered."

Chapter 12

Frisky Whiskey

Hammer's Jack-of-all-tradesmanship was most manifested during the period between the time of his return from Russia via Paris in 1931 and the day, twenty-five years later, when he made a serious attempt to retire. During that hyperactive span he persuaded tens of thousands of Americans to buy millions of dollars' worth of art, thus enriching their lives, and beyond that he emerged as a power in the whiskey and cattle businesses and dabbled in network radio, gold, and philanthropy. There were times when he juggled some or all of those balls simultaneously.

His serendipitous Midas touch did not automatically bring serenity. He and Olga broke up and in time were amicably divorced. It was a spontaneous combustion born of restless natures. Hammer's many business pursuits kept him flying around the country for days or even weeks at a spell. The Russian wife found her new life in their Fifth Avenue apartment and later at their subdued home in Highland Falls, New York, less challenging than the life she had known. She resumed her singing career, and so successfully that their separations grew even more frequent. After the divorce, Olga and their son, Julian, moved to Hollywood, where she occasionally appeared in films, type-cast as a gypsy singer. The handsome woman who had nearly died before a firing squad succumbed much less dramatically to cancer, after Julian had reached his maturity.

Hammer's second wife, whom he married in 1943, was Angela Zevely. She was a divorcee who maintained a small estate in the horse country near Red Bank, New Jersey, and was as vivacious as Olga was moody. Her family raced Thoroughbreds. A relative had owned one of the top American stake runners, Zev, winner of the 1923 Kentucky Derby and victor over the French champion, Épinard, in a match race at Belmont. Happy-go-lucky Angela loved life, parties, Armand's seagoing yacht *Shadow Isle* (named after their Red Bank farm), and the comfortable glow that emanates from a vigorous, versatile millionaire.

Hammer attempted to make the best of an unhappy alliance while at the same time moving on to another challenge that suddenly presented itself. His versatility was seldom demonstrated more clearly than by his successful assault on one of the nation's most formidable strongholds, the whiskey industry.

The doctor had pulled full many a rabbit out of a silk hat, figuratively. This time he altered his act. He himself popped out of a barrel, literally. His eye may have been on the sale of his Romanoff art as Franklin Delano Roosevelt neared the White House, but his ear was otherwise occupied. It picked up a clear signal: The New Deal, once in power, would repeal Prohibition and that would create an unprecedented demand for barrels to hold the beer and whiskey needed to slake the nation's thirst.

There were no barrels.

There had been little need for them since the Curse of Andrew Volstead had descended on America, October 27, 1919. Now there would be a loud cry for them, especially for those made of seasoned white oak, some for beer kegs, others charred, in which whiskey could age properly. The doctor knew exactly where to find the staves. Where else but Russia? He had lived there long enough to have inventoried in his fertile mind just about everything the Soviets had available for export. He ordered several shiploads of their staves and was only momentarily dismayed when the order was fouled up and the ships arrived not with shaped staves but blocks of air-dried white oak from which to fashion staves. Hammer set up an improvised stave-shaping plant on one of the piers of the New York Dock Company, Brooklyn, berthing place of the Russian ships. When that proved inadequate, he built a modern barrel factory in Milltown, New Jersey—the A. Hammer Cooperage Corporation, no less. His barrels came tumbling off the production lines just in time to reap the harvest of Repeal. They were eagerly snapped up at fantastic prices by Anheuser-Busch, Coor's, Schenley, and others.

For a time the doctor was content to be a supplier rather than a participant in what under normal conditions was a fiercely cutthroat industry. But then Fred Gimbel, best man at his wedding to Angela, gave him a stock-market tip as the two were leaving for Mexico on their honeymoon. World War II had broken out and whiskey was hard to get, since distilleries were not allowed to use badly needed grain. "Buy some American Distilling stock," Gimbel urged him. "There's no risk. They're going to give a barrel of bonded bourbon as a dividend to everybody who buys a share of their stock. We'll buy the whiskey from you, any or all of it. The law says we can't buy the stock ourselves because we're in the retailing side of the business."

Hammer bought 5,500 shares at $90 on the 10 percent margin that was permissible at the time.

It was a most unusual investment on his part, and not only because he was next to being a teetotaler. He had no stocks. Thus he had been one of the relatively few rich Americans totally unaffected by the 1929 Crash. He was a millionaire in the early 1920s and a multimillionaire through his years in Russia. Some happy pipeline to reality prompted him to stay away from the feverish speculation of the decade. Thus the Crash was just another news story for him to scan. If any person except Fred Gimbel had touted him on to American Distilling, he probably would have laughed at him. Now, having bought his stock in American Distilling, Hammer went off on a two-month trip with his bride and forgot the transaction until he returned to New York. There he discovered to his surprise and delight that the stock had jumped to $150 a share. He was ready to sell it then and there, but Gimbel interceded.

"Don't," Gimbel said. "You'll make more out of the whiskey that's coming to you and you'll still have the stock."

In Hammer's case, it was not a question of trucking 5,500 barrels of bourbon to New York. He left all of his fifty-gallon barrels in storage at the American plant, which agreed to bottle it and label it under Hammer's private brand. To his astonishment, he discovered that he could not obtain a wholesaler's license in New York City. But one could still be obtained in Buffalo. So he hurried there, opened an office, applied and got his necessary credentials. Then it became just a question of ordering Peoria to go ahead with the bottling and labeling. It was put up in fifths, 86 proof, and baptized "Cooperage" after Hammer's barrel company. Gimbels took it from Hammer, fast.

Gimbels took full-page advertisements in the New York papers. Lines formed almost all the way around the block occupied by the huge department store.

In short order, 2,500 of Hammer's 5,500 barrels had been drained. The remainder would have quickly disappeared, and in all probability the doctor would have sold out, locks, stocks, and barrels and left the whiskey business, except for one of those strokes of luck and perseverance that lace his life. He was busy with other ventures at his office in Hammer Galleries one day when his secretary announced that a Mr. Eisenberg wished to see him. He had met Eisenberg, a chemical engineer, in Russia seven or eight years before. Their paths had not crossed in the intervening years. Eisenberg was now employed as a business broker. Hammer welcomed him, hoped he would not stay long, and lent him an ear. The doctor's mind was largely on his art and other enterprises, but, through the slight fog in which he had immersed himself, he realized that Eisenberg was saying something of enormous interest. What the visitor was trying to explain to the slightly inattentive host was that straight whiskey could be stretched five times by adding 80 percent of cheap neutral spirits, and most of that day's drinkers would find the blend just as palatable.

Hammer's brain made a quick calculation: If this were true, his remaining 3,000 barrels would be magnified to 15,000 barrels, 9,500 more barrels than he had bought in the first place. And he still had his stock.

Eisenberg came prepared to prove his point. He had worked in vodka in Russia and knew his business. He had a sample of neutral spirits made from grain and another sample made from potatoes. Dr. Hammer had a bottle of Cooperage handy. Eisenberg poured a bit of it into two paper cups, then added his grain and potato potions to fill the cups, stirred each cup, and invited the doctor to test both. Hammer could not taste the difference between the grain blend and the potato blend; more delightedly, he couldn't taste the difference between the blends and the real stuff.

"So what do we do?" Hammer asked the man who had the idea of how to stretch spirits but no bonded and aged whiskey to go with it. Eisenberg was ready for that one, too.

"I've been in this country for two or three years and I've learned a few things," he said. "I know where there's an abandoned rum distillery. It's in a place named Newmarket, New Hampshire, just over the border from Maine. The people who ran it defaulted on a Reconstruction Finance Corporation (R.F.C.) loan and the government took it over. The government wants to get rid of it. We can pick it up for very little money and turn it into a potato alcohol plant. We won't have to worry about getting enough potatoes. Over in Maine they're a glut on the market. The warehouses are full of them. They're rotting and stinking to high heaven, but the government is still subsidizing the Maine farmers to grow more and more of them. *Time* magazine had a piece about it. It's terrible."

Hammer went about the purchase step by step. The newly formed War Production Board (W.P.B.) had placed a high priority on alcohol. There were dozens of needs for it in the war effort, not the least of which was the juicing of torpedoes. The doctor went to Washington and sought out the senator from New Hampshire, Styles Bridges, and the senator from Maine, Owen Brewster—both Republicans. Both welcomed the proposition, Bridges because it would bring industry to New Hampshire, Brewster because it would help the Maine potato growers. The senators arranged for the doctor to see Donald Nelson, head of the W.P.B. after his long and successful career with Sears, Roebuck. Nelson agreed that the surplus of Maine potatoes was "smelling up the whole countryside" and gave Hammer a letter of approval that would eventually compare with the one from Lenin. It stated that in view of the critical potato overproduction, the doctor and his associates were permitted to produce potato alcohol for beverage purposes. The law at the time permitted the production of alcohol only for industrial use.

Hammer then moved on to the R.F.C. office in Boston, which had control of the Newmarket fiasco. He asked the official in charge what it would cost to take the ghostly rum plant off the government's hands. The man said $55,000, the amount of the bad loan. The doctor took out his checkbook and wrote a personal check. The distillery and all its warehouses, some of them four or five stories high, were his. As it turned out, quite accidentally, he had made the deal scarcely hours in advance of a man who, on equal terms, would have swept easily into control, the former ambassador to the Court of St. James's, Joseph P. Kennedy, Sr. Apparently the ambassador thought the property was a good speculation, just as he had bought the Chicago Merchandise Mart for a song during the Depression, only to reap a harvest of millions when things returned to normal.

Following the rule to which he had disciplined himself from the time of the pencil adventure in the U.S.S.R., Hammer hired away from American Distilleries a German chemist named Hans Meister, an acknowledged master at transforming the honest spud into heady alcohol. He then bought thousands of tons of potatoes from the government at the bargain price of ten cents per hundred-pound sack and stuffed them into the warehouses of the former rum company until the walls were bulged like staves. He cut off all bottlings and sales of Cooperage until such time as he could cut it with the fermented potato squeezings, raw stuff that would need no aging.

It did not take long for the blend to flow. Gimbels was happy to accept it, though it contained only a 20 percent smidge of the doctor's good whiskey being slowly partitioned in Peoria, the minimum the law allowed for labeling blended whiskey. Indeed, Fred Gimbel gave the new product its name—Gold Coin—and the Gimbels ads hailing its merits caused new queues to form around the department store. Customers were rationed to two bottles and had to buy abysmal penalty bottles of Cuban gin to boot. Such was the permissibility of the nation's taste buds.

Almost at the exact hour that Gold Coin, the potato-based whiskey, went on the market, there came a disheartening decision by the U.S. Treasury's Alcohol Tax Unit. It ruled that beginning the following month, August 1, 1944, until further notice, there would be a "grain holiday" which would grant the distilleries of the United States the right to resume making alcohol for beverages with the ancient and honorable wheat, rye, and barley.

"There I was in Newmarket, up to my neck in those potatoes, which were now really beginning to smell to high heaven," the doctor later remembered. "Gimbel is on the phone. He says, 'You'd better close up shop and come home. Nobody will want potato whiskey if he can get grain whiskey.' It was a disaster. Cancellations for Gold Coin came in like a blizzard for the next few days. The roof was falling in on me. Gold Coin began to look like counterfeit money. I called a council of war with my technical people. Most of them were in favor of throwing in the towel, which was understandable. But I said that I had decided to go ahead with production of the potato spirits. I said to them, 'Just keep making the alcohol and store it in drums in the warehouses as we use the potatoes. We'll fill the whole place up with alcohol. *Somebody* will want it. *Nobody* wants rotting potatoes.' So we did just that. As the level of potatoes fell in the warehouses, the barrels of alcohol rose. In a way it was a relief to get rid of those damned potatoes, but on the other hand, nobody wanted the alcohol."

The doctor guessed right. The "grain holiday" lasted only one month. Potato alcohol was in high demand again, and Hammer had it. Countless gallons of it were shipped to Peoria to be mixed with his residue of aged whiskey. Gold Coin became golden coin more than ever before. It put the doctor in a good bargaining position with traditional distilleries. The doctor had the neutral spirits, they had aged whiskey reserves. He offered National Distillers four barrels of neutral (potato) spirits for one barrel of four-year-old straight whiskey. He succeeded beyond his expectations but realized that he was on thin ice. The government might declare another and longer grain holiday, and then his potato alcohol investment would decay like the tubers themselves. So he started buying idle grain distilleries. He bought nine before he was finished, and that enabled him to weather the parade of on-and-off grain alcohol directives from Washington. Hammer's grain quota during grain holiday periods grew in size with each acquisition.

One of the smallest of his purchases, rather typically, was his best. It was the J. W. Dant distillery in Dant, Kentucky, which produced about twenty thousand cases of a dozen fifths a year. The sour mash bottled-in-bond bourbon was priced the same as such better advertised brands as Old Grand-Dad, Old Taylor, and I. W. Harper, but held its own. There was a family connection between Dant and a neighboring distillery named Dant and Head in Gethsemane, Kentucky, owned by National Distillers, who wanted to unload its surplus distillery capacity. So the doctor bought Dant and Head too, plus the Baltimore Pure Rye Distilling Company plant in Baltimore, and a huge former molasses-processing alcohol plant from National in Gretna, Louisiana. It was not long before he—who had been reluctant to get into the whiskey game in the first place—was second only to Seagram's in the production of bulk whiskey in the United States. He called his company United Distillers of America, Ltd. The nation's wartime thirst kept all plants working overtime during the grain holidays. When the government prohibited the use of grain periodically, the doctor's various blends fell back on potatoes. When the bans on grain were lifted, he received his share of it without fail, and his distilleries produced straight whiskey for aging as well as grain neutral spirits. When aged whiskey was in short supply, Hammer, like his competitors, would cut it down to 20 percent of the contents of a bottle. When the supplies eased, he would up it to 30–35 percent. At the same time, he set about to improve the reputation of potato alcohol within the industry. He added a few bushels of carrots to a ton of potato mash and obtained a government ruling enabling him to label such mixes with the words "blended with vegetable neutral spirits," which seemed to him much more decorous than "potato neutral spirits." As a result of the government's imprimatur it was quite legal for Hammer to put out blends that were a mix of rationed grain and potato/carrot derivatives, plus, of course, the redeeming factor of snippets of the aged whiskey he was beginning to acquire in ever greater quantities, on his own and by purchase. The government permitted the doctor to divert part of his non-Kentucky grain quota to enable him to run his Kentucky distilleries even when there was no grain holiday, thus enabling the good doctor to build up his inventory of Kentucky whiskey, which sold at a premium over whiskey produced elsewhere.

After the government permitted continuous grain usage, Hammer found there was no longer any demand for his new blended brands, even those with grain alcohol. The public wanted old established brands and preferred straight whiskey at least four years old and bottled in bond.

The doctor's career as a whiskey baron peaked in the face of this seeming disaster, saved, however, as a result of a phone call from his brother Harry and a somewhat anachronistic contribution by his younger brother, Victor. Harry's call dealt with prices. He had just come from an illuminating visit to a New York liquor store, where, in his typically loyal way, he had asked for a fifth of bottled-in-bond J. W. Dant. The counterman said he did not handle that brand. (Actually, sales of the doctor's proudest product were originally confined largely to Kentucky and southern Illinois.) So Harry opted for a bottle of Old Grand-Dad, same price (about $7 at that time), same Kentucky sour mash bourbon. But instead of peeling a bottle of Old Grand-Dad off the shelf, the salesman did a remarkable thing for a whiskey storekeeper. He reached under the counter, fished up a fifth of something labeled Heaven Hill, a Kentucky sour mash bottled-in-bond, and poured a highly illegal shot glass of it. "Try this," he said to Harry. "We can't keep it in stock. We keep it under the counter and sell it only to our best customers. Usually we ask them to buy a couple of bottles of something else before we let them have a bottle of Heaven Hill."

Harry tried it and pronounced it every bit as good as J. W. Dant and other top bonded bourbons.

"How much do you charge for it?" Harry asked the man.

The man's voice dropped. "Four forty-nine," he confided.

Harry's resultant phone call to his brother created a bombshell in booze circles. By coincidence, the doctor was well along with what he felt would be a major breakthrough in the bonded bourbon field. He had decided to reduce the price of the four-year-old bourbon of his own aging Kentucky stocks and put out J. W. Dant for the joyous price (for bourbon drinkers, at least) of $4.95 per fifth. He was netting just under $20 a case on the limited production of the original J. W. Dant, 20,000 cases a year selling retail for $7 per fifth. He had decided to go for broke, slash the Dant price to what he considered the absolute bone, and hope within a few years to sell a million cases a year, to the consternation and dismay of the elder competitors who were crowding him out of business. But here was Harry on the pipe, telling him there was already in existence an equally good Kentucky bonded bourbon being surreptitiously sold for $4.49, the price of Seagram's 7-Crown blended with 35 percent grain alcohol. The doctor called his vice-president, Newt Cook, who was about to unleash the advertising program based on what he and Hammer had considered a master stroke, the $4.95 price.

"Change all the ads, Newt," Hammer directed. "The new price will be four forty-nine."

"You can't do that," Newt protested.

"Who says I can't?" Hammer demanded. He thought that would end it, but it didn't.

"I say you can't," Newt said. "Nobody ever sold a bond for the price of a blend. Nobody!"

"That's just the point," Hammer explained. "That's why we're going to put this thing over. The drinker will say to himself, "Hey, if I can get straight whiskey for the price of Seagram's Seven, why the hell should I buy a blend? Why drink something made of sixty-five percent alcohol when you can get the real aged stuff for the same price?' "

And so J. W. Dant, with the words "The Crown Jewel of Kentucky Bourbon," blown in the bottle in raised letters, was launched on a national scale. Victor provided the artistic hocus-pocus. He bought a bushel or two of Habsburg crowns and jewels—for later sale in the Hammer Galleries —and took them on tour, a J. W. Dant promotion tour. Local clubwomen were invited to model them at charity affairs. The somewhat unnerving sight of a noble Austrian hemophiliac's tiara cocked rakishly atop a bottle of $4.49 bourbon made the feature pages. The Hammers discovered something else: Retailers stopped exacting tribute from them for showing J. W. Dant bottles in their windows. Indeed, they began asking for sealed empties to lure not only J. W. Dant drinkers but potential buyers of other brands.

It took J. W. Dant only two years to jump from regional acceptance to the top of the national bourbons. The high mark of one million cases was reached simultaneously with the high irritation of Louis Rosenstiel, the chairman of the rival Schenley's. After considerable negotiation, some of it conducted when Rosenstiel's yacht would overtake Hammer's in Florida waters, Hammer sold him the J. W. Dant distillery and inventory for $6.5 million cash. Then the doctor unloaded his other distilleries, his old and young whiskey, his warehouses of "vegetable" spirits, his label rights and related alcoholic interests for additional millions.

He had had it with whiskey and wished he could say the same for Angela.

Chapter 13

The Golden Bull

Barrel staves led Armand Hammer into the whiskey business; his appetite for a good steak at a time when they were hard to come by beckoned him into another field in which he became an almost simultaneous success—a sphere as far removed from the world of art as were his dubious potato and carrot squeezings. He knew nothing about the cattle game except that breeders and feeders were good customers for a by-product of his distilleries—the nutritious residue of the mash. It made good feed, and a nice little profit.

For all his affluence at that time, during World War II, Hammer experienced the average American's difficulty in buying good beef at the market. Chicken was no problem. The Hammers' eleven-acre estate at Red Bank, New Jersey—they called it Shadow Isle—employed a part-time farmer to take care of its chickens and vegetables, mostly corn. One day the farmer, hearing Hammer longing for a prime steak, suggested that he buy a steer, have it slaughtered, and store the cuts in a freezing locker. He estimated that it would cost about $200.

The doctor gave him orders to buy such a creature and have it butchered. And forgot all about the incident until one weekend when he returned to the estate from his New York office.

There he beheld for the first time an Aberdeen Black Angus.

The farmer was apologetic.

"I'm sorry," the man said, "I couldn't find a steer, so I bought this cow for you."

Hammer shrugged. It was still meat, he thought. Two hundred dollars' worth of it.

The man coughed.

"She's been bred," he said. "She's going to have a calf pretty soon."

"Good God!" Hammer exclaimed. "I can't kill a cow that's going to have a baby. Don't have her butchered. Treat her nice. Let her stay here on the farm and we'll see what happens. I don't need a steak that bad." The calf was dropped, the cow's execution was stayed, and Hammer watched the calf grow to maturity. Later the cow was bred again to a neighbor's bull and dropped another female calf.

In 1947 a neighbor who was an authority on the Black Angus breed invited the doctor and Angela to accompany him to Trenton to witness an exhibition, competition, and sale of purebred examples of the hardy species. A cow from the extensive herd of Seymour H. Knox of Buffalo, a major stockholder and executive of the F. W. Woolworth chain, won the top ribbon that day and was offered at auction. The bids from the professionals on hand droned past the $500 level when, to his own astonishment, Hammer began bidding. The cow, ribbon and all, was suddenly his for $1,000.

Knox's manager strolled over to congratulate him.

"I don't seem to place you," he said to the unflappable gambler. "What size herd do you have?"

Hammer burst out laughing and told him.

"What made you buy our champion?"

Hammer had been wondering about that, too. But he had an answer of sorts. He explained about the by-product of his grain and vegetable mash, its yeast and vitamin yield as cattle feed, and then heard himself saying, "I'd like to show how good this feed is by raising the best purebred cattle in the country."

"That's very interesting," Knox's man said. He said it as if intrigued. Had he expressed skepticism that a man with two cows and a calf on eleven acres in New Jersey could ever make a dent in the Black Angus breeding world, Hammer probably would have retreated from his newly found aspiration.

The doctor's sixth sense gave off a soundless signal.

"Would you like to come to work for me?" he asked the manager of one of the richest Angus operations in the world.

The man paused, then said, "Mr. Knox doesn't take enough interest in what I'm doing. If you're really sincere about wanting to go to the top of the business, then I'll come to work for you."

They made a deal then and there at Trenton and began the ponderous task of realizing Hammer's impetuously expressed new ambition.

"How do you want to go about it?" asked the freshly hired manager of the country's smallest Black Angus herd. "You want to go fast or slow?"

"Fast, of course."

"Well," the man said, scratching, "at that rate you'll have to buy the best bull in the country."

Two prize bulls happened to come up for sale within a few weeks of the doctor's dip into the cattle business. The better of the two, Prince Eric of Sunbeam, was offered at an exhibition and sale at Chillicothe, Missouri. Hammer flew there and was well briefed before entering the bidding arena: Prince Eric, five virile years old, was being justly hailed among Black Angus breeders as the bull of the century. He had never been shown at the top exhibition of them all—Chicago's International—but he had won grand champion honors elsewhere and his get had already become legendary. To the practiced eye, there was no mistaking a Prince Eric calf, bull, or heifer, so dominant was his strain.

Prince Eric was owned by a lumberman named Ralph L. Smith, who had bought him as a calf for the then astounding price of $40,000. Now, after making a lot of money out of Prince Eric's offspring, but in need of quick capital for his lumber business, Smith had decided to part with his herd, including the block-shaped bullyboy.

As a kind of warmup for the main event at Chillicothe, Hammer bought two Prince Eric daughters for $5,000 each, then, as Prince Eric was brought in, raised a natural question:

"How high do you think I'm going to have to go?"

"How high do you want to go?" his manager countered.

"How about fifteen thousand?"

The manager just looked at him. By the time the spirited bidding reached $15,000, Hammer had not been able to get his hand up. But at that plateau he made himself heard. When the bidding reached $30,000, in $1,000 jumps, the only two left in the contest were the doctor and a Chicago hosiery manufacturer named Leslie L. O'Bryan. The pace slowed to $100 upgradings. At $34,000, Hammer began to sweat. But not because his money was running out. In the excitement of the bidding he had forgotten that he had recently borrowed $10 million from the highly conservative Chase Manhattan bank to finance an expansion of his whiskey interests. He worried over what the executive vice-president of the bank, Bill Dubois, would say if he read the next day that Dr. Hammer, who knew nothing about the cattle business, had purchased the most expensive Black Angus bull on earth. However, he stayed in the running a bit longer.

"Thirty-five thousand," he called, mopping his brow.

"Thirty-five thousand one hundred," O'Bryan replied easily.

Hammer stopped. It was all over. The "bull of the century" was consigned to O'Bryan's big herd, there, supposedly, Hammer thought, to reap a fortune for his new owner.

Hammer quietly cursed himself. He would have to settle for next best, Prince Barbarian of Sunbeam, winner of the International reserve championship the year before, owned by New York restaurateur Jack Solomon. In the Black Angus trade the noble creature was known as Willie. Solomon had nicknamed him that in memory of his late great friend Will Rogers. To ballyhoo the auction, Solomon brought a planeload of Broadway celebrities to his upstate New York farm and retained Ed Sullivan to M.C. the bipeds' performances. Willie was knocked down to a determined Dr. Hammer for $27,500.

The Hammer herd began growing. Its eleven acres expanded to three farms and nine hundred acres. The nonpracticing doctor who had become prominent in art, whiskey, and what not was finding growing acceptance among the hard-nosed inner circle of Angus breeders. His spending sprees had boosted Angus prices in general; his innovations were studied and often copied. At his early Shadow Isle auctions he discovered that he could sell a $500 or $750 cow with a calf in her by Prince Barbarian for as much as $3,000.

But the doctor's acceptance among his peers was not total. For his own pride (and profit for his feed business) he yearned to have a grand champion at Chicago's International Livestock Exposition. Hammer retained Solomon's former manager, Lee Leachman, to put extra pounds on Willie, who won grand champion ribbons in several shows that year. Hammer pinned his hopes on the bull and shipped him to Chicago for the main event. On the day before the judging began, Hammer learned to his indignation that he was still regarded by the traditionalists as an intruder. The news was broken to him by Frank Richards, secretary of the Aberdeen-Angus Breeders' Association.

"Don't put Willie in the show," Richards said with brutal frankness. "Take my advice."

"I don't understand you. Everybody knows Willie's the best you've got here."

The secretary wheezed unhappily.

"You're not going to win with Willie," he said. "You've made a great success in this business and you've helped the whole structure of it. But we've got some powerful old-timers around who say you've gone too fast. They're out to cut you down to size. One of them is the judge. You can't possibly win, and that will hurt Willie's standing."

"Well, I'll be damned," Hammer said angrily. "If that's the kind of business I'm in, I won't stay in it. But I can't resist seeing if what you're saying is true. I'm putting Willie in."

Willie lost to what Hammer's advisers considered a relatively unimpressive bull. Hammer had some hard things to say about judges of the livestock show and called for a reform that would designate neutral professors of animal husbandry as judges of future shows. But he swallowed his bitterness and stayed in the business for two reasons: His cattle feed and sales were booming, and he had fallen in love with his herd. If he could not beat the establishment, he would join it. He began making a point of showing up up at every important livestock show and meeting the young and old and rich and poor of the Angus set. He made purchases at every important breeders' auction sale. The logistics problem was not a serious one. Hammer owned a twin-engined Beechcraft Executive in which he had had built a comfortable bed, a bar, easy chairs, and galley. He could fly overnight from New York to California with only one stop, thanks to extra fuel tanks. He could make it from Denver to New York and New York to the cow country of Florida nonstop. He paid top prices, and then some, to breeders who had been less than hospitable in the past. He began taking the middle spread in the *Angus Journal*, and he was always a generous host when a breeder and his family visited him in New York or Red Bank.

"I became accepted," he has remarked of this period. "I was genuinely fascinated by the business itself, and not as a tax refuge, as some of my competitors regarded it. I got a real bang out of winning prizes and coming up with champions. It also filled a void in my life, the fact that I had never gone forward with medicine. The inheritance of a great bull's and a great female's characteristics became for me an absorbing study, and so did the job that never ends—keeping the cattle healthy and curing them when they're not. The experience of walking through pastures in the open air and climbing fences was great for me. Jack Solomon could breed and show his cattle and also sell their steaks and roasts in his restaurant. I couldn't, wouldn't. I sold to breeders, mostly, but sometimes to the big commercial herds, where my bulls and cows upgraded the quality of the herds and the quality and even quantity of the meat."

Dr. Hammer, cattleman, devotee of a breed developed in Scotland in 1808, ventured only once into another kind of cow pasture. In adding to his New Jersey holdings he encountered a neighboring farmer who would not sell him the land he wanted unless he also bought the farmer's herd of Herefords. Hammer agreed and, upon acquisition of the land, fenced off the white-faced English breed from his all-black Angus and went about his collection of other callings.

The fence was not strong enough. A Hereford bull burst through it and covered an Angus cow who was in heat. The doctor's manager was disturbed.

"Bloodlines," he lectured Hammer. "Records. We can't afford another headache like this. Make up your mind. Are you going to be an Angus man or a Hereford man? You can't be both."

It was not a hard decision for Hammer to make. He sold off his Herefords, the fence came down, and the Aberdeens moved forward and grazed. Willie and his sons, and other bulls of good breeding for which the doctor had paid dearly, ruled and multiplied until where there once had been one—intended for a food locker—there came forth several hundreds.

The Hammer herd became the envy of the Angus industry. It enjoyed fine grazing fields, the most modern and efficient barns, and, when being shown, the services of the top handlers in the business. The cattle were transported in the latest design of vans and, as a matter of good business, Hammer never let anybody in the trade forget for an instant that the feed that made his herd big, beautiful, and bountiful was Shadow Isle Feed—rich in what was left after most of the alcohol and whiskey had been pressed out of it.

The only cloud in Hammer's cattle-raising sky was that he did not own Prince Eric; that he had opted for timidity at the irretrievable moment when he had the opportunity to buy the bull of the century. It was a source of lingering distress to him even though by now his two annual public auctions at Shadow Isle were grossing $500,000 each. To that $1 million was added hundreds of thousands of dollars from private sales.

Hammer faced the grinding fact: He must have Prince Eric! He could not rest until he did.

Then one day he heard arresting news about the country's most potent bull. Prince Eric had become impotent at the age of eight!

Gossip spreads as fast in cattle breeding as in human procreation. The spreader of the dire news about Prince Eric was an itinerant veterinarian from Crystal Lake, Illinois, named Dr. Cropsey. He called periodically at Shadow Isle to check herd problems and enjoyed this stop especially because he saw in Hammer a kindred soul in the medical profession. Hammer made a point of being on hand for such occasions and dressed the part: boots, old clothes, and rubber gloves. He kept careful notes as he and Cropsey attended to vaginal examinations and discussed gynecological problems such as state of pregnancies and possibility of aborts. It was on one of these visitations, over dinner, that Cropsey revealed the plight of the bull Hammer so coveted.

"What happened to him?" Hammer asked, not knowing whether to be sad or relieved over the report.

"My guess is that Mr. O'Bryan overdid him," Dr. Cropsey said. "He let him run with fifty cows and that was just too many for any bull, even Prince Eric. He screwed himself almost to death, the way I look at it. Worse, there was a handler on that farm who would beat him with a bullwhip when he became hesitant about mounting a cow. So, the way I understand it, every time now that he's given a cow, he looks the other way. He associates her with being whipped. He's only eight years old. I think his problem is psychological, not physiological. I've been doing some work in artificial insemination as consultant to the herd belonging to the Curtis Candy Company in Chicago. I have a hunch this bull's semen may be as vital as it ever was. All I'd have to do to prove it would be to put a condom on him, go in his rectum, massage his prostate, and wait for the ejaculation. Then examine the semen and check its viability."

"That's a hell of an idea, Doctor," Dr. Hammer said. "Let's do it. I'll call O'Bryan. He'll probably sell Prince Eric to me for a song, now he's listed as a nonbreeder. Then we can experiment and get on with this artificial insemination. He's *got* to be still good. Imagine having the bull of the century working for you. And be able to produce as many of his offspring as you want, artificially. It would be better than a gold mine. . . . I'll call my good friend O'Bryan immediately."

Hammer went to the phone at the farm and reached O'Bryan in

Chicago. There was a cheerful exchange involving generalities for a minute or two, then Hammer closed in.

"Les, old friend," he said, "how would you like to sell me Prince Eric?"

"I'd like very much to sell you Prince Eric," O'Bryan said.

"Grand!" the doctor enthused. "You've got a sale. How much do you want for him?"

"One hundred thousand dollars," O'Bryan said.

Narrowly averting a heart attack, Hammer shouted, "Are you crazy? I just heard your bull is a nonbreeder; hasn't bred for a year and more."

"Then why do you want to buy him?" O'Bryan asked, devastatingly. Before the doctor could think up a reply, O'Bryan came back on the line. "I know what you want to do," he said. "People from the university have been over to see me. They tell me this bull could be made to breed artificially."

"Well, then, why the hell don't you do it?" Hammer asked testily.

"I'm just too busy with the women's underwear business to bother about my herd right now. So I'd just as soon sell him."

Hammer perked up.

"You paid thirty-five thousand, one hundred dollars for him," he said. "I tell you what I'll do: I'll give you your money back. I'll give you what you paid for him three years ago. After all, there's no guarantee that it'll work. I'll have to take a chance."

"One hundred thousand dollars," O'Bryan repeated.

"All right, I'll give you fifty thousand."

"One hundred thousand."

"Les, I'll split the difference with you. I'll give you seventy-five thousand dollars providing I can make a test."

O'Bryan was silent for a time, then said, "All right, come on out."

Hammer flew out the next morning in the Beechcraft with Dr. Cropsey and his farm manager, Bill Ljungdahl. The pilot put the aircraft down on O'Bryan's extensive fields of well-nibbled grass, and the owner of Prince Eric came out of a barn with a cheerful welcome. He led the party to a paddock where stood Prince Eric.

"He was the most beautiful Angus ever bred," Hammer still says, with much the same awe that overwhelms him when he speaks of a Rembrandt or of a private meeting with Leonid Brezhnev. "My heart skipped a beat. I just stood there gaping at him and wanting to kick myself for missing the chance to have owned him three years before. I thought of all of his get in that period. He was pretty old for a bull, at eight, but he looked like he had many more good years in him. The only question was his spermatozoa."

The matter of a test in that respect had been explored during the phone conversation. Dr. Cropsey went to work on Prince Eric. He had brought along the rudimentary gear, huge condom, rubber glove, smear glass, and small microscope.

The bull of the century came forth abundantly. Cropsey put a specimen on glass and focused his hurriedly produced eyepiece. He let out a low whistle.

"Look at this," he said to Hammer. Hammer squinted professionally at the slide.

"There were thousands, thousands and thousands of spermatozoa swimming around," recalls the man who knew any offspring of Prince Eric commanded a current sales price of $5,000. "All I could see through the microscope were five-thousand-dollar bills swimming around."

Cropsey quickly repacked his kit, and the two excited doctors went off in search of their host. They found him in his farmhouse.

"We're satisfied," Dr. Hammer said. "We inspected him and I'll buy him. Here's my check for seventy-five thousand dollars. I accept all your conditions: You don't guarantee him as a breeder. If he drops dead five minutes from now, it's my tough luck." (Actually, Hammer had found time early that morning before taking off for O'Bryan's farm to take out a $75,000 life insurance policy on Prince Eric. The premium was a fat $7,500 for one year. Lloyd's was wary of the bull's age.)

O'Bryan took the check and looked at it for a moment. Then he handed it back to Hammer.

"It isn't enough," he said.

Hammer was stunned. "What do you mean it's not enough?"

"I told you I wanted one hundred thousand dollars."

"No, you didn't! I told you I'd split the difference at seventy-five thousand and you said to come on out."

"Sure I said come on out," O'Bryan said, "but I didn't say I'd take seventy-five thousand."

Hammer was outraged. He has seldom used bad language in his extraordinary life, but on that occasion he said to his friend O'Bryan, father of a large brood of children, "You son of a bitch, I wouldn't buy that bull if it was the last bull in the world!" He turned to the others. "Come on, let's go home," he ordered, and they marched to the parked plane, a day and a scheme in shambles.

The following December, at Chicago, Hammer was convinced that he had a world's champion in a young cow by Prince Eric that he had bought at auction for $5,000 when she was a calf. She met all the requirements of Angus aristocracy. She was about as broad as she was tall, beautiful head, and a string of lesser but important championships behind her, in both the United States and Canada. He had bungled the early purchase of Prince Eric, he had been hornswoggled out of an international championship for Prince Barbarian, called Willie, but here clearly was a cow who showed all the class of her sire at his prime. This magnificent two-year-old could not miss. The grudges against Hammer had disappeared; he was a treasured and respected member of the fraternity. Even was sometimes asked to judge.

Hammer was seated in a box borrowed from his friend Gussie Busch at the Chicago livestock yards on what would be his day of days, talking shop to some of his friends, when one of them, an experienced hand named Cal Peterson, interrupted him.

"Hey, look!" Peterson said excitedly. "Is that your cow they're leading out?"

Hammer turned his head with confidence. Then a dumbfounded stare. It was not his pride and joy by Prince Eric. This one was magnificent, big, low slung, all the right configuration, plus an unprecedented harvest of hair. Hammer left the box and sought out the handler, who recognized him and prematurely sympathized with his dilemma.

"Where did that cow come from?" the doctor demanded. "I've been showing mine all year, all over, and we've never come across this one. She's the most magnificent cow I've ever seen."

"She's a full sister to your cow, Doctor," the handler said. "Both by Prince Eric out of the same mother. My boss kept her up at his place in Colorado, in the mountains. She got that wonderful coat of hair from the snow and cold. This is the first time she's ever been shown."

Prince Eric's Colorado baby was judged grand champion; his New Jersey baby made reserve grand champion, which means runner-up in less charitable language. It was the first time in half a century that full sisters had finished one-two at Chicago.

"I was sick," Hammer recalls. "I left the stockyards, went back to the Palmer House, and fell in bed. I couldn't nap, as I usually do at that time of day. It was just too much. There I was: so close to winning my first grand championship ribbon, only to lose out . . . lose out to a full sister of *my* cow. And both by Prince Eric. Prince Eric was making a fool of me! So I called O'Bryan. I told him I'd meet his price, but if he didn't come to the hotel immediately . . ."

"I'll be over," O'Bryan said.

The doctor rose from his bed of pain and went down to the lobby. He asked the desk clerk for a sheet of stationery. When his friendly foe arrived, he led him to a writing table in the lobby. There he wrote out a simple bill of sale: $25,000 down, $75,000 when the bull was picked up.

"I held my breath," Hammer says of the great showdown of his then current life. "He had doubtless heard about the grand championships the two daughters of Prince Eric had just won. It wouldn't have surprised me a bit if he had told me he had raised Prince Eric's price to two hundred thousand. But he signed and accepted the down payment of twenty-five thousand."

Three years and $64,900 after he had his first chance, not to mention the lost get, Armand Hammer owned Prince Eric.

That night at the traditional dinner and ball, the doctor was roundly applauded and congratulated. He had set a new world record price for an Angus bull, indeed an eight-year-old bull considered by the industry at large as incapable of breeding. The next morning Hammer chartered a DC-3 freighter, paid O'Bryan the $75,000 remainder, put Dr. Cropsey under contract on a full-time basis to manage the artificial insemination program, picked up Prince Eric, borrowed a little heifer to keep him company, and flew back to Shadow Isle.

What followed still remains difficult to believe. Prince Eric's injected semen produced a thousand calves in the three remaining years of his life. He earned $2 million for Shadow Isle. Before he died, he sired six international champions, several without ever having met the mothers. On auction days at the Hammer place in New Jersey, private planes landed and took off as if an air show were in progress. Breeders came from as far away as Argentina to contract for the get of a bull who hated the female of his species. Sales of Shadow Isle Feed (enthusiastically endorsed by Prince Eric in the cattle press) skyrocketed. So did the Angus business in general, and Hammer, the one-time Johnny-come-lately, became the acknowledged leader in the field. Rivals marveled. He sold the Prince Eric cow he had lost with at Chicago for $22,000, for a profit of $17,000. He seldom missed a show in the United States or Canada, never neglected an opportunity to sell or buy, never failed to plug his feed and its most renowned consumer, flew countless miles to be on hand to root for a Prince Eric cow or bull in competition.

"It was a fabulous time," he told a reporter. "It seemed as if nobody else in the business had a chance. I'd buy a cow for, say, five hundred or a thousand dollars, or sometimes as little as three hundred. I'd have her injected with the semen of Prince Eric and sell her, while she was still carrying her calf, for maybe five thousand. A cow with a calf by Prince Eric at side brought from seventy-five hundred to ten thousand dollars. Then I got the idea of 'three for one.' After a cow calved by Prince Eric's semen she could soon be made pregnant again in the same way, and I could sell the cow, the calf at side, and the one coming up for a single price, anything from ten to twenty thousand dollars, depending on whether the calf was a bull with indications of developing into a carbon copy of his sire. Thus a new owner could have a foundation to start a whole new Prince Eric herd.

"It was like being partners with a mint."

An interesting change came over Prince Eric when he reached the ripe old age of eleven, the equivalent of a human being's biblically allotted three score and ten. He became interested in compliant cows again. He apparently had forgotten the bullwhip. Management took a dim view of this. Artificially spent, his semen was more valuable than if naturally stimulated. It could, and did, impregnate many more cows. Moreover, Dr. Cropsey had been experimenting with freezing samples of it, with some assurance that it could be used a year or more after it had been ejaculated. Theoretically, Prince Eric might thus propagate his widely sought-after get for at least a year after his death. This was the limit imposed by the rules of the Angus Association.

Prince Eric died a sport. Sometime during the night of August 13, 1953, he shed his reputation as an impartial supplier of seeds and became enormously enamored of a heifer in heat on the other side of a high barbed-wire fence that separated him from a bevy of young cows who would be inseminated with his endless spermatozoa in the next day or two. He attempted to scale the fence, almost made it, apparently, and the wire prongs at the top ripped him down his middle. He crashed on his own side of the fence and was found in the morning, dead in a pool of blood.

Less than a year later, Hammer phoned his friend Frank Richards, the

American Aberdeen-Angus Breeders' Association secretary who had once warned him that his Willie could not win, and gave him some news that shook the industry. Richards asked him to put it in letter form, and the doctor did. The letter read:

Dear Frank:

It was with a heavy heart that I advised you over the telephone a few days ago that it is necessary, for tax reasons, to disperse the Shadow Isle Herd. The enclosed letter from our tax counsel is self-explanatory. I was trying to find some other way out of the dilemma caused by the fact that the cattle are owned by a family corporation, and my brothers feel it is essential that we follow the advice of our tax counsel. In so doing, we would be subject to a tax rate of possibly 26 percent at capital gain rate instead of a possible 90 percent on ordinary income. Fortunately, there is nothing in the tax law which prevents me from going back into the Angus business on my own accord after the dissolution of the partnership with my brothers. I realize that it will take years to build up a herd of such proven producing cows as comprise the present Shadow Isle Herd. The result of our last seven public auction sales, totaling $2,722,600 from 634 head, are an average of $4,294. And our outstanding show record during the past five years will attest to the quality of our brood cows, as well as our herd sires.

It is ten years since I acquired my first registered Angus. This has been one of the happiest periods of my life, partly due to the pleasure I derived in assembling the Shadow Isle Herd and watching the results of our constructive breeding program. Meeting so many fine people among my fellow Angus breeders has added immeasurably to the pleasure I have enjoyed.

Some of my friends tell me that this is a poor time to hold such a sale as prices are lower than they were a year or two ago. Even if this is so, I have no alternative as our tax counsel advises all possible speed. However, in this connection, I remember in the years back when I had a pleasant visit with you in your office in Chicago and you showed me a catalogue of the Andelot Angus Dispersion back in 1900. We both marveled at the fact that over 50 years ago good Angus cattle brought as high as $2,800 apiece when ordinary registered Angus cattle were selling around $75 a head. When one considers what $1 would buy 50 years ago, it makes one certain that the purchase of good purebred Angus cattle is still the best investment that one can make.

I want to thank you for the many courtesies shown to me by you and members of your staff. Our association of over 26,000 members is the best testimony of a solid foundation in the Angus business. I look forward to serving you as a breeder and a member of the American Aberdeen-Angus Association for the balance of my life.

Richards expressed himself as "shocked" in his return letter. "I hate to see such herds as yours scattered to the four corners," he wrote.

Hammer's 350-page, finely printed dissolution catalog, "Shadow Isle's Sale of the Century," compares as a collector's item with his book "The Quest of the Romanoff Treasures." That one lamented over the senseless destruction of so many great works of czarist art. The dissolution catalog wept over the "bull of the century," the bull who gave his all—and then some—for love.

(See Appendix C for a statement by Dr. Hammer for the dissolution catalog.)

The Shadow Isle dissolution sale lasted three days, May 10–12, 1954, and was the first to raise $1 million, a fitting climax to an offbeat adventure that began so casually when he expressed a wish for a good steak. He kept a few Angus for sentiment's sake, gave Prince Eric a permanent grave and headstone on what he kept of the New Jersey farm, and made gifts of the great bull's progeny to Angus fancier President Dwight D. Eisenhower and to a delighted Soviet dictator, Nikita Khrushchev.

The excitement and challenge Armand Hammer found in the cattle business died the day Prince Eric was found next to a barbed-wire fence. "The way he was, he might have lasted for years more," the doctor has said in his fond eulogies to this bravest of bulls.

Chapter 14

A New Sunrise
at Campobello

═══

Perhaps because of his nine years of residence behind the Iron Curtain, Armand Hammer had a peephole drilled through the wall near his desk on the mezzanine floor of the Hammer Galleries on Fifth Avenue. It commanded a gimlet-eyed view of whatever was happening in the show-room below. One day in 1952 Victor buzzed into Armand's eyrie excitedly and said, "Elliott Roosevelt's downstairs." Armand verified that announcement with a quick squint through the peeper.

"What's he want?" he asked his brother.

"He says his father left him Campobello in the will and he wants to sell it."

"How much does he want for it?"

"He's willing to sell it for a song, but it has been terribly neglected and will require a couple of hundred thousand dollars to restore it."

"Buy it," Armand said.

Armand's affection for the Roosevelt family was so great it even encompassed Elliott. He had been brought under the Rooseveltian spell by two mutual friends, Senator William H. King, Utah Democrat who had once been his guest at the Brown House in Moscow, and former Senator Henry Hollis, Democrat from New Hampshire, who had been Hammer's attorney when both were living in Paris. The Democrats spoke to F.D.R. about the doctor's versatility and availability. Senator King recommended that Hammer be appointed a consultant on various plans to help Britain in general and, in particular, on one of the White House's prickliest pre–Pearl Harbor crises: how to help Britain combat the German submarine menace without involving the United States in the war. Roosevelt invited him to Washington for a chat.

Hammer was ushered into the office of General "Pa" Watson, the appointment secretary, who told him there would be a delay: the President was tied up with a group of committee chairmen from Capitol Hill. Half an hour later, Hammer was joined in Watson's waiting room by William C. Bullitt, who had been the first U.S. ambassador to the Soviet Union. Bullitt's appointment was to follow Hammer's. In the course of the small talk that followed, Hammer admired a pair of outsized dice on Watson's desk. Watson said they had been a gift of General G. W. Goethals, builder of the Panama Canal, and had been carved from some of the lumber used in its construction. Then that least formal of presidential secretaries said, "While we're waiting, let's have a crap game."

The three of them got down on the rug, pulled out their money, and started rolling the dice. Half an hour later the committee chairmen filed out and Watson took Hammer into the Oval Office and introduced him.

"This man is lucky, Mr. President," Watson said. "Anything he touches gets lucky. While we were waiting for you to get rid of the congressmen, he took a couple of hundred dollars from Bullitt and me shooting craps."

In Hammer, F.D.R. found a strong supporter of the theory—not generally shared in isolationist-minded America—that some legal method must be found to bolster Britain against Hitler, short of a declaration of war. Hammer had originally devised a plan for giving Britain financial aid in return for leases of military bases in the Western Hemisphere. Hammer's plan was printed in pamphlet form on June 11, 1940, at Senator King's request, and copies were widely distributed. It was entitled "A Proposal for the Immediate Leasing of Military Bases in Certain Territories of Great Britain in the Western Hemisphere, Payment for Which Is to Be Applied in Full Settlement of the War Debts and Any Balance to Be Placed at the Disposal of England for Purchases in this Country." Hammer now strongly urged that the controversial U.S. destroyers bases ploy was preferable. It was, he said, a way of lessening the virtual stranglehold that U-boats were exercising against Atlantic shipping and would provide the United States with steppingstone bases it would need for its aircraft and Navy if it ever entered the war. The President assigned Hammer to Harry Hopkins, who put him to work developing the fifty-destroyer deal as well as the lend-lease program, which in due time Roosevelt implemented. It proved to be one of the early milestones of the Allied victory.

Here was Dr. Hammer urging immediate aid to Great Britain eighteen months before Pearl Harbor and pointing out the danger of eventual attack by a victorious Germany in alliance with Italy, Japan, and Russia. If Hammer were pro-Soviet, as he has been accused of being by his detractors, he would hardly be urging such action when Russia was an ally of Germany. This was a full year before Hitler suddenly reversed his policy of friendship with Russia and made a surprise attack on the Russians.

The Roosevelts, Hopkinses, and Hammers became fast friends. When Elliott set out to add the Campobello property to the list of family memorabilia he needed to sell, he chose a customer he sensed could not turn it down. The fact that F.D.R. had been stricken with polio at Campobello, had spent his honeymoon with Eleanor there, that Franklin Delano Roosevelt, Jr., had been born there, and that the family had spent time there even after Roosevelt had been elected President were sales points Elliott did not need to mention to Hammer.

With the artistic Victor in charge, the Hammers set about a major reconstruction of the rundown estate. It had deteriorated badly, Bay of Fundy winters being what they are, since the President's death in 1945. A new roof, replacement of supports, floors, and windows, and restoration of the gardens cost as much as or more than the original price. But when it was finished, the Hammers were justly proud, and Armand indignantly turned down a $500,000 offer from a syndicate that proposed to commercialize it. He preserved it for his own family and set aside a portion of it for Mrs. Roosevelt and her family, for use any time they wished. Mrs. Roosevelt and Victor refurnished the main house in keeping with what it had looked like when she first knew it. Fortunately, most of the original furnishings were found intact. Victor also scrounged memorabilia from F.D.R.'s youth—such as the rowing oars he used in a Harvard shell—and, in due course, it was once again what F.D.R. used to call "my beloved island." Nobody was more pleased than the widow Roosevelt, who spent most of her summers there amidst her bittersweet memories and in the company of the vivacious Mama Rose.

Mrs. Roosevelt died November 7, 1962. The previous August she had made what turned out to be her last pilgrimage to Franklin's "beloved island." On the nineteenth of that month she wrote Armand's brother Victor:

Dear Victor:

On this my last day at Campobello I want to thank you again for your great kindness in letting me stay in the cottage and for arranging everything for my comfort. I have had a most delightful time, topped off today with one of the most beautiful days the Island could produce and ending in a glorious sunset.

I am leaving much, much stronger than I came and I attribute the renewal of my strength to the peace and quiet I have found here.

Words cannot express my gratitude to you and Irene but I do hope you realize that it is deep and warm.

Looking forward to seeing you both very soon, and hoping you will come to visit at Hyde Park before long.

> Affectionately,
> ELEANOR ROOSEVELT

P.S. Your couple are wonderful. They could not have been more kind, and of course Linnea [the Roosevelt family's former housekeeper] was good as gold.

In that same August, President Kennedy, speaking in Maine after the dedication of a short causeway-bridge that linked Maine with the historic little Canadian island where so much of the Roosevelt saga had been written, told a rain-soaked airport crowd that he thought a park in the vicinity of F.D.R.'s old haunts would "further strengthen the bond of friendship between the two countries." The following May, the subject came up again at Hyannis Port, at a meeting between J.F.K. and Canadian Prime Minister Lester Pearson. Dr. Hammer happened to listen to a radio news report alluding to it. He promptly called his friend from Maine, Senator Edmund Muskie, whom he had supported in his Senate race, and told him of his intention of making a gift of Campobello to the United States and Canada. The Senator enthusiastically supported the idea. Hammer called R. A. Tweedie, the head of the Canadian Tourist Department, who had been trying in vain to buy the property from Hammer for the Canadian government. He too applauded the doctor's generosity. Finally, Hammer called his congressman, Jimmy Roosevelt, and asked him to relay a message to the President and the Prime Minister. For confirmation, he put it in a telegram:

FOLLOWING MY CONVERSATION WITH YOU, SENATOR MUSKIE AND R. A. TWEEDIE, THIS WILL CONFIRM AND REQUEST YOU TO INFORM THE PRESIDENT

THAT THE HAMMER FAMILY WILL DONATE CAMPOBELLO ROOSEVELT HOME
AND GROUNDS, ESTIMATED TO BE ABOUT TWENTY ACRES, TO THE UNITED
STATES GOVERNMENT AND THE CANADIAN GOVERNMENT FOR PUBLIC PUR-
POSE TO COMMEMORATE PRESIDENT AND MRS. FRANKLIN D. ROOSEVELT. GIFT
WILL INCLUDE ALL ORIGINAL CAMPOBELLO FURNISHINGS WITH ADDITIONS
THERE FROM WHITE HOUSE AND HYDE PARK.

The President called Hammer in Los Angeles the next morning to
check on whether the offer he had heard about was authentic.

"Yes, I meant it," Hammer told him.

"That's a very generous gift, Doctor," the President said from the
summer White House. "The Prime Minister is here with me at Hyannis
Port. We wanted to get your confirmation before we released it to the
press."

"Have you received the telegram I sent to Jimmy Roosevelt last night
to show to you?" Hammer asked the caller. Kennedy said he had not; that
evidently there was a delay in its transmission.

"Would you mind holding the phone until I get a copy of it to read
to you?" Hammer requested.

The President of the United States, commander in chief of the armed
forces and leader of the free world, said no, he wouldn't mind. Trouble
followed immediately. Hammer could not find the copy of the wire. He
searched high and low in the house, while the President held the phone.
When he returned empty-handed to the phone the first voice he heard
was that of his wife, Frances.

"Do you realize that you've kept the President waiting on the phone?"
she scolded him.

Hammer brushed that aside, picked up the phone, and said, "Here's
what I said in the wire." He repeated the longish telegram from memory,
writing it down as he spoke. Later, when he found the missing copy and
compared it with his note, he found he had not omitted a word!

On May 12, 1963, the President directed the State and Interior Departments to enter into negotiations with their counterparts in the Canadian
government to implement the Campobello memorial. Two days later, the
Senate and House of the State of Maine passed a resolution commending
the Hammers for their generosity. The following January, two months
after Kennedy's assassination, President Lyndon Johnson invited Armand,
Victor, and Harry to the White House for luncheon and the signing in
the Treaty Room of the intergovernment agreement. The following Au-

gust 20, after Queen Elizabeth II had added her signature to the agreement, the First Ladies of the United States and Canada officially opened Roosevelt Campobello International Park.

In her remarks, Lady Bird Johnson said, "Both Franklin and Mrs. Eleanor Roosevelt knew the meaning of courage sustained by compassion in every day of their lives. This landmark is an inspiration for all future generations. This island off the northeastern coast of our continent will always turn its face toward the sunrise of world events—the sunrise at Campobello. We owe a great debt of gratitude to the members of the Hammer family for their generous gift."

Armand, who had permitted producer-playwright Dore Schary to film portions of the moving drama *Sunrise at Campobello* on the spot, was called upon to respond for the Hammer family. In the course of his remarks over an international radio hookup, he said, "In one of T. S. Eliot's 'Four Quartets' he speaks of the 'still point of the turning world.' I believe that Franklin Delano Roosevelt would consider that today we have made a good beginning."

Armand Hammer appears destined to leave many monuments behind him. But Campobello he may consider in his heart of hearts to be his finest.

Chapter 15

Accidental Occidental

Armand Hammer's entrance into the oil business was as casual as his arrivals on the scenes of earlier triumphs. That it would become the central source of his power in assorted fields of activity could not have crossed his mind as he dipped a tentative toe in the chill of one of the world's riskiest trades. He originally thought of oil speculation as a tax shelter. The sales of his bountiful whiskey and cattle businesses, plus the modest but prestigious income from Hammer Galleries, had added several multis to the millionaire status of his schooldays at Columbia. It is one of the imponderables of his life that his busiest career—oil—had its origins in what was to have been the time of his withdrawal from the commercial world. He was fifty-eight, the year was 1956, and he had enough.

Aside from the concern over finding a shield against the prospect of astronomical income (and confiscatory inheritance) taxes, Hammer was undergoing at that time two emotional litigations: a murder charge in Los Angeles against his son, Julian, and his second wife Angela's demands for a colossal separation settlement in a suit she instituted in New York. He had moved out of their Red Bank, New Jersey, home, claiming he was unable to endure further the "public embarrassment and humiliation" caused by her drinking problem. On the advice of his attorney, Louis Nizer, Hammer countered by bringing a successful divorce action in New Jersey, on the grounds of cruelty, rarely granted in favor of a husband. Hammer made a generous settlement in favor of Angela. He also won the freedom of his son, and, as a kind of remarkable dividend, Hammer gained his third and present wife.

He met Frances Tolman through Victor about twenty years before, during the Romanoff sales at Marshall Field's in Chicago. Their paths thereafter had separated. But then, out of the blue, he received a letter from her. She told him that she had lost her husband some years earlier and that she had read about the doctor's divorce battle with the second Mrs. Hammer—in the *Police Gazette,* she added roguishly. She had bought a home in Westwood, near Beverly Hills, and found California enchanting after her years on the Tolman estate in Mundelein, Illinois. She had also read about the charge against Julian and asked if she could help him in any way.

They were married in January 1956, shortly after Hammer obtained his divorce from Angela, and settled down to a life that was intended to be as placid as the Pacific at sunset. They shared a love of the arts, as the wing of the Los Angeles County Museum that bears their names attests. Together they expanded and decorated her pleasant house with some of the French Impressionists from his art collection and joined together in philanthropic good deeds. Armand contributed his Old Master collection to the University of Southern California and made a multimillion-dollar grant to the Jonas Salk Institute to establish the Armand Hammer Cancer Center to research his belief that cancer might be controlled, as was polio, by immunization. Hammer was elected chairman of the Executive Committee. Hammer acquired a second collection of masterpieces valued at over $25 million and announced he had willed the paintings to the Los Angeles County Museum and the drawings to the National Gallery in Washington, D.C.

They were to live happily ever after, but not according to the original plan. No man who had done as much in so many worlds of endeavor, and seen as much, and hustled as hard, could sit for very long in an easy chair in the flowery back yard of that ultimate back yard named Westwood, one of the most attractive parts of greater Los Angeles. The seductive song of tax relief—number 1 on the hit parade among most mortals, particularly rich ones—was sung to him by an accountant he happened to meet at a cocktail party. The accountant suggested that oil investment, with its enticing prospects of failure—dry holes—would be his best bet.

Hammer's problem, when first he ventured into oil, was that he had trouble drilling a dry hole. An enraged competitor was to say in later years, "Every time he poked a hole in the ground, up came a gusher."

Hammer laughs off such barbs. He prefers another assessment of luck:

"Luck seems to come to the guy who works fourteen hours a day, seven days a week." It is an understatement.

But in 1956, ready to spend the rest of his days swimming, sunning, and giving away his trove, there came the temptation of oil, or rather the prospect of losing money in it for tax purposes. A friend brought to his attention a struggling California-based company named Occidental, born in the early 1920s and by then rated with the Edsel. Occidental's stock was selling at eighteen cents a share on the Los Angeles Stock Exchange at that point in its drab history, which meant the entire outstanding 600,000 shares had a market value of something slightly over $100,000. Hammer examined the balance sheet and after a brief scanning determined that the true worth of Occidental was $34,000. He turned down the offer to buy treasury shares at market. However, Hammer and his wife agreed to loan Occidental $50,000 for a 50 percent interest to enable it to drill two wells, figuring that if they were dry holes, it could be written off as a tax loss. Both hit, to the astonishment of Hammer, and one brought in a little field at Burrel, California, about fifty miles north of Los Angeles.

Hammer was hooked. The stock jumped to a dollar a share and Hammer started buying it in the open market. When Occidental was offered an opportunity to buy a small oil field with nine producing wells and several undrilled locations in Dominguez, a suburb of Los Angeles, from an elderly Texas wildcatter named J. K. Wadley, who was in need of a million dollars in cash, the company offered the Hammers the same kind of 50 percent participation. Hammer rushed to Wadley's hotel, the Beverly Hilton in Beverly Hills, accompanied by Arthur Groman, his attorney, and consummated the deal in the hotel lobby.

Groman picked up a piece of hotel stationery and scribbled a short note of agreement which the principals signed with alacrity. Hammer laid off 50 percent to one of his friends, New York builder Louis Abrons. Like Hammer, Abrons had never seen an oil well, but he was intrigued by Hammer's sudden success. This time Hammer took an option to convert his investment into Occidental stock at the then market price of $1.50 per share. The next day Hammer called Groman and asked him if he'd like to drive to Dominguez, where Occidental's newly acquired nine old-fashioned rocker-pump wells were located. Combined, they produced about a thousand barrels a day. On the way there, Hammer stopped at a drugstore.

"I want to buy a Polaroid camera," he explained to his lawyer.

"Why?"

"Because I've never seen a producing oil field up close in my life, and I want to get some snapshots to show Frances her oil wells."

Hammer saw a number of other Occidental wells over the next few years, some producers and some dry. He maintained a remarkable faith in the future of one of the world's least stable occupations. On Hammer's recommendation Groman was elected to the Occidental board and, a bit later, a new friend he had made through Frances since arriving in California, Neil Herman Jacoby, then dean (and, in effect, founder) of the Graduate School of Business Administration, U.C.L.A. In 1957 Hammer himself was elected president of the struggling company. He converted his loan into stock, which was later split 3 for 1, and became the company's largest shareholder, a position he still holds. Hammer's boundless optimism proved contagious. Friends and friends of friends bought hundreds of thousands of shares in private placements to help him fund continued exploration. Some sold out when the shares showed a modest profit; others, including Mr. and Mrs. Randolph Apperson Hearst, hung on.

Hammer was still an apprentice in this erratic new business venture, but he felt he knew enough about the game to send in a pinch-hitter to replace the driller with a drinking problem whom he had inherited from the old management. Typically, he inquired around as to where he might find and retain the best in the business. It was as naive a search as the quest of a new Hank Aaron by a minor-league club. But Hammer consulted Professor Nick van Wingen of the University of Southern California, a former Shell engineer whom Hammer had placed on his board. Van Wingen said, "When the majors have drilling problems they say, 'Send for Gene Reid.'" Reid generally commanded great sums for his services, but the drilling business was in a slump when Hammer approached him and he accepted Occidental stock in lieu of hard money for his drilling rigs, valued at $400,000 and heavily mortgaged. Reid said, "I've always wanted to be worth a million dollars, but after thirty years I've never made it. I have a feeling I'll make it with you." (Before Reid passed away in 1970, he was worth some $30 million, all made on Occidental stock.)

Hammer was moving. Also, he was being studied by Professor Jacoby.

"What attracted me to this man was his entrepreneurship," the distinguished educator said recently of those swaddling days of Occidental. "I had never known anyone of his enthusiasm, his vision. He has a truly extraordinary nose for sniffing out business opportunities and, what is more important, acting on them quickly. Takes courage. That's what I try to teach my students here at U.C.L.A. But, looking back, I suppose I had a selfish interest in association with Dr. Hammer because I felt that here was a marvelous case study on an entrepreneur at work. And, indeed, it has proved to be that."

The economics adviser to Presidents from Truman to Nixon was asked why Hammer, a very rich man at the time, had sought outside financing and what amounted to a partnership with Reid when he had the means to retain 100 percent of the company.

"I don't think any man is wise to put all his fortune into oil drilling," Professor Jacoby said mildly. "This is a very risky business."

It was an understatement. Oxy, as it came to be known on the New York Stock Exchange, had just about exhausted its $10 million exploration program for 1961 when Hammer made the decision to shoot the rest of the works on a hunch that had seized Bob Teitsworth, a fine young geologist who had offered his services to Reid. Teitsworth contended that Oxy should take up a group of leases surrendered by Texaco, which he felt had given up too soon on a likely gas field near Lathrop in the Sacramento River valley east of San Francisco. It had lain fallow for a few years, the last well drilled being a barren hole 5,600 feet deep. The Reid team moved its people and gear into the area and the geologist pointed to an innocuous-looking spot of ground about six hundred feet from the abandoned dry hole. The rig climbed, the bit bit, and Hammer tapped himself, his wife, his board of directors, and a group of western friends for the money to probe deeper than Texaco. It was the last well in the 1961 drilling program; do or die.

At 8,600 feet, little Oxy punctured the second biggest gas field in California, worth about $200 million.

A few months later it hit another bonanza at the Brentwood field nearby.

The joy of striking it rich was temporarily dampened when the doctor trooped off to the Pacific Gas and Electric Company, prepared, in his own mind at least, to sign a twenty-year contract for his gas. The huge utilities concern, Oxy's ostensible customer, brought him up short by saying sorry, it didn't need his gas. It had but recently gone to the heavy expense of building a pipeline from Alberta, Canada, to the San Francisco Bay Area. Hammer was flabbergasted, but not for long. He went to the City of Los Angeles, informed the city fathers that he planned to build a pipeline down from Lathrop, and would undersell Pacific Gas or any other bidders to supply the city's needs. Pacific Gas eventually threw up its hands and signed the contract. Oxy, with gas contracts in hand, had hit the jackpot and now began selling carve-outs for cash.

Prior to the Lathrop strike, Oxy had picked up control of the Mutual Broadcasting System for $700,000, and when its president had to be dismissed, Hammer somehow found time to serve as the ailing radio enterprise's chief executive, commuting from Los Angeles to New York. He pared management costs to the bone and got it to a point where hundreds of additional radio stations throughout the United States were using its news and entertainment—including Walter Winchell and Kate Smith, whom Hammer signed up personally. But the doctor soon sensed that running a network, even the largest in the United States, which owned no stations of its own was one ball he'd never learn to juggle. He wasn't cut out to be a peer of General David Sarnoff and William S. Paley. So in time he looked around and found an overzealous buyer, or a set of them: Hal Roach Studios, then controlled by Scranton Corporation, which was controlled by F. L. Jacobs Company, which, it leaked out, was controlled by the notorious international hustler Alexander Guterma. Oxy sold out with a $1.3 million profit a little more than a year after buying. Guterma cheapened MBS, a feat in itself, by making it a propaganda tool of the Trujillo government of the Dominican Republic. Eventually Guterma went to prison for S.E.C. violations and the network sank for a time in Chapter 11 reorganization.

Though its gas was not yet moving into Pacific's pipes, Oxy now had no great money problems. Its stock shot from around $4 a share to $15. The doctor had no trouble in selling a percentage of its gas in the ground to Mutual of New York (the insurance company, not the deflated radio chain) without any liability to Occidental, to be delivered as it was produced over eighteen years. This is known as a production payment, and Occidental accountants ruled that since this was not refundable except out of the oil, it could be taken into income. When the S.E.C. took exception, Hammer compromised by agreeing to treat this as deferred income in the future. Oxy paid its first dividend in the history of the company. Its accounting office, which consisted mostly of Paul Hebner, secretary-treasurer, was for a time uncertain about how to go about paying a dividend!

With radio and a brief unproductive flyer into Montana gold out of his system, Hammer concluded that he was not a conglomerate man. He henceforth would concentrate on putting together a complex based on natural resources. The first step in that direction was Oxy's acquisition of Best Fertilizers Company. Its ammonia plant was located within a short distance of Oxy's underground sea of gas. Gas being essential to ammonia, a basic ingredient of fertilizer, Best found it convenient to buy from Oxy. It was a good early customer, but wasn't satisfied. So in 1963, with the easy consent of the board, Oxy bought Best for stock then worth more than $10 million. Best's somewhat cantankerous owner, Lowell Berry, maintained his title as president of the fertilizer company and, in addition, was named an executive vice-president of Oxy and member of the board.

From a personality and legal standpoint, the merger was not destined to be harmonious. Best was hit with a strike and Berry adamantly refused to negotiate personally with the unions involved. The company fell idle just at a time when there was a worldwide demand for fertilizer. Countless orders could not be met. Hammer called a meeting with the union representatives to hear the complaints of the strikers. Berry refused to appear when requested to do so by Hammer and told him defiantly, "You settle it." He was fired from his two executive positions for insubordination by Hammer and removed from the board. He promptly sued Oxy for $12 million, which he said represented the value of his unexpired employment contract and stock options.

His preemptory discharge meant, at least to Oxy, that he had forfeited his thousands of low-priced options on the parent company's stock. Hammer's lawyers did not think they had a very good case. They offered to settle for $2.5 million. Berry balked, and the case went to court. That is when the doctor asked his friend and attorney Arthur Groman to look into the matter.

It became a landmark case in that it turned upon a single word. The word was "shit."

Groman:

"We were literally standing on the courthouse steps in Santa Monica the day of the trial when one of Berry's lawyers came up to me and said, 'Mr. Groman, Mr. Berry has decided to accept your settlement offer, but we have two additional conditions. First, he wants to go back on the board of Occidental, and second, he wants a fifty-thousand-dollar-a-year consultant fee for three years.'

"I told him that I certainly wouldn't accept those conditions. I said in the first place he could never go back on the Oxy board; that he had committed an act of insubordination, and that this wasn't a love feast. I added that I thought the fifty-thousand-dollar proposition was ridiculous. Berry had already become a multimillionaire through Oxy, and now he's being offered another two and a half million to go away. I told him that if I had been on this case sooner I certainly would never have offered any such preposterous settlement. It is overly generous, I said.

" 'Overly generous!' Berry's lawyer shouted. 'You're full of shit!'

"Well, I've been practicing law for many years, but I never heard a lawyer use that kind of language. And this was a very dignified and eminent lawyer in our community. So I then undertook a great deal of responsibility without consulting Dr. Hammer or anybody else. I said, 'If you feel so strongly about the merits of your case, why don't you walk into the courtroom and make your opening statement, because I'm withdrawing the settlement offer.' I had a lot of nerve to say that, and do that. After all, Dr. Hammer had only asked me to associate in the case, not take over from Phil Westbrook of O'Melveny and Meyers, his already assigned lawyer. We tried it jointly, after my unilateral decision. It was a very difficult and technical case that lasted a month. Berry claimed that he was an officer of Best, you see, and that Occidental's board did not have the right to discharge him because only the Best board could do that.

"We took the position that he was an officer also of Occidental, vice-president of Occidental, and that Best was a wholly owned subsidiary, and therefore we had the right to discharge him. It was a very, very close question. Anyway, at the end of the trial the judge ruled right from the bench. Not only did he give Berry nothing, but he awarded Occidental ninety thousand dollars in attorney fees.

"We were very pleased. . . ."

Oxy was saved by a $2.5 million four-letter word.

Hammer settled with the strikers and looked to broader horizons in fertilizers. He built another plant in Texas and then set out to acquire sources of the other soil-enriching ingredients. He had the gas and the ammonia; now he needed the other cards in the deck—phosphate, potash, and sulfur. He hit a veritable El Dorado by discovering phosphate in northern Florida, where none had been found before. Producers from central Florida, where the phosphate industry had been located for half a century or more, scoffed at the ridiculous idea promoted by a neophyte in the fertilizer business of finding usable phosphate in north Florida. Hammer got his sulphur by bad management—the other fellow's bad management. Jefferson Lake Sulphur Company in Texas was the third largest in the United States, behind Freeport and Texas Gulf. Unlike the prosperous holders of first and second place, Jefferson Lake was in deep trouble. Even in the midst of a depressed sulfur market it continued to pour much of its fortune into an unproductive asbestos subsidiary in Canada. Stockholders were angry, Jefferson Lake officials desperate. Hammer picked up the company for $15 million of Oxy stock and sold the useless asbestos operation for $1 million. In the deal, Jefferson threw in its 70 percent of Jefferson Lake Petro-Chemicals, a Canada-based company listed on the American Stock Exchange whose stock had a market value of about $12.5 million. Within weeks, the price of sulfur went into a climb that was to quadruple its value.

"Jefferson Lake was Hammer's biggest bargain," *Fortune* magazine would declare in one of its periodic inquiries into the Hammer phenomenon, which usually praises him with faint damns.

With limitless phosphates in his back yard in Florida, Hammer agreed with his experts to try something that was the reverse, in effect, of his adventure in the whiskey business. Instead of watering his product, he agreed to spend several million dollars to build a Florida plant that would concentrate the product of Oxy's phosphate rock combined with sulfuric acid. This produced superphosphoric acid, with the same potency in one shipload as three shiploads of phosphate rock and one shipload of sulfur. At destination, superphosphoric acid can be combined with potash and ammonia to form the customary fertilizer mixture, saving considerable capital investment for the buyer. Oxy gained a leading position in that field. This latest technology in chemical fertilizer helped Oxy land a stunning $8 billion contract with the U.S.S.R., which was later to escalate into a $20 billion deal. To obtain worldwide outlets for his innovative endeavor in fertilizers, Hammer bought Interore (International Ore and Fertilizer Corporation, world's largest marketer of fertilizer) for a modest $2.8 million worth of Oxy stock, which put him in business in sixty countries.

Potash he was content to buy. Seems that when God handed out natural resources, he decided (along with ruling that Israel didn't need oil) that the United States would never need potash. So Oxy bought it from Canada, which has a huge surplus.

The doctor's dip into real estate proved to be as much of a headache as the Best Fertilizer suit, as Groman explains it:

"Dr. Hammer decided that acquiring Kern County Land Company, the California real estate development company, which was greatly undervalued by the existing public, for Oxy stock would contribute a lot to earnings. We acquired more than ten percent of the stock for about eighty million dollars. But then the Kern people decided they didn't want to be controlled by Oxy, so they brought in the Tenneco Corporation in a defensive merger and it took over control through an exchange of stock. Considering what we were locked in for, we just didn't want to be a shareholder and have all that money involved. So Dr. Hammer negotiated an arrangement whereby, for a down payment of several million dollars, Tenneco was given an option to buy Oxy stock at a price that, if exercised, would yield us a nineteen-million-dollar profit. It was a brilliant maneuver. However, there's a rule in the S.E.C., Sixteen-B, to the effect that if you own more than ten percent of a company you are what they called an 'insider' and cannot change positions in a publicly owned corporation in a period shorter than six months. In other words, if you buy a stock and you're classified as an 'insider,' you cannot sell it until at least six months have elapsed, otherwise any profit you make belongs to the company. That's called the 'short swing rule.' "

Occidental and Tenneco were familiar with this rule, of course. When they negotiated this part of the agreement both parties understood that no exercise of the option or sale or exchange would occur within six months. But despite that, Tenneco went ahead and did bring about the merger with Kern County Land Company and Occidental was compelled to exchange stock. Then some individual shareholders brought an action to recover this profit on behalf of Kern County Land (which now belonged to Tenneco). Tenneco joined in the suit and, in effect, was trying to get back by this maneuver what they had agreed to pay in order to remove Occidental as a contender for Kern County Land.

The case was tried in New York before a Federal District judge. He entered a summary judgment in favor of the plaintiff, which meant Oxy had to return the $19 million plus interest and plus all accumulated dividends, some $28 million in all. Dr. Hammer, as is his wont, looked around for a special attorney who was known to have an excellent record for working complicated cases on appeal. He came up with the distinguished Whitney North Seymour, whose son was later the United States attorney for the Southern District of New York. Seymour argued the case on appeal in the Second Circuit before a court headed by Judge Henry Jacob Friendly. The Friendly court unanimously reversed the trial judge and ordered that summary judgment be entered on behalf of Occidental, "a remarkable decision," in Groman's view. Tenneco took it to the U.S. Supreme Court, which upheld Oxy 6 to 3.

It was all very heady for a retired gentleman, but Armand Hammer had hardly scratched the surface.

Chapter 16

Allah's Messenger

The colossal coup, the one that has been the prime source of both joy and trepidation for Hammer, for Oxy's 30,000 workers and executives, and its approximately 350,000 stockholders, has been Libya. Nothing quite like Libya ever happened to a company like Oxy and, from all we can discern, may never happen again.

"Allah sent you to Libya!" King Idris I exclaimed to Hammer in a 1966 audience for the doctor and Frances at his palace in Tobruk. He meant it, this old white-bearded Emir Mohammed Idris El Senussi, spiritual and then temporal leader of the Senussi tribesmen and recognized by Great Britain as Emir of Cyrenaica.

In the years of King Idris's rule, before he was overthrown and banished by Colonel Mu'Ammar El-Gathafi, Libya must have been a capitalist's dream, like the early Texas triumphs and disasters.

Some assorted memories of it:

Hammer's: "When we decided to compete for the concessions in Libya, we thought of various things we might offer to the government which would give us some advantage over our competitors. I had had the slight advantage of having been there before, on assignment by President Kennedy in 1961, and this was five or six years later. Concessions can be most sensitive."

Jacoby's: "You know the cultivation. If you want to get a concession from a foreign government you've got to cultivate that government, and it often takes years, literally, to lay the groundwork and make the contacts and negotiate. Considering everything, we moved with incredible speed."

Fortune's: When Hammer decided to send Oxy into Libya to find oil he moved in on what must have been a veritable miasma of deal-making. On any day when the *ghibli* wasn't blowing sand up out of the desert, the air was redolent of buying and selling, winning and losing. The rival capital cities of Tripoli and Benghazi offered the biggest floating bazaar and crap game anywhere. The participants were oilmen (governments, majors, independents, and would-be's from all over the world). Cabinet ministers and subordinates, ex-Cabinet ministers and ex-subordinates, relatives and friends, two-bit drifters trying to parlay a handshake with a politician into access to the King's ear, a fake French general, and a leading American academic administrator, formerly on the staff of Columbia University, all trading in concessions, geological survey data, and assorted tips, secrets, and inside dope.

Hammer's: "Until it hit oil, Libya had nothing much to support it except what the United States was paying to keep up our bomber base there. Mussolini had spent about ten million dollars looking for oil during the Italian occupation period, but nothing happened. Esso was about to pull out when they hit on their last exploratory well, after spending millions of dollars with no encouragement. Shell had sunk about fifty million in noncommercial wells. So had the French National Oil Company. Some wild Esso geologist came up with the idea that all the majors had been drilling in the wrong part of Libya—near the Algerian border. Naturally oil had been found in great quantity in Algeria. Well, this geologist suggested that Esso, and everybody, look in the direction of Egypt, where nobody had thought of finding oil. So Esso Standard of New Jersey's Zeltin bonanza came in, and that was the beginning."

Fortune's: When Occidental came to Libya, the government was preparing to award a second round of concessions, tracts largely relinquished by the companies that had obtained Libyan concessions earlier. Under Libyan law, oil companies are encouraged to explore their concessions as quickly as possible, because they must return portions of them to the government if they don't find oil. The second round included land with dry holes, but it also included many pieces of desert adjoined by producing wells. . . . More than 40 companies from nine countries entered the bidding. Some apparently were little more than shells that hoped to get a concession and then peddle it to a qualified outfit in exchange for an overriding share of production. Others, including Occidental, though light on money, at least had oil-industry experience. The Libyan Government permitted the smaller companies to enter the bidding because it was even more concerned about avoiding domination by majors and big consortia than about limited capital.

Jacoby's: "Looking back, it's hard to believe the conditions our people worked under. Tripoli and Benghazi are familiar cities, but most of Libya is pretty much as it must have been a couple of thousand years ago: little mud villages, endless stretches of desert, Bedouins in their tents, massive illiteracy, and poverty in the midst of oceans of oil. The Libyans are the most orthodox Mohammedans. They adhere to the Koran and its mode of life most religiously. They don't use alcohol, and since the Colonel took over, no visitor can, either. Women's Lib would find Libya intolerable. The Libyan women are kept in *purdah*, and when they venture out of doors they are allowed to reveal only one eye in their veiled faces."

Hammer had his own problems. In time he came to be on intimate terms with King Idris I, but in the rush for second-round concessions he was just another bargainer and a relative minnow in a swarm of corporate barracudas. His only previous oil exploration outside of California had been a short-lived partnership with Texas oilman John Mecom in a futile, money-losing venture in Nicaragua. Now he was in the oven heat of Libya, jousting with giants who could buy and sell him, weighing the boasts of self-professed intermediaries who claimed to own the King's ear.

After proper consultation with his own people, he had flown over from Oxy headquarters in Bakersfield, California, in a beat-up converted A-26 Douglas bomber. Hammer bid on four concessions. He bid colorfully and shrewdly. He had the bidding documents done in the form of sheepskin diplomas, rolled and bound with silk ribbons of red, green, and black, the national colors of Libya. In the text of the bids he added a clause to the standard terms: Oxy would give Libya 5 percent of pretax profits to be used for agricultural development. Moreover, it promised to search for water near the oasis village of Kufra, which by no coincidence happened to be the birthplace of the King and his queen and the site of the King's father's tomb. One additional carrot was dangled before the noses of the selection board: Oxy would do a feasibility study on an ammonia plant and build it jointly with the government if oil was struck.

Hammer was granted two concessions in March of 1966, to the surprise of better-known competitors. The first of these, surrounded by producing wells, had been given up as hopeless by Oasis, a consortium consisting of

Shell, Amerada, Marathon, and Continental. Oxy was one of seventeen bidders. The second area to which Oxy won rights attracted only seven bids. It had been relinquished by Mobil after the spending of millions of dollars in dry holes.

The properties soon became twin albatrosses around Hammer's neck. The first three holes Oxy drilled were bone dry, and they had devoured $3 million in addition to $2 million spent on seismic work and untold bonuses to the Libyan government.

Several members of the Oxy board began mournfully referring to the ambitious project as "Hammer's Folly." Of deeper concern to Hammer was the attitude of Gene Reid, who had given him Lathrop and Brentwood and who was now Oxy's second largest stockholder.

"We don't belong in Libya, Doctor," Reid told him bluntly at a board meeting. "Only the majors can make it here. It's just no place for a small company like Oxy. We ought to pull out."

It was the voice of experience speaking, but Hammer's sixth sense prompted him not to listen. Some weeks after this confrontation between finder and financier, an Oxy drill chomped its way into oil at a site abandoned by fainthearted giants. After the original strike in mid-November, eight additional wells were drilled in this Augila field, as it was known, and Oxy was in business—the field had a potential of 100,000 barrels a day. It was an unusually high-grade crude with very low sulfur content. What is more, it was flowing west of Suez. That meant it could be delivered in ten days or less, via the Mediterranean and Gibraltar, to oil-hungry Europe. Later when the Suez Canal had been sabotaged, the bulk of the Arab oil was forced to round the Cape on voyages of nearly two months.

Esso got the message and Hammer received a caller, the president of Esso-Libya. The man's pitch interested Hammer and sent his board of directors into ecstasies. Esso-Libya's man laid it on the line: He said it was nice to have hit in the Augila field where others had failed, but wait till you try to market it! You have no refineries and no retail outlets. You are at the mercy of the majors, who have a surplus of their own oil to sell. He offered Oxy a $100 million profit and a half interest in the Esso-handled production, refinement, and distribution.

It was enough to make even a man like Hammer waiver, particularly when he heard the whoops of joy from Gene Reid and his friends on the board as well as from the swelling numbers of stockholders. So with vague misgivings, he entered into negotiations with one of the world's richest corporations. And, in short order, he accepted the attractive proposition. But when the president of Esso-Libya presented the deal to the board of Standard of New Jersey, it was turned down. Period.

Meanwhile, there had been some highly sophisticated inspections of Oxy's second site, the barren reaches Mobil had given up. Hammer's geologists had become interested in a new seismographic technology that had just been developed and in effect took soundings and submitted findings to computers oriented to render judgments. They got Hammer's consent to retain the seismic company's people with the new techniques to study the Libyan concession areas even before the concessions were granted. The gamble paid off. After the success at Augila they reported on the former Mobil concession. Their report evoked both enthusiasm and scorn in the Oxy camp. Hammer sided with the enthusiasts and ordered the drilling of a million-dollar wildcat at once. The first well spouted 42,000 barrels a day. Oxy had hit what is called a reef, the first discovered reef in Libya. Geologically, a reef is a concentration of oil so bountiful that it will flow almost indefinitely without use of pumps. With the puncture of a nearby second reef, Oxy came up—or Libya did—with a 72,000-barrels-a-day hit, the largest well in Libya.

Hammer engaged Bechtel Corporation and ordered a crash $150 million development program and a $150 million pipeline 130 miles long and 40 inches in diameter, the largest in Libya, capable of transporting a million barrels a day! Considering that Oxy's total net worth was only $48 million, this was utter daring. However, credit was available after Hammer was able to get a DeGolyer & MacNaughton report confirming that the reserves were in the order of two billion barrels.

Esso came back to him, this time in the form and shape of a director of Esso with a full team, who said that he had the board's full authority and endorsement to make a deal. Hammer offered much stiffer terms, but a multi-multimillion-dollar deal appeared to be imminent. But once again, astonishingly enough, New York headquarters backed off. It distressed most of Oxy's board and, one would think, a majority of the shareholders. But Hammer had been looking around for options, an exercise of his which stimulates him almost as much as his daily swim. He told Esso where it might deposit on its corporate anatomy its later offer and opened talks with Forrest Shumway and Bill Walkup, president and chairman respectively of Signal Oil, which had a good setup in Europe: refineries, service stations, tankers, terminals, and so on. The problem with Signal Oil was that it had no oil. It was looking to get out of the daft business. Hammer said to the Signal people: "Look, take our oil. We've got plenty of it. We'll pay you a commission for the use of your terminals, tankers, refineries, and retail outlets in Germany, Belgium, Holland, and the United Kingdom—particularly that big one-hundred-thousand-barrel-a-day refinery you've got in Antwerp. We'll pay you a commission on every barrel of oil you sell."

Hammer had a backup proposal at the last minute.

"By the way," he said, "will you give me an option to buy your whole marketing setup? I understand you offered it for a hundred and ten million." Signal's people said that was right. They told Hammer he could have such an option for such a price, half five-year notes and half preferred stock, which he could exercise only when the first ship was loaded with oil under the commission contract. But by the time the first ship was filled to the brim with Hammer's oil, Signal had closed enough solid sales for future delivery that it had the firm expectation of $200 million in commissions.

"So all I did was exercise the option," Hammer said later with a pleased smile. "I got the whole thing for nothing, let's say, and I saved a hundred million dollars. Overnight, we had our own marketing setup with our own tankers, our own refineries, and our own service stations in Europe."

Later, when asked why Esso had muffed an opportunity to buy into Hammer's phenomenal fields in Libya, an executive of the company replied, "We tried on two occasions to make a deal, but the trouble was 'Hammer doesn't understand the oil business.'"

It must have been quite a day in April 1967 when Oxy's black gold reached the sea. *Fortune* reported:

Red, green, and black national flags snapped in the breeze. Camel troops patrolled the dunes around the installation, scarlet-coated bandsmen stood in formation with their instruments shining in the midday sun, and the blood of sacrificial lambs stained the desert sand. Some 800 Cabinet ministers, robed local chieftains, religious dignitaries, diplomats, a U.S. Senator and other assorted guests and attendants filled a splendid pavilion erected solely to house a half-hour ceremony.

The celebration cost Oxy a cool million dollars.

The accompanying picture showed Hammer standing next to the

berobed, white-bearded king. By that time, scarcely nine months after the concessions had been signed, they were fast friends. Hammer had made good on his pledge to bring water to Kufra and in such a bountiful way that the King offered to name his ancient birthplace and that of his forebears after Hammer. Hammer politely declined: It was "too much of an honor." Simultaneously, Hammer asked if he might name the huge strike at the ex-Mobil concession the Idris Field. The King consented.

The water strike was, in a way, more spectacular than the oil hits, which eventually reached 800,000 barrels a day. It had not rained in the Kufra Oasis area for at least a quarter of a century. What made Kufra an oasis was that it was moistened by the emission of brackish water. But there was never enough of even that.

Professor Jacoby still is impressed:

"It was about a million-dollar gamble, I'd say. We took a drilling rig and crews five hundred miles inland across the burning desert to Kufra, started the drilling, and found an underground reservoir estimated to be as big as the flow of the Nile for two hundred years! It was beautiful, clear spring water. The people couldn't believe it, and I don't think we could either. We found it at only two hundred fifty feet below the surface. The doctor flew in some San Joaquin Valley farming experts, ordered miles of aluminum irrigation pipes, sprinklers, and chemical fertilizers, and we taught those people how to make the desert bloom. We planted alfalfa and it sprang up from the sand as if it had taken root in the richest soil on earth." After the revolution, Hammer made a gift of Kufra to the new government in a meeting with Colonel Jaloud, the number-two man in Libya and recently named Prime Minister.

The price of Oxy's stock reflected the good news of Oxy's vast discoveries of oil reefs in Libya. It soared to over $100 and after being split 3 for 1 climbed to a high of $55 in 1968. Hammer decided this was a good time to use Oxy stock as currency and diversify into coal and chemicals.

So, in January 1968, Oxy bought the Island Creek Coal Company, third largest in the United States, for $150 million. It had annual sales of almost that much, with reserves that it owned or controlled of over 3.5 billion tons of coal. In 1974 the earnings of Island Creek approximated $100 million!

Previously, in 1966 and 1967, Oxy had purchased the Permian and McWood Corporations for $88 million in stock. There followed the acquisition of Garrett Research and Development Company, Inc., which among other tricks can change garbage into oil and has developed the unique patented process for the economical gasification of coal and recovery of shale oil "inside the mountain" without ecological problems.

Then Hooker Chemicals and Plastics was acquired in July 1968 for a staggering $800 million in preferred stock, said to be the largest acquisition of any company up to that time. Its products are such that they touch the lives of all Americans. Your car contains about 150 pounds of chemically based plastics that have replaced heavier, less reliable, or more costly metal parts. In all probability, the fruits and vegetables on your table were grown to plump maturity with the aid of its chemical pesticides and weed killers. Your garden flowers are protected by a Hooker miticide named Pentac. Rats in your neighborhood—New York City has a rat population of 8 million, one for every man, woman, and child—are held more or less at bay by Hooker rodenticides containing zinc phosphide. Hooker's influence is worldwide.

How wise and farsighted the acquisition of Permian, Island Creek and Hooker proved to be was vividly demonstrated when the coup of Colonel El-Gathafi and his Revolutionary Command Council, which overthrew King Idris on September 1, 1969, for a time placed Oxy's concessions in jeopardy.

The doctor did not share the tremors that swept through a portion of the oil industry when Libya's Revolutionary Command Council nationalized its oil. Oxy had gone through that shock wave a month earlier, and Hammer was certain his company could live with the hot-blooded colonel's demands: Libya henceforth would own and sell 51 percent of all the oil Oxy's expensive machinery sucked to the surface of the Sahara and pumped through its pipes to the sea. The doctor's man in Libya, George Williamson, given full authority to sign on the best obtainable terms after the 51 percent nationalization decree, immediately acquiesced in the 51–49 split and then asked for and received $136 million in cash, the book value of 51 percent of Oxy's assets—drilling equipment and a gas liquefying plant, mostly.

There was some weeping and gnashing of teeth among the major oil companies, the doctor's rivals in Libya. Hammer was accused of capitulating at the expense of the other companies doing business with the difficult El-Gathafi. As evidence, his critics pointed to an interview he had given to a Dow Jones reporter during one of his trips to Moscow just prior to the Libyan settlement. The reporter quoted Hammer as saying, "We are negotiating with the Libyans for a fifty-one–forty-nine deal. We will soon reach an agreement which will include compensation." Actually, the doctor meant "the industry" was negotiating, not Oxy exclusively. (As a matter of fact, the doctor had suggested at an industry meeting a few weeks before that the industry offer the Libyan government a 50–50 deal but be prepared to accept a 51–49 split, in an effort to stave off a 100 percent takeover.) He put out a quick denial of that portion of the news story. The Oasis group of Continental, Amerada-Hess, and Marathon promptly followed Oxy's lead and agreed to the Libyan terms for a sale of 51 percent of their assets without waiting to be nationalized. Shell, a part of the Oasis combine, refused since its parent was among the majors. The Colonel soon dropped the other shoe on the heads of Esso Standard Libya, Mobil Oil Libya Ltd., Texaco Overseas, Asian Standard Oil Company of California, and the Libyan-American Petroleum Company by nationalizing 51 percent of their holdings, along with his announcement that they would be compensated.

"Some of them said about me that I had dealt with Libya behind their backs, or that I must be clairvoyant," Hammer said of the new pinch in Libya. "Neither was true. It was just my opinion that if the industry offered the Libyans fifty-one percent control, Libya would stop suggesting it was going to take a hundred percent. That's what it earlier did to British Petroleum and Bunker Hunt of Texas. We came out well, on the whole.

At the time of the Bunker Hunt nationalization, the Colonel was quoted as saying that it was time that he gave the Americans a "slap in the face." His controlled Tripoli radio had more to say in the course of announcing the September 1 take-overs, on the fourth anniversary of this coup that dethroned old Idris I, who had once praised Allah for sending him Hammer. The radio barked:

"The decision has ended an era of domination exercised by the monopolistic companies at the expense of the Libyan people."

"I think one of the things that depressed our stock was the dire predictions made by analysts that Occidental would be nationalized without compensation and that we'd lose our entire Libyan investment," the doctor diagnosed at that time.

He drafted a reassuring letter to Oxy's army of stockholders, then changed his mind and expanded his September 12, 1973, speech to the New York Society of Security Analysts not only to include his optimism about Libya, but to announce new high grosses in Oxy's other divisions and to answer skeptics of his deals with the Soviets.

Things would have been simpler if Idris had prevailed, but Hammer is philosophical about the Colonel.

"People have said that he is a wild man," the doctor says. "But it seems to me that he is a combination of uncanny cleverness, idealism, perhaps fanaticism, and he certainly wants to raise the living standard of his people. He's apparently bugged by the fact that he has only two million people and Egypt, right next door, has thirty million. Nasser was his idol. I think he'd like to take Nasser's position in the Arab world, which he can't very well swing with only two million people. Nasser always had a dream of unifying the Arab states; the Colonel has the same vision, an Arab union with himself at the head of it. One of his problems with Egypt is that he is a much more diligent disciple of the Prophet. He lives by the spirit and the letter of the Koran, whereas many Egyptians have drifted away. I was pleased that he accepted our blueprint for the best way to use the water we found at Kufra. The Colonel is making a huge agricultural development there, raising hundreds of thousands of sheep. Pretty soon now, Libya will be able to stop importing meat from Australia, Yugoslavia, and some of the East European bloc countries. The Sahara will supply all the meat the Libyans need. That water we found is still a miracle. It may prove more valuable than their oil."

Chapter 17

A Man of Many Faces

This, too, is Armand Hammer:

"I was doing pretty good in the whiskey business, in the cattle business, and in the art world. I had gotten a lot of publicity during the Hearst Collection disposal. I was an active member of such well-known groups as Cardinal Spellman's Committee of the Laity for Catholic Charities, President Truman had appointed me to the International Food Committee, President Eisenhower had appointed me a member of the Council for the Study of Peace in the World, and President Kennedy appointed me to the Eleanor Roosevelt Memorial Foundation. So I found it slightly irritating when somebody I'd meet seemed to take it for granted that I was connected with, or owned, the Arm and Hammer Baking Soda Company.

"Maybe I helped bring it on myself. Sometimes I'd fly an ensign on my yacht showing an arm and hammer.

"Anyway, I mentioned this irritation of mistaken identity to my brother Harry one day and he said, 'Why don't we buy Arm and Hammer Baking Soda and then you won't have to disclaim ownership when you're asked.' That seemed like a pretty good idea at the time, so I looked into it.

"Well, the company was owned by two nice old brothers in their seventies who had never had to issue a financial report on their business. They purchased bicarbonate of soda by the carload from Allied Chemical Company, where it was a by-product, and put it up in little boxes. They seemed surprised that anybody would even think of trying to buy them out. Besides, their company was not for sale. And for good reason: They didn't owe a cent and had ten million in cash in the bank. So I realized

that I'd have to go on living and being mistaken as the 'Baking Soda King.'
"But I guess there are worse things to be called."

Hammer's Greenwich Village home in New York, which he has owned since attending Columbia more than half a century ago, once was the carriage house of a fashionable Villager. It is a faceless place, for security reasons. It has no street number or name plate. The neighborhood has long since gone to pot—figuratively and literally. A procession of young and old kooks and addicts of all genders passes Hammer's home day and night and never gives it a glance, unless his rented Cadillac limousine with uniformed chauffeur is parked outside. Inside, the sentimental redoubt has great charm and variety. A balcony that looks down on the high-ceilinged living room and connects the upstairs bedrooms was once the stable's hayloft. A large-screen Sony TV, which the doctor remotely controls from his favorite chair near his two favorite telephones, casts its assorted colors on the nearby Steinway baby grand that Hammer bought as a millionaire undergrad and on which he sometimes plays Russian gypsy laments.

The paintings he has chosen for his hideout in the jungle of the Village are not likely to be selected for another exchange with the Russians. Featured artist is Frances and her copies of her favorite masters, including a good replica of a Gauguin. There is an original Vlaminck and an impressionist painting of that very street in the Village, executed about 1900 and showing Hammer's house—found in some obscure shop by Victor. The dominating, huge-framed painting over the living-room fireplace is almost as great a source of pride to Hammer as the oil painting of the head of Prince Eric in the California home. It is Sir Thomas Lawrence's portrait of the children of a titled Englishmen named Best, done in the 1800s. Hammer picked it up for peanuts at a Parke-Bernet auction where it had been consigned by the Metropolitan Museum in a sale of unauthenticated masters. The Met's curator was skeptical of it because the two Best daughters were not centered on the canvas. Hammer had checked the records of the Metropolitan and had found out that the picture had been sold in 1900 at the highest price ever brought by a Lawrence to Charles Pratt, a partner of John D. Rockefeller, and had been bequeathed by Pratt to the Metropolitan. Hammer had the picture cleaned and the figure of a beautiful boy appeared when a red pillow clumsily covering him had been cleaned away, hence the bargain price.

The Best family had had the figure painted over after his early death so as not to remind them of their loss. (Hammer has willed the now quite valuable work to Fairleigh Dickinson University.)

The tiny bar at the Greenwich Village place is as bleakly stocked as if Hammer were observing Colonel El-Gathafi's Koran-directed abstinence. The little kitchen, on the other hand, brims with goodies either collected by Frances in the aromatic neighborhood shops—she's a diligent cook when in New York—or brought in by Mike Brignole, Hammer's faithful friend and house guard since 1920. Mike was the son of the owner of an Italian grocery store a few doors down the street when Hammer moved into the then gentle neighborhood. He delivered groceries to young Hammer, took care of the log-burning fireplace, and ran errands for the student tycoon. Mike has been looking out for Hammer's place ever since. Shortly after Hammer gained control of Oxy, Mike came to him with a grievous problem: He had invested his life's earnings of $50,000 in a company that turned out to be Mafia-ruled. When he learned this, he tried to sell his shares. The listed market value on the curb had been rigged to three times what Mike had paid for them. He was promptly called on by a couple of "hit" types and told that (1) he could not sell his stock, and (2) if he went to the police and told what he had discovered, he'd be killed. Hammer advised him to write a letter describing his dilemma, giving names and dates, and tell his family to mail it to the District Attorney's office if anything happened to him. When next threatened, and acting under Hammer's advice, Mike told the hoods what he had done.

Mike got his $50,000 back, plus $100,000 profit, the market price of his stock. Without asking the doctor's advice, Mike promptly bought 20,000 shares of Occidental at the then quoted price of $1.50 per share. What with a 3-for-1 split and a market value that shot past $50, Mike's 60,000 shares became worth more than $3 million.

"At that point, I suggested he sell off a million dollars' worth, put it in a bank with good interest, and live happily ever after," Hammer told a reporter recently as Mike, still dressed as a delivery boy of old, puttered about the little kitchen in the Village. "Now the stock's down to ten, but Mike's shares are still worth six hundred thousand dollars. Tell him why you didn't take my advice, Mike."

Mike toweled his hands and said to the reporter, "If the doctor himself didn't sell at fifty, why should I? I'm wit' him all the way."

143

Dorothy Prellwitz has been Hammer's private secretary at Occidental's Los Angeles headquarters since he took over in 1957, when the entire staff consisted of vice-president and secretary Paul Hebner, Gladys Loudenslager, who was office manager and accountant, and herself. Among a dozen regular chores, Miss Prell, as she is known, is the traffic director of the doctor's memento-laden *sanctum sanctorum*. While handling his incoming and outgoing phone calls from all points of the globe, she routes in a steady stream of the executives who have appointments and, after a given time, routs them.

"Dr. Hammer's a hurricane, isn't he?" a reporter once said to her.

She shook her pretty head. "No," she said firmly. "He's the *eye* of a hurricane."

Louis Nizer had some thoughts on his sometime client Hammer. The latter-day Clarence Darrow or Max Steuer intoned:

"He is really one of the most remarkable men I've ever met, certainly as a business executive but more than that. He has a grasp of so many difficult and varied projects. His lucid mind, his personal strength of discipline which enables him, while ordinary mortals would be harassed by one-tenth of what he has to face, to be calm and laugh quickly and easily and at the same time create calm and a kind of contagious serenity all around him. It's a remarkable trait. American executives are wonderful creators, but the statistics show that about one man in every ten occupies a bed in a mental hospital at one time or another, or else is a nervous wreck with or without a hospital. That's true because we haven't learned how to achieve the greatest conquest of them all, the conquest of oneself. He has mastered that and I don't think very consciously. I don't think he has made any special effort to do so. He wants to be efficient, instinctively. And the best way to be efficient is to be calm and serene—and he's not going to let anything interfere with that.

"He made that—or was born with it—part of his personality. That enables him, like an athlete who is loose instead of muscle tense, to do about two times what any other top executive does. When you're not tense, you don't wear yourself down. And that explains to me why in an important case he reads every brief; I've never had a client who ever studied a brief presented to him—complicated, sixty or seventy pages— who comes back and says, 'On page twenty-eight, I studied that footnote

144

The bare facts of Armand Hammer's early life.

Teenage exile in
Meriden, Connecticut, 1910.

Dr. Julius and
Mama Rose, 1910.

The doctor sometimes takes a musical
break. A painting of Frances by Luigi
Corbellini looks over his shoulder.
(NBC Photo)

The doctor slips quietly into his
hideaway in Greenwich Village.
(NBC Photo)

and I don't think we should put in that footnote, do you, Lou? And on
page sixty-three I think the word should not be *and,* it should be *but.'*
I'm not exaggerating. He goes through every brief that way. And at the
same time he's calling his expert accountants and saying, 'On line fourteen, you've got the following figure with the following footnote on
contingent liability, and you know that part of that could be different.'
At the same time, he's receiving an international call concerning some
very involved matter and he shows his knowledge of the basic fact and
asks whether the suggested solution would run contrary two years from
now when the cancelation clause takes effect. And at the same time all
this is going on, he has the vision of large affairs which you would think
would come from complete rest and quiet thinking. Kind of a think-tank
thing where you go for one month and you come up with an idea like,
'Well, I'll spend fifty million for exploration in the North Sea.' And, while
all this is going on, he has seen the vision of large affairs, large horizons,
which is evidenced by the fact that he now deals with governments and
prime ministers, and what not, while at the same time he's taking care
of legal briefs, affidavits, firing and hiring executives. I've seen him negotiate with an executive he wants—charm him out of his skin.

"Nothing frightens him. No giant in any industry can intimidate him.
If he feels they've done him wrong, he sues them. Or if they sue him and
he thinks he's wrong, he'll settle, but he's ready to defend himself if he
thinks he's right. He wins them all! I'm not speaking of myself; there have
been other lawyers who have tried cases for him. He takes on Gulf Oil,
Armour, Tenneco, or anybody. As you know, the only way to be popular,
not to be criticized, is to say nothing, do nothing, and be nothing. He says
something, does something, and is something. Naturally, he has enemies.
That's true of lawyers, true of writers, too.

"He makes quick decisions, like all great executives. He's not torn by
indecision. He doesn't procrastinate and say, 'Well, I'll think it over for
a week.' When he wants more facts, he gets them firsthand. He picks up
a phone and calls London, Tripoli, Tokyo, or hops in his plane and flies
to Moscow. It's a schedule that could kill a hundred strong young men.
The reason he can stand that schedule is because of this constant cushion
of serenity. With that goes a personal trait. Thomas Edison had it: the
ability to nap. Sometimes when we're going over a case and it comes down
to four or five in the afternoon he'll say, 'I have to make a call. Will you
excuse me for a few minutes? Do you have a room where I can do it?'

145

I know what that means. I give him a room with a couch. He'll come back in fifteen minutes completely refreshed, and we might work through the night.

"Then there are his late-night calls. I don't permit other clients that privilege, but I'm such an admirer of his. He called his vice-president, Bill McSweeny, one night about three-thirty A.M. Los Angeles time, or six-thirty A.M. Washington time, and said he had a little problem he needed some advice on. Bill said, 'What are you doing, Doctor, at three-thirty in the morning?' Hammer said, 'Oh, is it that late? Well, I'll sleep on it and I'll call you later, let's say at seven.'

"He is in one sense naive. You'd think that such sophistication would make a man with some very hard layers within him; sophistication develops calluses, a protective or offensive hardness. The man loves a joke, especially the jokes of Victor, who is a master storyteller. Victor can tell him a story and he'll laugh heartily, even though he may have heard it before. I'll tell him something that happened to me in court, some jest or gesture, and he'll start laughing before I get to the punch line. Most important men are not easily touched that way.

"But with it also goes a fault that he has, and that is while he has an enormous breadth of interests, his real interest is what he is achieving for Occidental. At dinner, while he'll participate in international discussions that don't touch his field, there is no passion in him until someone touches on his principal drive in life. He can discuss general subjects for hours, but anybody who knows him well knows that he's saying to himself, 'Do I have to go through all this?'

"But he's a loving, affectionate man to the people around him. And that, too, is part of his naiveté, because it's quite contrary to a good many men whose bigness, hard-boiledness, has killed some of the simpler emotions in them."

Dr. Hammer graduated from Columbia's College of Physicians and Surgeons in June 1921. He began practicing his profession in May 1972. He is not a man to be rushed into anything.

It happened in an odd way. He was presiding over Oxy's annual stockholders' meeting, held in the ballroom of the Beverly Hilton in Los Angeles, when an elderly woman shareholder tripped on a step and was knocked out by the fall.

"Is there a doctor in the house?" another stockholder yelled into a floor microphone.

There was.

The chairman.

Hammer threaded his way through the crowded hall to the place where the woman lay, revived her, and, as he had been taught half a century and more before, called for an ambulance.

"Never thought I'd get a chance to practice," he said later, wistfully.

The purchase of Campobello from Elliott Roosevelt was not the only deal Armand and his brother Victor had with the son of the creator of the New Deal and leader of the free world. Early in F.D.R.'s first term, a well-known Midwest businessman was sentenced to federal prison for tax evasion. There he was befriended by a fellow inmate named Charlie Ward, who was in the pen on a manslaughter conviction. The murderer became the rich inmate's bodyguard, protecting him from other convicts who would have molested him. The businessman was so grateful that he promised that when he got out, he'd take care of his protector for life. Roosevelt in time pardoned the businessman, who resumed control over his properties, and when the bodyguard also was eventually sprung by F.D.R. he was made a partner in the business. The rich man, grateful to the end, willed the business to his friend.

The new owner, beholden to F.D.R., searched for a suitable gift he might send him. He found it at the Hammer Galleries, a twenty-four-inch gold, platinum, and silver model of a Volga steamboat created in 1913 by the incomparable imperial court jeweler, Karl Fabergé, as a present to the Czarevich Alexis on the occasion of the three hundredth anniversary of the Romanoff dynasty. The Hammers had bought it from a Moscow commission store in the late 1920s and it reached America with the rest of the ornaments of the Brown House. Victor priced it at $25,000, one-fourth of what he estimated it cost Nicholas II. Even at that reduced rate, he assured the purchaser that it was "the most expensive toy in the world."

Boat enthusiast F.D.R. was delighted to add it to his collection of models, which included a fabulous seventeenth-century model of an ancestor's China clipper from the Hearst collection, previously presented to him by Armand. Maxim Litvinov was invited to attend the formal presentation in the Oval Room of the White House. Thus, aside from the somewhat painfully obvious connection between the presidential pardon and the ornate Fabergé, there was the happy thought of strengthening the new entente with the Soviet Union. The entente, however, was slightly jarred by an accident. Someone pushed the button that turned on the Volga boat's music box. It promptly tinkled out "God Save the Czar"— the same czar that Litvinov's establishment had executed. Roosevelt relieved the tension by laughing uproariously.

After Roosevelt's death, Victor met his one-time client, still proud about the $25,000 gift, and happy that it would now be a permanent part of the Roosevelt museum and library at Hyde Park.

Victor's face made a wince.

"What's wrong?" the donor asked.

Victor swallowed.

"Elliott didn't send it to Hyde Park," he said with a sigh. "He said it belonged to him, and he sold it to another dealer."

Today it rests on a pedestal in Brandeis University.

One work of Hammer art that was routed to the White House actually remains there, and probably will forever. It is a magnificent bronze by Charles Russell showing a pack of mounted Indians charging a stampeding herd of buffalo, titled "Meat for Wild Men."

It happened this way:

At a State Dinner for the Shah of Iran in 1967, President Johnson boasted to Senator Mike Mansfield and the doctor about a fine bronze by Frederick Remington that had been presented to the White House by Amon Carter, the Fort Worth publisher.

Mansfield, an old friend of Hammer who knew the doctor had one of the top collections of Russell sculpture, said archly to L.B.J., "Wouldn't it be nice if you had a Russell to go with your Remington?" The Senate majority leader and Russell were both from Montana.

While Johnson was heartily agreeing, Hammer said, "I'd be glad to give you one of Russell's greatest, 'Meat for Wild Men.'" He said it without a suggestion of a sigh. It was worth about $100,000.

The President thanked him warmly and suggested that he speak to Lady Bird, who was thrilled by the acquisition, especially when Hammer gallantly promised another Russell as well, the "heroic" size "Bronco Buster" (valued at $75,000), for the soon to be completed Lyndon Johnson library.

The Hammers have had perhaps more than their share of offbeat customers. James Crichton, one of the richest men in the United Kingdom, for example. Whenever he was in New York, Crichton was a constant visitor at the Hammer Galleries on Fifth Avenue, buying whatever caught his fancy. But he was attracted chiefly by the Hammer brothers themselves. At one point he gave Armand his power of attorney and whipped off to California. The next Armand heard from him was that he had fallen into the bottomless hole of a notorious floating card game in Los Angeles run by a black-sheep brother of Fanny Brice, the talented comedienne. Crichton was stuck for $200,000 in IOUs. He wrote a check for that amount on his New York bank and asked Hammer to see that it was honored. Hammer, strongly suspecting that the game had been crooked, offered to go to the police and save Crichton the money. Crichton was shocked by the suggestion.

"I couldn't do that," the Englishman said. "It's a debt of honor." Hammer notified the Los Angeles police anyway. They caught the crooks red-handed with their marked cards and arrested them. Hammer persuaded the bank to stop payment on the check, even though the con men had had it certified. It was something the bank had never done before. It broke with its tradition, however, when Hammer gave the bank the alternative of being liable for the $200,000 or accepting his agreement that he would indemnify the bank if it was ever sued by the crooks. It never was, of course.

Out of gratitude Crichton strolled into the Hammer Galleries after the case was closed. His eye fastened on a small Frans Hals sketch.

"I'll give you two hundred thousand dollars for that," he said to Victor.

"Too much," Victor said. "We've priced it at one hundred thousand."

Crichton was hurt. "If you don't sell it to me for two hundred thousand," he said crossly, "I'll never speak to you again!" Victor apologized. Crichton wrote out a check for $200,000, took the Hals off the wall, put it under his arm, and walked back to his hotel.

The doctor is as proud of his acquisition of the more than century-old Knoedler's gallery in New York as he is of any other property in his far-flung empire.

Like other art dealers, he was concerned for years about the diminishing fortunes of one of the pillars of the American art world, when he learned, to his surprise, that the owners were considering the sale of their fading treasure house. Hammer immediately made a multimillion-dollar bid on the recommendation of Dr. Maury Leibovitz, his financial consultant, and it was his. He then took Leibovitz in as a junior partner to look after the business.

"And it makes a lot of money, too" he says contentedly.

A London newspaper carried an interesting geriatrics item during the summer of 1973:

> Two of the richest and most ebullient figures in the world art market held a reunion last week after an interval of exactly 60 years.
>
> One was Julius Weitzner, whose coups include buying Titian's "Death of Actaeon" for more than 1,500,000 pounds and the unrecognized Rubens, "Daniel in the Lions' Den," for a mere 500 pounds.
>
> The other, Armand Hammer, chairman of Occidental Petroleum, recently lent his great art collection to the Royal Academy for a special show which included a van Gogh the doctor had just bid in at auction for $1,200,000.
>
> Last time they saw each other was at the Morris High School, New York, in 1913.

Then there was Farouk I, King of Egypt (1936–1952). Somewhere in the course of pursuing his prime occupation, slobhood, he was told that whatever he longed for in the way of costly baubles might be found for him by Hammer Galleries, New York.

His order involved extraordinary logistics.

He wanted one of the Russian crown jewels, a platinum and diamond Easter egg about the size of the kind laid by an ostrich. It was one of the fabulous jeweled eggs created for Nicholas II by Fabergé as an Easter gift for the czarina in 1906. It opened to reveal inside a platinum swan afloat on a miniature lake of aquamarine. A concealed spring, when wound, caused the swan to move about, spreading its wings and moving its head and tail. Farouk ordered it in an odd way. His agent had seen it at the Hammer Galleries and brought back to Farouk a movie in color and a description. Farouk cabled: SEND IMMEDIATELY SWAN EGG.

That posed two problems—how to get it to him and how it was to be paid for. The price tag was $100,000, World War II had begun, and German submarines were torpedoing Atlantic shipping. So Armand, who was too busy to make the trip himself, assigned his unsinkable brother Victor to the job with strict instructions to deliver the egg and get the $100,000—or, more precisely, vice versa.

The doctor had done some research on Farouk and learned he was an amateur magician whose great joy in life was to confound his fawning court. So when Victor took off with the egg, his luggage included a suitcase filled with tricks of all types, plus an assortment of additional Fabergé jewelry and knickknacks that might catch the monarch's jaded eye.

Peering out the window of the plane on the last leg of his journey, Victor wondered what dignitary was among its passengers. There was an honor guard drawn up in front of the terminal and a committee of what looked like Egyptian dignitaries. To Victor's astonishment, the committee advanced on him and presented him with a solid-gold hammer encased in velvet. The hammer was inscribed, "Welcome to Egypt," and signed by the King. He was whisked to Abdine Palace with a police escort and spent a week in Cairo as Farouk's guest. The tricks he brought with him were a huge success with the King, who ignored everything else—including the approach of Rommel's tanks—to play them on his ministers and others. Victor lunched with the royal family on a barge on the Nile and received a royal mandate:

"When you return, tell your brother Armand that I have heard about him and I am going to appoint him my financial adviser and personal representative in the United States."

One subsequent order from Farouk was for a secondhand deluxe land yacht valued at more than $100,000 which Armand arranged to have shipped as wartime cargo. Farouk will hardly be remembered with Ptolemy in the annals of Egyptian history. He was, in short, a royal oaf whose idea of art was concentrated mainly on watches whose working parts simulated round-the-clock copulation. Farouk also had a garage filled with red Rolls-Royces, at least one of them equipped with a horn that imitated the scream of a dog being run over.

151

Before Egypt's Society of Free Officers forced Farouk's abdication on July 23, 1952, the King sent Armand Hammer two orders. One he was unable to fill, for a change.

The first was a simple cablegram. It read: BUY ME A BAKELITE FACTORY FAROUK.

The second came in an airmail letter that contained a bosomy clipping from a movie magazine and a short note. The note said: "Send me Lana Turner."

There is the following assessment by Armand's friend and associate British financier John Burton Tigrett:

"Doc has always reminded me of that lovable character 'The Little King,' which Otto Soglow draws. His clothes sometimes look as though he had slept in them for several days. He moves with a rather shuffling glide and he always seems to look at the world in complete wonderment. As an aloof sophisticate, he is at least a failure.

"My associate, Jimmy Goldsmith of London, and I were in Los Angeles on some negotiations—not connected with Oxy—and one day lunched with Fran and Doc at their home. As we were leaving, he asked what we were doing the next day, and I said we had engagements with officials of the Union Bank. 'Put them back a day, John—I have something I want you and Jimmy to help me on. I'll pick you up at ten o'clock tomorrow morning. Bring the girls too—they'll enjoy the trip.'

"Jimmy and I figured it must be at least a one-hundred-million-dollar deal we were being cut in on, though we had no idea where it was or whether we were driving or jetting to it.

"Fran and Doc picked up the four of us at the Century Plaza promptly at ten and away we went. We kept driving with no mention of our destination and Jim and I, by this time, were afraid to ask.

"Suddenly we turned in at Disneyland and Doc said, 'I thought we'd all enjoy spending a day here. I love Disneyland.'

"When we left at nine that night, we had ridden on everything that moved, seen nearly every show, and eaten continuously. Doc did not touch a telephone, nor once mention business (he told his staff he had to go out of town on some important secret negotiations). No six people ever laughed any more or had a happier day.

"Doc's use of the telephone is prodigious. At least forty or fifty percent of his working hours are spent on it. I have heard stories that his annual personal telephone bill is near a million dollars. I don't know the facts—but I can believe the story. Except for that day at Disneyland, I have never been with him in an airport or on a street anywhere in the world for more than ten minutes that he didn't find a telephone and call someone about something. Some of my more amusing moments have been spent listening to him try to conquer the telephone system in foreign countries. If it can be done, believe me, he has done it. He uses every possible device to get through—some most ingenious—and there's always a new one. 'It's an emergency—this is Dr. Hammer,' is a common one, and in some foreign countries, 'Get me the Prime Minister—I want to use his line to the United States.'

"The telephone is Doc's way of cutting across organizational lines (if he ever knew there were any such lines). A fellow on a rig in Nigeria or in the North Sea is just as liable to get a call from him at an odd hour as one of his executives. He frequently will have four different executives working on the same project—not one of them knowing what the other is doing. But he monitors all of them by telephone. That tiny, beat-up, two-by-two-inch book he carries in his pocket has in penciled scribbles the private lines and unlisted numbers of everyone from rig operators to shahs to presidents.

"Doc makes notes on a pad in his own shorthand of nearly every telephone call—even standing up in a phone booth. Whatever this does to his memory discs is unique, for he has the finest memory in the world for every detail of a transaction and every conversation months or years afterward. At seventy-six, I will stake his memory against anyone alive at any age.

"I have never seen Doc tight or tough about money. Some of his best deals have been made when his executives thought he was giving the company away. He hardly ever has any money in his pocket. In fact, sometimes I've wondered if he knows what it is.

"Doc and I were working on a Persian Gulf deal with Lord Thomson, the mighty press lord, in Roy Thomson's office in London. About noon Lord Thomson said, 'Let me take you all to lunch.' Doc said, 'No, you come to lunch with us.' We got in Roy's Rolls and started to the West End.

" 'Where do you want to go?' I asked. With that, Doc put his hand in his pocket and drew out a one-dollar bill. 'It's going to have to be a pretty cheap place,' he said. 'How about you Roy?' I asked Thomson. 'Well, I've just a pound in cash, but I do have one of those Diner's Club cards,' he replied. 'That's great,' I said. 'Do you know where it's good?' 'No,' he answered, 'I've never used it.'

"We ended up lunching at the Clermont Club, where I could sign the check.

"Doc has never been able to recognize a stone wall. When he has come up against one, he has simply turned and gone in another direction. His friend Norman Vincent Peale wrote a book on 'positive thinking' but Doc put the idea fully into practice. Through 1972 and the first month or so of '73, Oxy went through some difficult times. When the true situation was pointed out to him several times in detail, he never admitted once that it existed. To his executive mourners who described the situation with long faces, he said simply at the end of their explanation, 'I tell you, boys, we're going to get a big strike in the North Sea.' At that moment, Oxy had just drilled the third dry hole there, at two and a half million a hole. But sure enough, the next one hit a zillion barrels of oil."

If a man is known by the autographs he keeps, Hammer must have had a broader range of famous friends than any other man alive. On the walls and tables of his office are the inscribed photographs of Lenin, Khrushchev (who envied him for knowing Lenin personally), three camera studies of Brezhnev, Presidents Hoover, Roosevelt (and Eleanor), Truman, Eisenhower, Kennedy, Johnson (plus one of Lady Bird), Nixon and Nixon's family. Also King Faisal of Saudi Arabia, Major General Yakubu Gowon, head of the Federal Military Government of Nigeria, King Hassan II of Morocco, President Habib Bourguiba of Tunisia, President Carlos Andreas Pérez of Venezuela, Lester Pearson of Canada, Adlai Stevenson, Senator Ted Kennedy, and Ronald Reagan.

Also, the pens President Kennedy and Prime Minister Pearson used in sealing the two-nation deal for Hammer's Campobello, a model of Gene Reid's drilling rig that opened a whole new world for the doctor when it hit gas at Lathrop, and a framed quotation from Lincoln that Hammer particularly admires:

> If I were to try to read, much less answer, all the attacks made on me, this shop might as well be closed for any other business. I do the very best I

can; and I mean to keep doing so until the end. If the end brings me out all right, what is said against me won't amount to anything. If the end brings me out wrong, ten angels swearing I was right would make no difference.

Chapter 18

Back to the U.S.S.R.

Armand Hammer's lives overlap like a Reuben sandwich.

Less than a month after John F. Kennedy's entrance into the White House he appointed Armand Hammer as a roving economics emissary, without portfolio, and dispatched him overseas in search of ways and means of balancing the ebb and flow of dollars. The United States was generally running second in that field. The young President and the international business wizard had been introduced some years earlier by their mutual friend Representative Jimmy Roosevelt (Democrat of California). At the January 1961 inauguration Hammer and his wife Frances were again close to J.F.K. and Mrs. Kennedy. They were the guests of Kennedy's good friend Senator Albert A. Gore, the Tennessee Democrat whose herd of Aberdeen Angus cattle had been enriched by several bulls and heifers produced, by remote control, by Hammer's Prince Eric. On Gore's enthusiastic recommendation, the President gave his imprimatur to Hammer and ordered Secretary of Commerce Luther Hodges to arrange an itinerary and to see that he was properly received. Hodges decided that Hammer should take a look at the United Kingdom, France, West Germany, Italy, Libya, the Soviet Union, India, and Japan.

The European phase of the Hammer mission was bland. Libya was more interesting. But Hammer's days in Moscow—his first trip back in thirty-one years—were paramount. The visit proved so productive that he was ordered to return to Washington with his report, dropping his Indian and Japanese trips.

The doctor's first interview in the Soviet Union was with V. M. Vinogradov, chief of the Administration of Trade with Western Countries,

156

and M. N. Gribkov, chief of the American Trade Section. He had never heard of either of them. They were in knee pants when he left Russia with his fortunes.

In light of what one day would happen in U.S.–Soviet Union trade relations, and Hammer's own multibillion-dollar deal with a succeeding generation of Russian officials, the doctor's meeting with the Foreign Trade Ministers on February 14, 1961, could only be described as exploratory. A "Memorandum of Conversation" dictated immediately after leaving the meeting at the Ministry of Foreign Trade recalls the scope of the gap that existed between the two powers in the wake of the abrasive Khrushchev visit to Eisenhower, the Khrushchev–Nixon "kitchen debate," the shooting down over Sverdlovsk (Ekaterinburg) of C.I.A. U–2 pilot Francis Gary Powers, his public trial and sentencing before a military court in Moscow, the breakup of the scheduled Eisenhower–Khrushchev–De Gaulle–Macmillan summit in Paris, and Khrushchev's harsh rescinding of his invitation to Eisenhower to visit the U.S.S.R. and speak to its peoples by radio and television.

The memorandum noted:

> I opened the meeting by describing my previous experiences in the Soviet Union and my American business activities during the past thirty years. . . . In the course of these remarks it was emphasized that improvements in [U.S.-Soviet] trade would take time but that it would be helpful to make some small beginnings. Changes which require administrative action probably could be effected more easily than those requiring legislation. As a businessman I studiously avoided political questions and sought only to explore areas which offered some promise for improved trade.
>
> There was a very brief discussion of the prospects for an air link between the U.S. and the U.S.S.R. but this brought no significant response from Vinogradov as this subject does not fall within his field of responsibility.
>
> It was interesting that nothing was said about credits and that Vinogradov seemed to recognize that an improvement in trade relations would take time. I recognized a number of Soviet misstatements, propaganda points, and old arguments, but I felt it would be inappropriate in this kind of exploratory discussion to argue or to belabor these points.

The next day, Hammer was shown an embassy list of other prospective Soviet officials he might meet with. He pushed it aside as politely as possible.

"These people were boys when I left here," he said. "I want to see Mikoyan."

An embassy aide laughed nervously. "That's impossible," he said. "Mikoyan is the deputy prime minister. He doesn't see *anybody,* especially American businessmen. You must be joking."

"I met him in 1923, the day I brought the Fordson tractors into Rostov," Hammer said, controlling himself. "He was secretary of the local soviet at the time. I'm going to send him a note right now, tell him I'm here in Moscow, that I want to see him, and why I'm here." It must have sounded like an order to the aide. The note was delivered to the Foreign Office and to the surprise of the aide, and apparently all others around the American embassy, Mikoyan's office called within two hours and said that it was sending a car for the deputy prime minister's friend of old.

The Mikoyan-Hammer talk went a little more easily than the meeting with Vinogradov. There was much to talk about after nearly forty years, and the talk was in Russian. When the amenities were done with, the exchange of views came down to what Hammer considered the singularly inconsequential matter of the U.S. ban on Russian crabmeat. He soon gathered that it was not an unimportant topic in Mikoyan's mind. The politically indestructible Armenian, Comrade Anastas Ivanovich, gravely resented the continuing American embargo on Soviet crabmeat on the ground that it was produced by "slave" or "forced" labor.

"Do you think we'd eat this crabmeat ourselves if it were produced by what you call slave or forced labor?" he asked Hammer. "That would be unsanitary and dangerous. Why don't you ask your Japanese friends? They crab side by side with our vessels. They would surely know, and tell you, if we were using slave or forced labor."

Hammer's report observed:

Mikoyan stated that major problems such as a Lend Lease settlement [the United States contributed an estimated $11 billion to Russia during World War II], credits, and the granting to the U.S.S.R. of most-favored-nation treatment required legislation and will take time. He believes that even [John Foster] Dulles before he died favored the granting of credits, settlement of Lend Lease, and the expansion of trade between the two countries. If Lend Lease could be settled and credits arranged the U.S.S.R. could place orders in the U.S. in the amount of $1 billion. In this connection, Mikoyan said that these orders would not include military items. In his words, "After all, we can make these better than you can. For example, we are ahead of you in rocket development."

He was critical of former Secretary of Commerce [Lewis L.] Strauss, "who only wanted to discuss the religious issues in the U.S.S.R."

The U.S.S.R. only a few days ago placed an order with Sweden for delivery of 135,000 tons of steel pipe and with the Italians for 240,000 tons. No long credits were involved. "Orders like these," he said, "could have been placed in the U.S. and it would have helped to solve the U.S. unemployment problem, when the U.S. steel industry was operating at only 50 percent of capacity."

I pointed out that in my opinion settlement of the Lend Lease debt would go a long way toward creating the proper atmosphere for changing the "mfn" situation and obtaining credits for Russian trade. He said that Mr. Khrushchev had given orders to settle the Lend Lease debt when he was in Washington. However, he said, the Russians wanted the assurance that they would be treated in the same manner as the English were in this regard, namely the parallel negotiations he conducted regarding the granting of credits and a trade agreement. . . . Mr. Mikoyan said, "How can we make our payments under a Lend Lease debt settlement, and pay for the orders we would want to place, if we did not receive credits and if we could not sell our goods on the same conditions as other countries sell to the U.S.?"

I said that improved relations could be assisted by increasing tourist trade both ways and cultural exchanges. In this connection, I made the suggestion to Mr. Mikoyan that Russia send a representative collection of their art treasures from their leading museums to the United States. The impact of a representative group of paintings from, for example, the Hermitage Museum in Leningrad would be enormous. In order to make it strictly noncommercial and nonpolitical, I suggested that Mrs. Eleanor Roosevelt be appointed chairman of a committee to supervise this undertaking and that any benefits from admission should go to the Eleanor Roosevelt Cancer Foundation. I said [Hammer wrote with some special prescience] that I believed the first exhibition could be held at the National Art Gallery in Washington, D.C., and then at the larger cities in the U.S., such as New York, Chicago, Los Angeles, etc. Mr. Mikoyan said he thought this was a very good idea and said he would speak to the proper authorities.

The next morning, the Hammers were preparing to leave for the airport and the doctor's scheduled meeting with Prime Minister Nehru in New Delhi when he received a call at his hotel from Ambassador Thompson's office. He must not leave; Mikoyan obviously had spoken to Khrushchev about Hammer, and Khrushchev wanted to see him the following day. Nehru was stalled and eventually dumped, as was Hammer's scheduled Japanese host. The opportunity to sit down with the ebullient heir to the mantle of his old friend Lenin took precedence. When Hammer met Khrushchev on February 17, 1961, at Khrushchev's Kremlin office, there was no question about who ruled the U.S.S.R. It was a remarkable meeting that lasted more than two hours. The doctor's subsequent memo to Washington is a long and often revealing footnote to the history of U.S.-Soviet relations and to the biography of a Russian leader who will be remembered for more than his obstreperous declaration "We will bury you."

Memo excerpts:

Subject: U.S.-Soviet Trade Relations
Place: Khrushchev's office, Kremlin, 6 P.M., 2/17/61
Participants: N. S. Khrushchev
                A. F. Dobrynin, Chief of American Countries Division,
                Ministry of Foreign Affairs
                Hammer

Khrushchev dismissed the interpreter. He felt that my Russian was sufficiently clear to permit the entire conversation to be held in Russian. He had in his hands a copy of my Angus sale catalogue I had left with Mikoyan two days before and stated that he had spent last evening reading it with the help of an English-speaking member of his staff. He said that meat was a major problem facing the U.S.S.R. and indicated that Soviet cattle were yielding only about 50 percent of their gross weight in usable meat. In the U.S., on the other hand, he understood that we were getting 65–70 percent. He also said that from his personal experience the quality of U.S. meat is better. He said that while he was in our country he enjoyed our huge steaks, eating every last morsel, and would like the Soviet people to have meat that good. He had received a Black Angus heifer from President Eisenhower and one from the former Secretary of Commerce. I said, "You can't do much with two heifers. I'll send you an Angus bull, a son of my famous Prince Eric." (Later Hammer kept his promise and through Amtorg dispatched one of his bulls and two females to keep him company.)

Khrushchev indicated that his country had learned much from the U.S. and is eager to learn more in fields where we excel. Ford, for example, had taught them how to make automobiles. He thanked me for bringing Ford to Russia and enabling the first modern plant to be completed. He continued that although the U.S.S.R. had made a lot of mistakes and its workers had broken a lot of machines through ignorance or otherwise, his country excels the U.S. in several fields.

He said that a group of American engineers had expressed admiration, even envy, of Soviet hydro-electric installations. He stated that his country can now make synthetic rubber directly from gas without first making synthetic alcohol. He said the U.S.S.R. had produced 65 million tons of steel in 1960, would produce 71 million tons in this year [1961], and from 76 to 78 million in 1962. In 1965, he predicted, they would produce from 86 to 95 million tons, and in 1970 "we will beat you in steel output and in 1980 we will produce double what you will be producing."

He continued, "Now we want to put more into agriculture than in the past because we are no longer afraid of the United States. We want to improve the conditions of our people. We want to strengthen our chemical industry in order to provide more clothing for our people. Other countries in Western Europe have no hesitancy in selling us this equipment and giving us credits. If some people in the U.S. think that by not trading with us they can crush us, they are mistaken. We now turn out three times the number of engineers you do. We don't want you to sell to us unless it is profitable for you to do so, and profitable for us. We'll buy what we need. Your man Dillon [C. Douglas, Eisenhower's Under Secretary of State] spoke about selling us shoes. I showed him my shoes and said they were better than his, and made in Russia. There are many things we want to buy —if we can get them we don't have to develop our own industries. If we work together, our economies will thus be tied in together. If you give us credit, you should do so because it is to your benefit and not as a favor. You will earn interest, you will make a profit on the goods you sell, and it will keep your plants busy. There has never been a case when we have failed to pay our commercial obligations and there never will. We will not buy on credit, even for five years, unless we know we can pay for it."

I repeated to him substantially what I had told Mikoyan, namely, that there had been a deterioration of goodwill toward the U.S.S.R., both in Congressional circles and among the American public, since the collapse of the Paris summit. As a consequence, prospects for improved trade relations had worsened. The process of regaining the support of American public opinion would be slow. Before any new legislation could be enacted, I stated that it was my opinion that Lend Lease must be settled. Khrushchev said, "I gave orders to settle it but U.S. authorities did not wish to treat us as well as they had treated the British; just treat us as you did the British, and we will be satisfied."

Khrushchev brought up the subject of the U-2 incident. He stated that

U.S. authorities had sent a U-2 across Russia in April of 1960. It was not shot down and the man responsible for that failure was punished. Khrushchev then said, "I was awakened early in the morning, May 1, when the second plane was sighted, and was told. I personally gave the orders to shoot it down. This was done with our rockets. I also laid a trap by withholding the announcement to see what U.S. authorities would say. When they lied, I exposed them. We caught them as you would a thief with his hand in your pocket." He said Eisenhower later admitted that they had lied but would continue to send U-2's over Russia. "This was too much for us to stomach," Khrushchev said. "Remember that Mr. Eisenhower had an invitation to be our guest. It was as if a guest in your home was saying, 'I'm going to destroy you.'"

Khrushchev continued, "I believe that while Mr. Eisenhower may have been consulted, and approved the general plan for the U-2, and had known of the flight in April, he was not consulted in advance about the May 1 flight. This was authorized by Allen Dulles or those under him in your C.I.A. I think their purpose was to embarrass me by showing Mr. Eisenhower that we were unable to defend ourselves. I tried to give Mr. Eisenhower an opportunity to apologize but when he refused I would not speak to him in Paris. Mr. Kennedy said, during the campaign, that he would have apologized. This shows that he is an honorable and clever man. However, the matter is now forgotten and we do not require any apology. Both Senator Fulbright and Mr. Stevenson took an attitude similar to that of Senator Kennedy." He added, "I also like your ambassador, Thompson. In our talks, Thompson presents the capitalist view, of course; but I understand him and he understands me. We get along as representatives of two great powers should."

Khrushchev volunteered the statement that he still had a high regard for Eisenhower, who, he remarked, was a noble and dedicated man who sincerely wanted to bring about peace in the world. However, he thought Eisenhower delegated too much authority to others and was "lazy."

In the course of Dr. Hammer's two-hour talk with Khrushchev he suggested to the Premier and party leader an exchange of each power's art treasures for exhibition purposes and a Mikoyan-Hodges meeting to study trade. Khrushchev promised to attend to both proposals. His fascination with comparing the powers intruded into his every thought:

"If we cannot give our people the food, shelter, and cultural benefit that you provide under the capitalist system, we know that communism cannot succeed. However, we are convinced that we can, and our performance over recent years is proof of this. We are perfectly willing to leave it to history as to which system is the best for mankind and which will survive." Apropos of this, Hammer had brought with him a copy of the book he wrote in 1932 after his years in Russia. He asked that the interpreter be recalled to translate the final chapter, which contained his conclusions. Khrushchev listened attentively as the man read, in Russian:

> I make bold to summarize my opinion of conditions in Russia. . . . As far as anyone can tell, the Soviet Government appears to be entirely stable. It not only has invariably met all its obligations but, according to all indications, will continue to do so. The new regime is, of course, not universally popular—what government is?—but it rests upon a much wider and more solid foundation than is generally believed abroad. Instead, as most people think, of a relatively small group who have seized power and hold it through the army and the secret police, that is by force, the Soviet Government has behind it over ten million organized workers who are the most vigorous and energetic element in Russian national life. . . . The nation-wide campaign of education and help to the poorer peasants, who are being grouped into collectives and supplied with seed, tractors, and implements and taught how to develop their land to the best advantage, will, I am convinced, bear fruit before long.
>
> There is, too, a psychological element of stability which seems to have been somewhat overlooked by the outer world in its estimate of conditions in Russia. This country has had its Revolution, has realized the wildest dreams of the wildest strike leader or labor agitator. The working class has seized power and attempted to put into being the theory of integral communism as a practical system of politics and economics. The attempt failed, and it was found necessary to revert to NEP, that is, to a system more nearly approximating the capitalist development of other countries. Under NEP, communism was replaced by a form of state socialism which permitted private profit and for a time encouraged individual initiative. As the socialist state has felt itself getting stronger in recent years, it has gradually suppressed the private trader through excessive taxation and other means. During all these years the workers have been flattered to think that the power is in their hands. They have no incentive to strike for that would injure their interests. In short, by a curious paradox, Soviet Russia, the country of Revolution, is today the least revolutionary of countries.
>
> It is still too early to say that the Russian experiment of government ownership on a vast scale is or will be successful. Will the Soviet leaders find it possible to stimulate private initiative and responsibility by sufficiently increasing the material reward for the individual? This is dangerous ground for the Communist because it tends to create class distinction.

163

Nevertheless, some progress seems to have been made along this path as, for example, the almost universal introduction of piecework among the workers, and the increased salaries and privileges to the engineers, the so-called "Specialists," who were formerly discriminated against and in some cases even treated with contempt. Mistakes are made, but it is to the credit of the Bolsheviks that they seem able to learn from their mistakes. During the past few years industrial progress has been rapid, real, and continuous. New factories are constantly being built and new industries developed.

In 1929 the Soviet embarked upon an ambitious Five-Year Plan of economic development in which every branch of production, finance, and commerce had been minutely surveyed with a view to its improvement and development to the greatest possible extent. Considerable progress has been made under the stimulus of reaching this goal, but there is no doubt that Russia will need many more five-year plans before the needs of her people will be satisfied.

Whatever may be said of a socialist system, the centralized control of the sources of supply and production has much to recommend it. Will some scheme of such centralized control be evolved to take the place of our [U.S.] present wasteful and planless system of overproduction? The present world-wide economic crisis would seem to indicate that we may yet have to borrow a page from Russia's Five-Year Plan.

I am betraying no secrets when I say that Russia looks to the United States for assistance in working out her gigantic program—perhaps unique in history, if one excepts the less sharply coordinated but equally grandiose schemes of Peter the Great. American technical advice and equipment, perhaps later, it is hoped, American financial support, will be welcomed. Not only is there a gratitude in the hearts of millions of Russians who owe their lives to the generous aid of America in the work of the American Relief Administration, but also it is realized that Americans have success-fully conquered the same difficulties of developing the natural resources of a vast territory which face Russia today.

Khrushchev was delighted. He complimented Hammer on his "consid-erable understanding and farsightedness."

It was time to leave. Hammer asked, "Is there any message you'd like me to take back to President Kennedy?"

"Yes," Khrushchev said. "Tell him to take off the ban on our crab-meat."

Hammer had been briefed that this relatively inconsequential but sensi-tive matter was certain to come up. The doctor gave the routine answer, the official U.S. position that the ban was based on the belief that slave labor was employed. Khrushchev fumed with anger.

"There is no slave labor any more in Russia," he almost shouted. "Not since Stalin died! There are no slave camps any more. They've been disbanded since Stalin."

Hammer shrugged. "All you have to do is let us send an inspection team or a representative to check on this and bring back a report that what you say is true. After that, there will be no problem. The ban will be removed."

Khrushchev reacted indignantly.

"I know what you're suggesting," he said. "Your officials want to send some of your spies. Your government wants to slip its agents in among us on a pretense."

Hammer's laughter cooled him and gave Khrushchev an idea.

"I'll let *you* go and see for yourself," he said. Hammer thanked him for the trust shown, but said he was sorry; he didn't have the time. Khrushchev then said the Soviet Union would accept any individual or group Hammer might recommend. Hammer said that he'd report that upon his return to the United States. The ban was lifted on President Kennedy's orders shortly after Hammer arrived back in Washington with his report and Kennedy verified with Secretary of the Treasury Dillon that our intelligence knew from the Japanese there was no slave labor used in the Kamchatka crab packing industry.

Hammer learned of the President's action by the following letter from his old friend Senator Albert Gore:

March 17, 1961
Dear Armand:

On day before yesterday, Secretary of Commerce Luther Hodges telephoned me and said he thought I would like to know that he had personally discussed with President Kennedy your conversation with Premier Khrushchev and particularly the emphasis he placed upon the banning of Russian crabmeat on the grounds that it was processed by slave labor. Thereupon, President Kennedy, according to Secretary Hodges, contacted the Treasury Department to remove the ban.

In the broad spectrum of the struggle to find a way for the East and the West to live in peace on one planet, this may not appear to some as a major item, but when one considers the dangers to mankind involved in war today, any step that moves toward better understanding and peaceful relations is important. Just as Rome was not built in a day, peace will not be achieved in one cataclysmic event, one major conference or one international concert. Instead, it will come step by step, little by little. I am hopeful that an exchange of exhibits of art treasures which you discussed with Premier Khrushchev may be arranged.

With the kindest of personal regards, I am,

Sincerely,
ALBERT

As Hammer said good-bye and *mir i druzhba* (peace and friendship), Khrushchev stepped over to his desk and gave him a present, his personal automatic pencil on whose crest sat a small red ruby set in a red star.

"This is in return for what you did in establishing the first pencil factory in my country," he said.

It was a cue for Hammer. After thanking Khrushchev he said, "You could do me a great favor. I've been here for several days and I've been trying to visit my old pencil factory. But every time I ask the Intourist people they give me an evasive answer. I think I'm getting a runaround."

Khrushchev turned to Dobrynin, soon to be Soviet ambassador to Washington, and said, "See that he sees his pencil factory—immediately."

Hammer was back at the embassy giving his verbal report to Foy Kohler, acting ambassador in Lewellyn Thompson's absence, and Frances was waiting patiently, when a phone call came in from the Kremlin about 9:30 P.M. saying that a car was coming over to take the Hammers to the pencil factory.

"It used to be on the outskirts of the city," Hammer remembers. "By that time, 1961, it was in town. Moscow had grown up around it. But it was just as it was when I left it, more than thirty years before. The snow was falling on the factory, falling on the schoolhouse, the recreation hall, and those little cottages I built there in the old days for the German workers. The white birches had grown taller and thicker. Soft lights glowed everywhere. It was the most romantic setting you can ever imagine.

"We walked in on the night shift. Except for several new machines, they were still using some of those I picked up in Germany years before. They took us through all the divisions—it must have taken an hour out of the middle of the night—and finally we came to the executives' offices.

My office was still there, nothing changed. When the tour ended, they led Frances and me to the boardroom, which had been set up for a party. There was caviar, champagne, vodka, the works. All the executives of the pencil factory had been invited, and, I'd guess, half a dozen or more of the old employees who had been there when I was there. It was just like a prodigal son coming home, a great, great night. One little old lady came up to me. There were tears in her eyes. Her sadness was based on the fact that Frances and I had not been led through her division of the plant, now named the Sacco Vanzetti.

" 'Armand Yulevitch, when your brother Victor Yulevitch came to work in the plant, I was the one who saw to it that he learned to operate every machine,' she said. And then I remembered her.

" 'Oh, my, how you've changed!' she said. Remembering her as a buxom young girl, I felt like saying the same to her but decided to spare the dear old soul's feelings.

"About fifty people were seated around the table and one toast followed another first with vodka, then with various wines, and finally with cognac and champagne."

It was a most rewarding send-off. Khrushchev made a reference to it in a speech later on which was duly reported in *Pravda*, in journalese peculiar to the Soviets. It read, in part:

> Hammer went to V. I. Lenin and said that he had decided to apply for a concession for the manufacture of pencils. V. I. Lenin looked at him with surprise and said, "Why do you want to take a concession for the manufacture of pencils?"
>
> "Mr. Lenin," said Hammer, "you have set a goal that everybody should learn to read and write and you haven't any pencils! Therefore, I will manufacture pencils!" (Noisy applause in the hall.) Some of the old employees were still there to greet Hammer. "See how pleased our old boss is with our progress," they said (laughter and applause).
>
> So, you see, V. I. Lenin went even further than we by granting concessions to foreigners.

Hammer returned to Moscow twice thereafter during Khrushchev's tenure. On the second trip, early in 1963, he put together a multibillion-dollar fertilizer deal that would depend on British credits. But before it could be implemented, Khrushchev was removed from his post as General

Secretary of the Communist Party and Prime Minister.

Nine years later, a new group of Russian leaders in the Politburo, headed by Secretary General Leonid Brezhnev, Prime Minister Aleksei Kosygin, and President Nikolai Podgorny, remembered the Khrushchev-Hammer agreement, found it viable, and escalated it astronomically.

Chapter 19

Grandma Leads the Parade

In 1961, on the occasion of the trip to Moscow that had the imprimatur of President Kennedy, Hammer suggested to Khrushchev that an exchange of art works might bring the two hostile powers a mite closer to detente. Khrushchev had promised he would take up the suggestion with his Minister of Culture, Yuri Zhukov, former *Pravda* editor and common scolder of most things American. Nothing came of it. However, near the end of Khrushchev's reign, Hammer was back in Moscow. There, on June 10, 1964, he met with Zhukov's successor, Mme. Yekaterina Furtseva, the first woman to achieve a high post in the Soviet hierarchy. This time his approach was more substantive. He offered that sturdy minister a well-nigh irresistible American institution: Grandma Moses.

Hammer could not have strummed a more responsive chord. Mme. Furtseva had recently returned from Copenhagen, where she had been enchanted by an exhibition of Grandma's bright primitives. The Danish showing was a huge success, she reported to Hammer in their Russian-language dialogue. She said she was certain the exhibition would attract even larger crowds and appreciation in the Soviet Union. But could he arrange it?

Hammer could. Hammer Galleries, had a joint venture agreement with the Galérie St. Étienne, which controlled the works of that dear old lady who had painted up to the time of her death on December 13, 1961, at the age of 101. The Grandma Moses exhibition was held at the Pushkin Museum in Moscow and proved to be a great success. People stood in lines extending around the museum in subzero weather waiting their turn to view the works of "Babushka" Moses, as she was affectionately called.

The second half of the bargain was not so easily arranged.

The ministry would select its own artist to exchange for Grandma. With that as her springboard, the spirited Minister of Culture asked with a twinge of indignation why the United States had barred a proposed tour by the Red Army Chorus. The chorus, she said, had performed all over Europe to great acclaim and now was being invited to make a second tour of Canada.

Hammer guessed that the group's Red Army uniforms were the reason for the action by the State Department; that civilian clothes might make the choristers more acceptable. Mme. Furtseva had a testy answer to that.

"Canada is not as strong as the United States, and yet the Canadians are not afraid of the Red Army uniforms," she said. "You have a very famous band, the Navy Band. We would have no objections to their coming here in their American naval uniforms." Hammer coughed, in Russian, and promised the dynamic lady (whose university training was in chemistry) that he'd speak to President Johnson about this cultural crisis.

The matter was finally settled, much to the satisfaction of the State Department, when the Russian Government agreed to send, in exchange for Grandma's works, a selection from the works of Pavel Korin. Korin had been trained from childhood as a painter of ikons and possessed one of Russia's greatest collections, which he willed to the Soviet government on his death. Victor was permitted to make the choices. Korin and his wife, both in their seventies, came to the Hammer Galleries for the opening on April 5, 1965, as the guests of the Hammers. The press acclaimed the exhibition as a great artistic success, devoid of any propaganda.

After their Grandma Moses–versus–Red Army dialogue, Mme. Furtseva and Armand became fast friends. Out of that friendship, based partly on her inherent awe of any person who had actually known Lenin, emerged an unprecedented relationship in the arts.

Their paths crossed again in 1971 when on a tour of the United States Hammer invited Mme. Furtseva to a Los Angeles exhibition of his extensive collection of American and European masters. The collection had been scheduled to be shown in London's Royal Academy of Arts the following June and July, after which it would be sent to the National Gallery of Ireland, Dublin, from August 9 to October 1, 1972. Mme. Minister, greatly impressed by the doctor's assembly of works by Cézanne, van Gogh, Renoir, Degas, Monet, Pissarro, Moreau, Gauguin, Corot,

Modigliani, Toulouse-Lautrec, Chagall—and Americans including Gilbert Stuart, Sargent, Eakins, Prendergast, Harnett, and Andrew Wyeth —asked her friend to include the Soviet Union on the tour. He quickly consented. It remained in the U.S.S.R. from mid-October 1972 until nearly a year later, attracting literally millions of fascinated viewers in museums as renowned as the Hermitage, Pushkin, and down the line to cultural places in Kiev, Odessa, Minsk, and Riga.

There were 104 oils, watercolors, and drawings—plus the Soviet Union's lone Goya. This was a gift from Hammer, since Mme. Furtseva said rather wistfully that there was not a single Goya in the U.S.S.R. Hammer said he happened to have two, so he could spare one; the figure represented is that of Doña Antonia Zarate, an actress and friend of Goya. Its first American owner was Marshall Field, who purchased it from the Knoedler Gallery in 1940 and exhibited it for a time at the New York World's Fair. Field willed it to his daughter, the Contesse de Flers, who in turn sold it back to Knoedler's.

The presentation was made by Hammer to Mme. Furtseva and other officials of the Soviet government at the Hermitage on October 22, 1972. It went on public display the following day.

It was now Mme. Furtseva's move. What, she asked Hammer, could her ministry do in return?

Whatever Hammer may be accused of, shyness will never be among his faults. After consulting with Victor and fellow officers of Knoedler's, he sent Mme. Furtseva a breathtaking and probably implausible list of thirty-six Impressionist and Postimpressionist paintings hanging in the Hermitage and Pushkin Museums. Many had never before been shown outside of Russia, and none had ever been shown in the United States. Madame's answer came back in the affirmative. Upon his return to the United States, Hammer was talking to J. Carter Brown, director of the National Gallery of Art, Washington, D.C., and told him of his coup. Brown said, "Couldn't we have this collection for the National Gallery?" Hammer said, "Let's dream a little." When they finished talking, Hammer had agreed to request that the exhibition be shown first in the nation's capital. Hammer had a warm spot in his heart for the National Gallery, as he had already agreed to bequeath all the drawings from his collection to the museum. Brown also asked Hammer to try to get five additional famous Impressionist paintings which he selected, thereby bringing the list up to forty-one canvases. Hammer cabled Mme. Furtseva, asking for permission to show the collection at the National Gallery as well as Knoedler's and to include the paintings selected by Brown.

On the audacious list were seven works by Matisse, seven by Gauguin, six by Picasso, five by Cézanne, three by van Gogh, two each by Rousseau, Renoir, Monet, and Derain, and one each by Braque, Sisley, Léger, Vlaminck, and Pissarro. These masterpieces covered the achievements of Impressionism from the dawn of the style in 1867 ". . . through its early lyricism in the Sisley of 1872 through Renoir's most classical and pure moment of the mid-1880s, to the late style of Pissarro in the last years of the nineteenth century."

They had been seen by only a handful of American art critics and connoisseurs who made their ways to the Hermitage and Moscow's Pushkin. The art world in general knew them only through photographs unable to do them more than casual justice. Once they belonged to and in some cases were commissioned by two of czarist Russia's richest merchants and rival collectors, Ivan Morozov and Sergei Shchukin. Each on his own shopped the humble studios of Paris and elsewhere, buying, shipping, and then harboring the output of enormously gifted rebels who left an indelible mark on Western culture. The Russian patrons also encouraged their own young native painters to learn from the Impressionists of the West. Their mansions became personal museums to which the public was invited each Sunday, and art students were welcomed any day during the week.

The Bolsheviks nationalized the lot. Morozov, whose museum possessed 430 Russian and 240 French works, was named "assistant director" of his rich collection and permitted to live in quarters of his mansion. He and Shchukin were allowed to leave Russia in 1919. Morozov died in Carlsbad in 1921, Shchukin in Paris in 1937, both in poverty.

That the forty-one paintings Hammer asked for had survived was something of a miracle in itself. During Stalin's twenty-year dictatorship they were relegated to the cellars and attics of Russian museums because Stalin's tastes in art did not appreciate Impressionism. In 1955, two years after Stalin's death, under Mme. Furtseva's leadership the Impressionists and Postimpressionists made a modest comeback in Moscow. The word spread and the crowds were huge. Thereafter, they were split between the Hermitage and the Pushkin. Art critic Carol Cutler, who fretted over these abused jewels while living in Russia during the years 1956–1958, told of their troubles in an article in the *Smithsonian* (April 1973):

Visiting art scholars who knew about them could ask to see them. Sometimes permission was granted, sometimes not. By late 1956 part of the collection was at last on view in the Hermitage; the Pushkin's went up later still. The Hermitage paintings, at the time, were difficult to find, being tucked away in a badly lighted corner of the top floor. The display improved slightly over the next few years, but it has always been in an out-of-the-way area.

Mme. Furtseva's answer to Hammer's bold request was a ringing yes. The forty-one works, thirty-nine of which had been the property of Morozov or Shchukin, were crated and shipped with all the fanfare and reverence that marked the transit from the Vatican to the New York World's Fair of Michelangelo's *Pietà*. Mindful of what a crazed man had since done to that ultimate in religious art, Hammer and Carter Brown arranged for the forty-one masterpieces to receive sturdier frames and to be shielded behind blow-resistant clear plastic.

The exhibitions in Washington and New York were ecstatically received. Driving by Knoedler's one morning in a whipping snowstorm, before the gallery's opening hour, Hammer noticed a line of art lovers a block long patiently awaiting the opening of the doors. He turned to an aide and said, "Get a picture of that. I want to send it to Madame Furtseva."

Madame approved Hammer's subsequent request to show the Impressionists at the Los Angeles County Museum of Art, the Art Institute of Chicago, and the Kimbell Art Museum, Fort Worth, Texas. Record crowds attended each show, and many came away with not only memories for a lifetime but an impressive catalog that has become a collector's item. Its slick-paper color prints are superb, its contributors impressive. Leonid Brezhnev wrote:

> The exhibition in the USA of paintings from Soviet museums is a concrete manifestation of the growing ties between our countries. The Soviet people regard exchanges and contacts in the field of culture along with cooperation in other areas as important factors in strengthening mutual understanding between nations. Therefore, Dr. Armand Hammer's initiative in promoting not only economic cooperation but also exchanges of artistic value between the USSR and the USA deserves full support.
>
> In extending greetings to the visitors to this exhibition on behalf of the Soviet people, I express my sincere hope that Soviet-American relations will

continue to develop in the interests of the people of both our countries and for the benefit of consolidating peace through the world.

President Nixon's page in the catalog was a reproduction of his February 26, 1973, letter to Paul Mellon, the president of the National Gallery, thanking him for providing that magnificent stage for the exhibition. He, too, had a special word of appreciation for the role Hammer played, and concluded:

"The American people are grateful to the leaders of the Soviet Government and the directors and staffs of the leading museums, and we look forward to the continuing cultural awareness and mutual understanding that derive from efforts such as this." He also thanked the Andrew W. Mellon Foundation for sponsoring (along with the National Endowment for the Humanities) a public broadcasting film produced by WNET/Channel 13 in New York of the arrival and keen reception of the collection.

Of all the treasures Dr. Hammer arranged for, the gifted creators of the catalog chose for its cover Matisse's subsequently defaced, if that's quite the word, *Nasturtiums and "The Dance"* (1912). John Richardson, vice-president of Knoedler's and author of the catalog, describes this in the following words:

"As he had already done in 1909, Matisse sets his still life against the famous *Dance*, commissioned by Shchukin for the stairwell of his Moscow palace. The *Dance* had been rejected for a time by Shchukin, because he thought the huge nudes would shock his Russian friends, not to mention his two adopted daughters. Eventually, the pictures were accepted, although one rather explicit passage was repainted in Russia." (A blob of Russian blue paint took care of the "explicit passage" in the case of the central, legs-spread nude in this superb work, and a splash from the same palette, or obscene bucket, gave the separation of a male dancer's buttocks the startling suggestion of a narrow well-kept grave.)

Hammer had insured the collection for $25 million. ("I would be delighted to be able to buy it for that," he said at the time.) (The *Pietà*, incidentally, was insured for $10 million by the Vatican and the Archdiocese of New York, during its stay outside St. Peter's.) The color film, shown throughout the United States and elsewhere as part of the National Gallery's Extension Service Program, has been and will continue to be seen by countless millions, now that the exquisite works have been returned to the Hermitage and the Pushkin.

If Hammer had accomplished nothing else in his life, he might well be remembered for this extraordinary coup. *Time* magazine said of it (April 2, 1973), "It is an event not only for the National Gallery but also for Knoedler's, whose chairman, Occidental Petroleum's Armand Hammer, was instrumental in persuading the Soviet government to show these spectacular works in the U.S." The International edition of the *Herald Tribune, New York Times,* and Washington *Post* reported (February 7, 1973), "Securing the loan was another of the Soviet-American coups of oil tycoon and art collector Armand Hammer, whose dealings with Russia date back to the days when he did business with Lenin." *The Times* of London added (February 7, 1973), "Dr. Hammer, one of the great impresarios of American business, had pulled off another coup with the Russians."

One day while Hammer was negotiating his fertilizer deal in the Soviet Union, he was called to Mme. Furtseva's office. "I have a surprise for you," she said. "We understand you do not have a Kasimir Malevitch painting in your collection. We have selected what the curators at the Tretiakovsky Gallery consider his finest Suprematist period work, and the Soviet government wishes you to have it." Hammer was visibly moved by this gesture of goodwill and thanked Mme. Furtseva and asked her to convey his deep appreciation to Mr. Brezhnev and the members of the Central Committee who authorized this gift, valued by Knoedler's John Richardson as at least a million dollars. Mme. Furtseva died in October of 1974 after her fruitful years as a promoter of better Soviet-American relations through the arts.

When Hammer's collection returned to its native habitat and the Impressionists were flown back to Russia (after a last-minute appeal from Henry Ford II and Richard Gerstenberg, chairman of General Motors, arranged for a showing of them at the Detroit Institute of Art), a question asked in U.S. art circles was "What can Hammer do for an encore?"

When asked, Victor said, "He's already got something in the works. The Russians have more Old Masters than most of the world museums put together. The Hermitage has rooms and rooms of Rembrandts, Rubenses, Van Dycks, and others. A showing of them in this country would have to be one of the greatest events in our art history, with the possible exception of a showing here of Leonardo's *Mona Lisa.*" Victor shrugged and added, "As you may have noticed, the Russians will give my brother just about anything he asks for!"

Chapter 20

How to Deal with Ivan

There are several paths to the heart and pocketbook of Ivan, that proud and sometimes perverse Communist. Capitalist Armand Hammer has traversed those paths so often that he rarely makes a wrong turn. President Nixon, who was no mean authority on how to get along with the current Soviet leaders, called Hammer to the White House on July 20, 1972, when Watergate still meant only a building complex, and asked him to report on his latest coup. Hammer had just returned from Moscow after signing the first trade agreement between a U.S. firm and the Committee for Science and Technology of the U.S.S.R. In the course of the forty-five-minute meeting, the President thanked Hammer for having told newsmen upon his arrival back in the United States that he could never have swung the deal for Oxy if the President had not paved the way during his summit meeting with Brezhnev in May.

Hammer wanted to express his gratitude to the Russians, but what could one give them as an encore after giving a million-dollar Goya? He found the answer unexpectedly in the pile of mail and telegrams that had been sent to him in the wake of the trade agreement. One letter was from a fellow art dealer who claimed he owned two letters written by Lenin. His proposition was a novel one: He would give the letters to Hammer (to give to the Russians) provided Hammer persuaded his Kremlin friends to present the dealer with a masterpiece from the Hermitage or the Pushkin.

The two dealers met to discuss the terms.

Hammer was shown the letters, one of them addressed to Clara Zetkin, the German feminist and Communist who knew both prison and a seat in the Reichstag, where she became its senior member during the Weimar regime. She worshiped Lenin, stumped articulately in behalf of his Revolution. Mrs. Zetkin died in Arkhangelskoe, near Moscow, in 1933. The dealer obtained the letters from her son in exchange for several paintings.

Hammer was shrewd enough to bring to the meeting with the dealer photostats of the letters he himself had received from Lenin. He compared the handwriting. They were genuine, as far as he could discern. But he had to be sure. The dealer gave him permission to make photostats, which he airmailed to Mme. Furtseva to show to the experts at the Lenin Institute. The word came back by cable that they were indeed genuine.

Now it was Hammer's task to explain the obvious to the dealer: The letters rightfully should be at the Lenin Institute, but the proposal that they be paid for by a work or works of art from the Hermitage or Pushkin was preposterous. The doctor offered the man several select paintings from the Hammer collection, and after months of bickering the deal was made, sweetened by what Hammer called a "substantial amount of cash."

Hammer flew his expensive prizes to Moscow in October 1972 and delivered them to Jermen Gvishiani, who is a son-in-law of Premier Kosygin and deputy chairman of the Committee for Science and Technology of the U.S.S.R. Council of Ministers, with this covering letter:

Moscow, October 27, 1972

The Honorable Leonid Ilitch Brezhnev,
General Secretary
Central Committee of the Communist Party
Moscow, U.S.S.R.

My dear Mr. General Secretary,

It is my great honor and pleasure to present to you two original manuscript letters written by Vladimir Ilitch Lenin. The letters were addressed on October 28, 1919, to his friend Comrade Loriot (in French) and on April 16, 1921, to Comrades Zetkin and Levi (in German). Both manuscripts are granted herewith as my unconditional gift to the government and people of the U.S.S.R.

The existence of the letters in the hands of a private individual was brought to my attention several months ago. Realizing their great historical significance to your country, I spared no effort to acquire them from their previous owner.

177

It may interest you to know that both items were bought 25 years ago from Konstantin Zetkin, son of Clara Zetkin, to whom one of the letters was addressed.

This offer of Vladimir Ilitch Lenin's personal writings, Mr. General Secretary, is intended to express my good will to the leaders and the people of the Soviet Union and my appreciation of a friendship with a great man whose memory will always remain sacred to me.

Respectfully yours,
ARMAND HAMMER

Several days later Gvishiani told Hammer (in Hammer's "Lenin Suite" at the National) that Brezhnev was out of town. The letters, he said, had been turned over to Mikhail Andreevich Suslov, the most mysterious member of the Politburo and secretary of the Central Committee of the Party. Gvishiani added that Suslov would like to see Hammer at the headquarters of the Central Committee. This was astonishing news for even as old a Kremlinologist as the doctor. Suslov never received foreigners. Hammer later told a reporter about his experience:

He is not the austere, forbidding individual he has often been described as in the foreign press. Instead, I found him to be a shy, extremely modest man; very friendly, in spite of what seemed to be an impassive countenance. He is a scholarly-looking individual with a kindly smile and his intelligent face lit up with animation when he spoke of Lenin.

I noticed that he had on his desk several volumes of Lenin's published papers which I recognized, and there were slips of paper inserted in the places where Lenin referred to me. Obviously he had been reading this correspondence and knew all about me and my early activities in the Soviet Union. He read to me a resolution of the Central Committee of the Communist Party thanking me for my gift of the Lenin letters.

Mr. Suslov then presented me with a beautiful engraved portrait of Lenin made of silver and other metals found in the Urals, where I had signed the barter deal bringing grain to the Russian workers of that area in the famine of 1921. A photographer entered the room to record the occasion. Mr. Suslov then read to me a release prepared for the press and asked for my approval.

Hammer was elated. He told the press:

Mr. Suslov escorted me through his secretary's outer office and pointed out Mr. Brezhnev's office in the Central Committee which opened into the same secretariat. He remarked, "Secretary General Brezhnev regrets he could not be here but he will write you on his return to Moscow and will also receive and thank you personally on your next visit to the U.S.S.R." The account of my meeting with Mr. Suslov and the complete text of the release appeared prominently the next day on the front page of *Pravda* as well as in all other Russian newspapers.

Shortly thereafter, the doctor heard from Brezhnev:

November 10, 1972

Dear Dr. Hammer,

Let me express my sincere gratitude for your gift to the Soviet people—two original letters by Vladimir Ilyich Lenin. It is unnecessary to tell you at length how dear to the Soviet people is everything that is directly related to the life and activities of the great founder of our Party and the Soviet State.

The leadership of the Soviet Union attaches great importance to the present positive turn in the Soviet-American relations. The development of contracts and mutually beneficial peaceful cooperation between our peoples in different spheres is considered by us as a matter of great importance. A highly significant role in that belongs to the economic relations and you, Dr. Hammer, are making an active contribution to their development.

Please accept my wishes of good health and successes.

Sincerely,
L. BREZHNEV

On February 15, 1973, Hammer had a two-hour meeting with the Secretary General in his office in the Kremlin. He told reporters:

I found Mr. Brezhnev a man of great humanism and vast warmth and understanding, enormously intelligent and sophisticated in the ways of the world.

We met in his office in the Kremlin, alone except for his interpreter, Viktor Sukhodrev. Initially, we spoke through the interpreter, but I found I could keep up with him in Russian, so I began to answer directly without waiting for the English translation.

Brezhnev said, "Well, Dr. Hammer, you apparently can understand my Russian very well." I answered, "Yes, I can understand you—but it's more important to know, can you understand me?" He laughed and said he could.

We spent two and a half hours together, talking about a wide range of subjects.

I told him: "You remind me very much of Lenin, whom I met in this very building fifty-two years ago."

His eyes filled with tears, which showed that he is a very human person who is trying to do good for his people just as Lenin tried. Fifty-two years earlier when I described the wheat deal to Lenin, and the help I was trying to bring to the starving people of the Urals, Lenin's eyes filled with tears as well.

Both men were the same kind, human and warmhearted. From that moment I had great faith that under Brezhnev's leadership we did have a chance for a lasting detente. We are never going to change their ideology any more than they can change ours, but there is no reason why the two nations cannot coexist. That is better than dropping atomic bombs on each other.

Hammer brought to the meeting a framed reproduction of the two original Lenin letters which he had given to Mr. Suslov.

Brezhnev said, "I want to give you something too," reaching into his pocket and taking out his thin gold watch and chain made in the U.S.S.R. "It was just a warm, human thing for him to do," Hammer recalled later. "It wasn't a protocol matter or anything. He just wanted to do it, and I was deeply touched. I still have the watch and chain and still wear it in my watch pocket, and sometimes I tease our American technologists by bringing it out and saying, 'See, it was made in Russia, but the workmanship is excellent, and it keeps very good time.' "

In this period, Hammer was in an unusual position, one of the few international industrialists meeting with both of the world's most powerful men. President Nixon had insisted on presenting Hammer with a set of special presidential cuff links and now Brezhnev had given him his watch, the unique set being perhaps the most unusual jewelry collection then in existence.

Hammer's next meeting with Brezhnev took place in Washington during the summit conference of 1973. Hammer met earlier in the day with Brezhnev at Blair House, the diplomatic residence for visiting chiefs of state across from the White House. That evening, entering the White House for Nixon's state dinner, the three men had their own brief summit conference. As Dr. and Mrs. Hammer came through the receiving line, Brezhnev held it up for about five minutes while he and Hammer conversed in Russian with Hammer interpreting into English for the benefit of the President.

The doctor is understandably proud of his way with Ivan, but he periodically puts on the brakes.

"I am a capitalist, and anyone who knows me knows what an ardent supporter of capitalism and America I am," Dr. Hammer said in a New York speech to the Society of American Business Writers, May 9, 1973.

> But I think a capitalist can deal with a Communist. We will never change their system. They will always be Communists, and they will always believe that our system is not as good.
>
> They say, "Well, you have your system and it works for you, but we don't believe in it. But it seems that the time has come when we can work together, you in your way and we in ours."
>
> Thus, there is a relatively cheerful prospect for coexistence, cooperation, and strong competition through commerce. President Nixon recognized this and, I think, deserves enormous credit from us for the way he moved steadily to the very center of the issue. If the Iron Curtain has now been lifted, it is President Nixon who has done it.

Hammer was uncommonly frank with the business writers, for a man in the throes of signing what Tass had termed the month before an $8 billion deal and the *New York Times* had called "the largest commercial agreement in the history of Soviet-American trade." He laid it on the line:

> The Hot Line, my friends, is no longer only in the basement of the White House. The hottest communication right now is the steady flow of negotiations between American businessmen and Russian commercial representatives. . . . Very candidly, I have been around too long and have been involved in too many episodes of international business not to recognize that the two great powers can still break apart. Ideologically we are never going to be partners.
>
> . . . We Americans must never lose sight of the fact that in our transactions with the Soviets we, as competing companies, are dealing not with a corresponding company, but with a government.
>
> . . . There are many trading organizations registered in Russia, but there is only one Chairman of the Board—and that is Mr. Brezhnev.
>
> . . . If it were that I could provide only one sentence of advice to all American businessmen, I would sum it up in this fashion: "Draw your contract carefully because once you sign it, the Soviets will make sure you live up to it, just as they intend to live up to their commitment."

... Their Deputy Minister of Foreign Trade, Alkhimov, tells a story about the Russian press that you may find instructive. In Russia, the word for "however" is "vsyahtekey." Minister Vladimir Sergeivich Alkhimov says the best way to read *Izvestia* and *Pravda* is to follow the story to the sentence which you will find beginning with the word "Vsyahtekey." And then from that point on pay *very close attention.* The same tip applies to contracts.

Even the business writers found Dr. Hammer's rapid ticking off of some of the details of Oxy's Soviet agreements somewhat mind-bending. Writers, half or even one-third the doctor's age, were given pause as the septuagenarian said:

Personally, I am confident that our fertilizer agreement will go forward as planned and will be fully operative in 1978. . . . This agreement calls for us to provide the Russians with American technology and equipment for a complex of ten plants, eight ammonia and two urea, having a total annual capacity of approximately four million metric tons of liquid ammonia and one million metric tons of urea. . . . This construction project is a vital part of our overall agreement, which also includes our twenty-year agreement to sell superphosphoric acid from 1978 to 1998. . . .

Dr. Hammer will be about 100 years old on that happy day when the fertilizer agreement ends. As of this writing, nobody on either side of the Iron Curtain he did so much to rend asunder is in any mood to bet him even money that he won't make it.

The "$8 billion deal" strained even the articulate doctor's power of delineation, particularly when trying to explain it to newsmen who thought urea was something floating like ambergris off the southern coast of Korea, useful in the manufacture of margarine. One reporter aimed a microphone at Hammer at his place in California and asked for a blow-by-blow:

Q. When did you start working on this deal?

A. In '61, with Khrushchev and Mikoyan. I made several trips back there after that, and in '63 it looked good. We could get all the credit we needed in England. Khrushchev was all set, but then he was removed, lost his job. When I went back in '72, after the Nixon-Brezhnev Summit, some of the Russian officials remembered the negotiations I had had with Khrushchev, and they suggested reviving our deal.

Q. Tell me something about the deal.

A. Well, now the deal. The way it's now been signed, it's for delivery of 1 million tons a year of phosphates, a superphosphoric acid. It comes from Florida and it will amount to about $200 million per year. And for twenty years that'll be about $4 billion. In return, we will purchase to an equivalent value ammonia, urea, and maybe some potash.

Q. What the hell is urea?

A. Urea is an ingredient of fertilizer made out of ammonia, which furnishes the nitrogen. Together with phosphate and potash, the mixture constitutes the complete fertilizer. We call it NPK. K is for potash, N is for nitrogen, and P for phosphate. So, since these nitrogenous fertilizer materials, urea and ammonia, are made out of natural gas, and the Russians have such a surplus of gas, this will be a product of export for Russia. . . . They will do the actual building of the eight ammonia and two urea plants. We'll supply the equipment and the know-how.

Q. Then we'll buy the product from them?

A. Yes, the value of the finished products will equal the value of what we sell them. So that will give us another $200 million of purchases from them. And this $200 million worth of ammonia and urea, and some potash will be used here. . . . It's a complete balance of payment, plus, for the United States to be able to have ammonia and urea available since we have a shortage of natural gas and otherwise would have to buy these products abroad for dollars.

Q. But how does Oxy make a profit?

A. Well, our first profit is on the sale of the superphosphoric acid. We take our normal markup on the sale. The second profit we will make will be on the marketing of the ammonia and urea through our International Ore and Fertilizer Corporation (Interore) Division. . . . So it's $4 billion in one direction and $4 billion in the other direction. That's what I tried to explain to the London reporter who woke me up in the middle of the night—I was on the way home from Moscow after signing the deal—and asked for an explanation of the Tass report.

Q. Sounds like a Mexican standoff.

A. It's not. As I said, on the phosphates we make our normal markup. We own the phosphates, we have them in the ground. We mine them at our Florida mines and make superphosphoric acid out of them and sell it. On the ammonia and urea we buy from them, we will make a commission on the sale of it, and they'll give us a discount on the world prices. Then we'll make a profit on the equipment we'll supply them. . . .

The scope of the deal, already signed or being readied, gets a bit too large for life, beyond that.

Amazingly, the "$8 billion deal" had dizzily inflated to $20 billion by 1974. That was apparently a little too much for even as canny an observer of mammoth transactions as *Business Week* to swallow or fully comprehend. It dispatched its editor in chief, Lewis Young, to Hammer's curio-crusted hideaway in Greenwich Village. The question-and-answer grilling, printed in the July 13, 1974, issue, sheds unfiltered light on the doctor's special way with the Russians:

Q. Why did the fertilizer deal seem to change from the time it was first announced until it was signed last week?

A. It's very complex to deal with Russians, different from dealing with anyone else. You have to go through a whole series of steps before you finally make your agreement. At any one of these steps, you might have thought that Occidental was out of it, that somebody else was coming in. We signed the first protocol in July of 1972, and now it was the spring of 1974 and we were still in the talking stages. This is the way you do business with the Russians. The Russians are good businessmen. They will never make a deal without getting competitive bids. They start with a protocol. That's an important step because unless you sign a protocol, you have no status there. You can't get visas, you can't talk to anybody, you can't implement your deal. When they sign a protocol, they are letting you in so you can move on to the next steps.

Q. Which are?

A. In our case it was a letter of intent. Then the third step was the global agreements, in which the principal terms of the understanding were set forth and paved the way for the implementing agreements signed last week. It took almost two years to complete this deal. If you have patience, if you stick to it and you are competitive, if your deal makes sense—it has to be a good deal for both sides—the results are rewarding.

The astronomical agreement, reports the Occidental Petroleum house magazine, *Oxy Today,* is actually the second contract between Occidental and the Russians under a five-year scientific and technical cooperation agreement signed in July of 1972 in Moscow, covering five areas: exploration, production, and usage of oil and gas; agricultural fertilizers and chemicals; metal treating and metal plating; the design and building of a hotel and trade center; and disposal of solid wastes. *Oxy Today* went on:

> The first contract involved the sale of metal-finishing equipment, processes and products to the Soviet Union and the purchase of nickel in return. Based on present market prices, the sale of the metal-finishing equipment will amount to some $40,000,000 over a five-year period, and the purchase of nickel, of which Oxy Metal-Finishing is a large user, will also amount to approximately $40,000,000 making a total of $80,000,000 for both transactions.

In the report, Dr. Hammer is quoted as saying, "The negotiations on our contracts to date have taken much bargaining and much patience."

But once Dr. Hammer got an invitation from Premier Kosygin to come to his office in the Kremlin, the doors of the Soviet ministries opened, all heads nodded as if with affirmative palsy. It is Hammer's uncanny ability to get an audience with the top leaders, and later with Suslov and Brezhnev, that is the mark of his highly refined art of dealing with Ivan.

Hammer's way with Russian leaders had long since become legendary, whether his latter-day peers and competitors acknowledged it or not. Asked by *Fortune* magazine why El Paso Natural Gas had included Oxy in its proposed huge deal to import Soviet gas, chairman Howard T. Boyd replied, "There were advantages to having Hammer in," referring to the doctor's Russian experiences and El Paso's desire to split the risks on an enormously costly project.

Hammer had a less complicated answer when the man from *Fortune* called. "El Paso was talking with the Russians and getting nowhere, so we stepped in," he said laconically. "I felt with our experience we could help them cut through the red tape."

It is a deal involving sums and amenities that would have been incomprehensible to both sides during the decades of mutual suspicion, a cold-war period that involved a host of frictions, including the Berlin airlift, the Korean and Vietnam wars, the Cuban missile crisis, the U-2 flights, the Berlin Wall, threats of economic "burial," etc. The et ceteras extended all the way to Khrushchev's shoe-pounding at the United Nations and his indignation over not being allowed to visit Disneyland, where he might have met a young "jungle guide" named Ron Ziegler, later Nixon's press secretary.

Fortune, which lately tends to take a dim view of Hammer, that almost ostentatious darling of fortune, spoke of the Soviet gas deal in its July 1973 issue as follows:

> Last month, Hammer and Boyd signed an agreement of intent with the Soviet government to import Siberian natural gas, worth $10,000,000,000 at current prices, to the U.S. West Coast over 25 years, beginning around 1980. Much remains to be done before this deal becomes reality: Russia needs Western loans of $2,000,000,000 for a 2,000 mile pipeline and a gas-liquification plant; the companies need another $2,000,000,000 to buy 20 tankers. And neither government is expected to approve unless Congress grants the U.S.S.R. most-favored-nation status.

The "$8 billion deal" would be paled by the much more ambitious Oxy–El Paso plan to tap the gas and oil of Siberia. Dr. Hammer sees a day coming when a dozen western states of the United States will be energized by gas that originates beyond the Urals, passes through a 2,000-mile pipeline, is liquified, put aboard tankers built for that purpose, returned to gaseous form at U.S. Pacific coast plants, and piped to millions of American consumers.

Gas-hungry Japan would be another prime customer and provide some of the capital funds needed to bring the enormous venture to fruition.

By comparison, the doctor's negotiations with the Soviets to provide Moscow with a world trade center are modestly scaled, hardly much more than $100 million. But he is as enthusiastic about that one as any of the other far-flung endeavors to pump new life into Oxy stock and bring more muscle to the corporation's "bottom line."

Given the awesome scope and potential worth of the deals Hammer swung with the Russians, or is in the process of completing, the speed at which some were consummated continues to be hard to believe. He is a man who literally jogs through life. But sometimes he steps up the pace. He sprinted through one important phase of the accords with the Kremlin. That was the day he was called to the office of Gvishiani.

"Gvishiani handed me a draft of the proposed five-point agreement," Hammer chuckles. "It was written in Russian, of course. I looked it over and it seemed all right with me. So I took a pen and struck out the word 'draft' and signed it. I handed it back to him and he was nonplussed. He had been brought up during a period when his country dealt more or less exclusively with other countries, other governments, not with a private company. He said, 'Don't you want to show it to your lawyer?' I said no, that I didn't need a lawyer. Then he said, 'Don't you want to think it over?' I said there was nothing to think over. It was his draft, I pointed out, not mine. And I hadn't changed one word of it.

"So he had a little conference with his own people and then he said, 'All right!' He took a pen and signed it. And that was the basis of our eight-billion-dollar fertilizer barter deal."

During the taping of NBC's hour-long documentary on the doctor, "Russian Connection," produced in 1973 by Lucy Jarvis, narrated and partly written by Ed Newman, and directed by Tom Priestly, it was clear to one and all that the colorful show needed a final act. Hammer booked it. He was in Brezhnev's office one day, discussing trade, when he found an opportunity to bring up another matter. The NBC team, working through the layers of Soviet officialdom, had been trying for some time to get into the Soviet leader's inner sanctum. Without succsss. Hammer dropped a word about the team's problem, Brezhnev snapped his fingers, secretaries emerged from the woodwork, and within minutes the phone in Lucy Jarvis's room at the National was ringing. She was instructed to "come right over" and bring along the rest of the members of the production.

It made a jolly finale for a video account of Hammer's long years of association with the Russians.

Brezhnev boomed through his interpreter, "I would like to give my warmest greetings to the American people. My advice and good wishes to President Nixon. We have formed a very solid basis for good relations between our two peoples."

Newman, who later had an exclusive interview with Brezhnev, came on —off camera—with "Just as in the 1920s Lenin used Hammer to promote trade with American businessmen, so in the 1970s Brezhev is using Hammer in the same way."

Brezhnev, back on to say a final word, said, "Armand Hammer has expended considerable effort. I help him, he helps me. It is mutual. We do not discuss secrets—just business."

Newman had the last word: "And Hammer, with half a century of practice behind him, uses Brezhnev. It is a classic transaction. It is the Russian Connection."

Then, as the credits rolled before the eyes of a TV audience estimated well into the millions, Armand Hammer strolls on the icy promenade along the Moscow River outside his first home in Soviet Russia, the Russian Sugar King's Palace, sporting a jaunty sable hat, the golden onion domes of the Kremlin appropriately sparkling in the background.

Chapter 21

The Doctor and His Public

An enthusiastic Oxy stockholder who nominated Dr. Hammer for the post of U.S. ambassador to the Soviet Union at the 1973 annual meeting found a somewhat unprecedented seconder. Late in August of that eventually somber year the doctor's jet swooped into Washington and picked up Soviet Ambassador Anatoly Dobrynin and his family and flew them to Palm Beach, Florida, for the weekend. It was before the Yom Kippur War, the U.S.-U.S.S.R. "alert," and the massive Arab oil squeeze that crimped such carefree travel. At a dinner given for the group by gracious Mrs. Loy Anderson, wife of a prominent Florida banker, Dobrynin proposed a toast endorsing his friend Hammer for the ambassadorial post, then still vacant.

"I'm one hundred percent behind him," the courtly Communist diplomat said of the rich capitalist. "He's my candidate."

Hammer was pleased, but said later to a reporter, "My first duty I owe to my stockholders."

He often speaks of his "duty" to bring about a turn-around in the market value of Oxy's stock. Hammer has given so much of himself to that crusade that an unusual intimacy has developed over the years between himself and the several hundred thousand co-owners of his manifold operation. It seems highly unlikely that very many holders of stock in General Motors knew Thomas A. Murphy, its chairman, sufficiently well to accost him in public or even write him a letter, good or bad. That must be true, too, of the relationship between the multitudes of A.T.&T. shareholders and their chairman, John de Butts. Hammer's people applaud him, lecture him, sometimes get very angry at him. But in times of corporate stress they tend to feel for him, as in the nationalization in

189

1973 of 51 percent of Oxy's Libyan oil, and the troubles there and elsewhere following the war in the Middle East, and his spanking by the Securities and Exchange Commission at year's end.

Oxy stockholders have been writing him what amounts to fan letters for years, especially after such strikes as in the North Sea, Venezuela, Nigeria, and Peru—as if he had personally pointed to the right spot to drill. Hence such mail as a letter from Michael and Gayle Smriga, of Hobart, Indiana:

Dear Mr. Hammer:

As satisfied stockholders of Occidental since 1969, we wish to express our belated joys to you personally. We have experienced Occidental selling at its highs and lows. We have seen you blasted and revered. We have thought to ourselves: how could we show our appreciation for the dynamic job you have done and are now doing for Occidental?

We have honored you by naming our son, who was born May 19, 1973, Chad Armand Smriga. He was baptized on June 17, 1973, with this name. It was also recorded that you are his honorary Godfather.

Realizing you are a very busy man and not wanting to take up your time with a long letter, we have enclosed a picture of your Godson along with a picture of ourselves and daughter Ginny.

We hope that you will accept the honor bestowed upon you. It is a gift to a dynamic man that we try to use as a model and hope someday Chad Armand Smriga will set his sights upon the same level.

We leave you with the thought of "Occidental throughout the World."

Another stockholder, somewhat better known, wrote to the doctor:

Sutton Place
Guildford, Surrey
19th April, 1968

Dr. Armand Hammer
President
Occidental Petroleum Corp.,
10889 Wilshire Boulevard,
Los Angeles,
California 90024,
U.S.A.

Dear Dr. Hammer,

I appreciate your sending me the most interesting Annual Report for 1967

The Doctor and His Public

of Occidental. It is an amazing story of what one man can do today. We all know there were Titans in the past but most of the present generation believe that conditions today do not permit a small independent to become a great major oil company. You have proved that it still is possible and I congratulate you. I send you my best wishes.

Sincerely yours,
J. PAUL GETTY

C. Duke McDougall, a philatelist in Washington, Pennsylvania, chimed in:

I certainly enjoyed reading a recently received progress report for the six months ended June 30 [1968]. The last paragraph, which advised that the government of Libya had honored Occidental by commissioning a new series of postage stamps, was particularly interesting. I was happily amazed at the thoughtfulness of my company's officers in providing stockholders with three First Day Covers commemorating the significant event.

This gesture just has to convince your stockholders that Occidental is a very, very human company.

A number of stockholders advised the doctor on what to do about Colonel El-Gathafi's coup, including Jerrold W. Watson of San Antonio:

Just a note and suggestion from an interested and concerned stockholder. With the new government in control of Libya, King Idris I is probably a "very bad" word. I would think that if the company gave new names to Idris A and Idris D oil fields it would probably serve our purposes better.

These fields have since been renamed Intisar A and D.

Dewey J. Forry of San Rafael, California, directed a terse note to Hammer during Oxy's dog days, in regard to his hundred shares of common: "Chairman of the Board: Your report looks good, but when does the shareholder get a break?"

Hammer himself, the largest stockholder by far, was wondering the same thing at the time. He had confidently predicted that Oxy stock would take off like a rocket when the news of his 1972 multibillion-dollar deal with the Soviet Union hit the front pages of the entire world.

Matter of fact, the stock did zoom. But, like other rockets, it fizzled before it could get into orbit. Hammer has no doubt about the person who caused it to swoon.

"For a time the Stock Exchange went wild," the doctor remembers. "Old-timers on the floor of the Exchange said they had never seen anything to equal it. Millions and millions of shares of Occidental were traded in a few days. Brokers were swamped with orders and the stock started to jump. But then Secretary of Commerce Peter Peterson arrived in Moscow and was met by the American correspondents. Naturally, he was asked about our announced deal. For some reason that's still hard to explain, Peterson played it down. He pooh-poohed it as if it was so much hot air. I had flown to Morocco to brief him about the agreement immediately after I made it. He was on his way to Moscow and I felt it was common courtesy to fill him in on what I had been able to do to supplement the President's and Brezhnev's wishes for expanded trade. I felt this was an important first step which laid the foundation for the implementing contracts which were to follow, as later events proved. Still, Peterson took that negative position in his press conference, and it killed what was probably the greatest movement in the history of the New York Stock Exchange. Later on in an interview with *U.S. News and World Report,* Peterson tried to rectify what he had said. But the damage had already been done. [See Appendix D.]

"So, in the long run, the price of our shares failed to reflect historic trades and potentials, despite the fact that the implementing contracts provided for in the overall agreement are now being carried out one by one. We've signed an eighty-million-dollar deal involving the sale over a five-year period of forty million dollars of metal finishing equipment and the purchase of forty million dollars of nickel. The eight-billion-dollar fertilizer deal, now a twenty-billion deal due to escalation of world market prices, has already been signed, the financing has been arranged and is being carried out. Then there's the Occidental–El Paso–Japanese gas deal, signed in November 1974, which, if approved by Congress, may eventually exceed ten billion dollars. The fourth one is the hundred-and-ten-million-dollar trade center, signed on September 18, 1973, between the Russian Chamber of Commerce and Occidental, which is completely funded. The design and technical supervision will be done by the Bechtel Corporation of San Francisco in conjunction with Welton Becket, the architect who designed Century City in Los Angeles, and the Garrett Research and Development Company, a wholly owned subsidiary of Occidental. The last is the conversion of municipal waste, which is under consideration, depending on the successful outcome of two prototype plants under construction by Occidental in San Diego, California, and Bridgeport, Connecticut. All that! I think it's just a question now of the market's watching and evaluating the things that are being carried out."

Hammer found himself engaged on other fronts beyond his dialogue with his shareholders. At seventy-five, the doctor was retiring or firing younger executives inherited from some of the companies Oxy had acquired whom he considered not up to scratch, in an effort to make Oxy stock more responsive to what the company was achieving in its widely varied ventures. Thus he was understandably offended when what he called a "young, half-baked writer" from *Forbes'* called upon him to retire himself and make way for new blood; it would bolster confidence in the Oxy stock. The irritating young man also wondered in print how Hammer could be so ruthless in shelving sainted old chieftains of firms Oxy merged with during its burgeoning years.

Answering the charge, Hammer explained, "It's the history of all acquisitions that you inherit a lot of executives and you discover that they are not able to do their jobs properly. You've simply got to let them out. That's your duty to the stockholders. I think Occidental has been able to get along fine with new teams in every division."

Professor Neil H. Jacoby came to the doctor's defense in a letter printed in a succeeding issue of *Forbes'*. He wrote James Michaels, the financial magazine's editor, on December 1, 1971, in part as follows:

Dear Sir:

As an outside director of Occidental Petroleum Corporation for the last twelve years in which Dr. Armand Hammer has been its chief executive, I can categorically say that the article in your November 15th issue contained incorrect statements and inferences injurious to Occidental, its 400,000 shareholders and Dr. Hammer. It appears that Forbes' got much of its information from disgruntled former employees and directors.

Louis Nizer had more to say on this continuingly sensitive subject:

"There's been a rap on him for a long time about his being ruthless in firing executives he feels have not lived up to his expectations. That's just not true. There has not been a large turnover at Occidental in relation to its size and number of executives. He has critics in the financial press who write about him as a tyrant because they claim that as a one-man corporation he must be a tyrant per se. He's the last thing from a tyrant.

He listens to anybody. He's open to suggestions night and day. He's the most open-minded man I know. The reason for this occasional hostility to him is that he has taken over so many companies and, automatically, all their executives—good, bad, indifferent. There must be changes made because some of those executives just don't want change; don't want to be swallowed into a bigger organization with fresher ideas and broader vision. Many of these people who have grown wealthy in the merged companies or have put in a great number of years with their corporations choose to retire, and have done so even when the doctor implored them to remain. That, too, has contributed to the sum of the criticism directed against him, unjustly. You'll find less of a turnover in Occidental than in most big corporations."

Forbes' subsequently ventilated a point no member of the Oxy family cares to discuss:

"Armand Hammer won't be around forever, a fact that encourages competitors and haunts his Occidental associates. 'There are plenty of men around here who can take over,' Hammer insists."

Nizer describes one situation when Hammer was put to the test before a group of financial people and reporters in London:

"Hammer spoke with ease and grace and no elocutional devices. Then came the question period. There is his real skill when he is called upon to speak. The questions were courteously asked, but piercing. For example: 'Dr. Hammer, you look like the youngest man in this room, and your vigor and vitality demonstrate that you may very well be. But, after all, we're all mortal. What is the future of Occidental's leadership after you, ah, well, *retire?*'

"He was ready for that one. He said, 'Lots of people ask me that one. I consider it part of executive efficiency to have in each department men who are the most able and most capable, most vigorous and very young, so that they can be trained when they are young and, when called upon, take over not with any loss of efficiency but rather with increased efficiency. Now let me tell you who I've got.' And he went through the whole list of the top men in all of Oxy's scattered interests. He gave a short biographical sketch of each of them, without referring to a note; their schooling, previous jobs, marital status, number of children—it was a feat of total recall."

But is there another Armand Hammer?

That question never goes away. One night in Washington, after a long session at the Securities and Exchange Commission, another *bête noir*, Hammer was stricken with a groin pain that doubled him over. With the aid of his attorney, Arthur Groman, he was able to reach a doctor's office in a building not far from the White House—a providential break. He was given an injection that numbed the pain and enabled him to get to his plane and fly back to Los Angeles during the night. He consulted Dr. William P. Longmire, Jr., one of the founders of the U.C.L.A. Medical School and one of the country's leading surgeons, indeed, past president of the American College of Surgeons. Since X-rays did not show up the stones in his gall bladder and the pain and other symptoms had disappeared, Dr. Longmeier left the decision of whether to operate up to Hammer. The then seventy-three-year-old doctor promptly said, "Let's see what's there. Go ahead."

"They found this big walled-off abscess full of pus and stones," the doctor relates. "It could have burst into the abdomen at any time, and caused peritonitis if they had not operated." The operation took five hours. A year later Dr. Longmire and Dr. Willard E. Goodwin, professor of urology, discovered Hammer had a stone in the duct leading from the kidney to his bladder too large to pass and was causing considerable pain and inflamation. This meant another operation, whereupon they discovered a diverticulum in his bladder. They had to sew it together, then go up into the ureter to get to the stone. The operation took almost six hours. The doctor laughs about it today. "I can play tic-tac-toe on myself, the way the scars are arranged."

Groman remembers that second operation: "I tiptoed into his hospital room the next morning, figuring he'd be out of action for six months or a year. He was sitting up in bed, telephoning all over the world. He made and took so many calls that the hospital had to install a special line because he was tying up the switchboard. I've never seen such a demonstration of vitality in all my life. I've been around some other rugged characters, such as Howard Hughes and Norton Simon, but the doctor's energy is limitless. In all the years we've been associated I've never known him to take a vacation. He works at least fifteen hours a day, seven days a week. His ability to grasp new problems in areas that he's never been before is astonishing. It's no accident that he has achieved what he has achieved."

The above deposition by the devoted attorney was made in Hammer's office in Los Angeles. The doctor had taken two or three phone calls as Groman spoke, but he must have had a spare ear tuned in on the tribute. As Groman finished, Hammer wheeled around in his swivel chair. "I guess I must be a pretty tough old bird," he crowed happily. It was an exclusive understatement. And reassuring news for share owners holding Oxy at $9.

Chapter 22

A Law unto Himself

There are occasionally brief periods in the success-studded life of Armand Hammer when he wishes he were a licensed lawyer along with his other skills. He believes he would have made a superior attorney, and this opinion has been bolstered by assenting statements from several renowned members of the profession. Louis Nizer once pleased the doctor by telling him that he possessed the prime essence of a first-rate lawyer, a keen sense of strategy. In fields as incommensurable as pencils, pipelines, and Picassos, Hammer has been operating on high-octane strategy for a very long time, including the fuel shortage of 1974.

He has retained the services of an army of astute attorneys and also sometimes of spectacular witnesses: Eleanor Roosevelt, for example.

In 1960 the Internal Revenue Service demanded $750,000 of Hammer, in connection with a tax assessment of his sold-out whiskey interests. It claimed an understatement of income. To save time and a troublesome court case, Hammer offered to settle for $500,000. He referred to it as a "nuisance case." I.R.S. said no. So the case was set, and Hammer, as is his wont, looked around for the best possible attorney to represent him. He keeps a list of specialists in laws applicable to all of his many fields of endeavor. But, on a hunch, he chose his friend and Occidental board member Arthur Groman to handle this tax litigation. Groman was not generally regarded as a tax lawyer, and the summons took him by surprise. He told about it years later in his wryly humorous way:

"The doctor called me up one day and said, 'Arthur, I'd like you to go back to New York and try a case in the Tax Court of the United States.' I tried to plead ignorance of that phase of the law. But he knew better:

197

I had started out in life as a tax lawyer. When I got out of Yale in '39 I went to Washington as an attorney in the General Counsel's Office of Treasury, then transferred to the Bureau of Internal Revenue. For two years, they sent me up to New York to try cases in the tax court, and when I joined my Los Angeles firm it was as a tax specialist. But I had always wanted to be a general trial lawyer. I made it, and forgot about tax law.

"Still, the doctor insisted. Stubborn man, you know.

"I asked him when the trial would begin, and he said, 'In two weeks.' I said I couldn't possibly prepare my case in such a short time. The case had been going on for years. He said, 'You can do it,' so I flew to New York, reviewed the files, and came back and literally worked night and day, cramming. By the time I returned to New York I was convinced that the case would come down to the question of credibility. So I said to the doctor that he must come up with the best character witnesses he could find. He said to me, in what I thought was a very offhanded, cavalier fashion, 'Well, who do you want?' And without really raising the hackles on my neck, I said to myself, 'I'll fix him.' So I said—trying to stump him or put him down—'I'd like Eleanor Roosevelt.' The next morning at nine o'clock I was interviewing Eleanor Roosevelt.

"I guess she was the greatest witness in my thirty years in court. There's not really much a character witness can do, on direct testimony, really, except say that the defendant can't be all bad. Mrs. Roosevelt made a mountain out of that. In her unique voice, she said yes, she knew Dr. Hammer, and that his reputation for truth and veracity in the community in which they both lived was 'excellent.' Then I turned her over to James Aloysius O'Toole, representing the majesty of the U.S. government. He had the reputation of being the finest trial lawyer in the I.R.S. He was a real bulldog of a man. He stood up to face Mrs. Roosevelt and I sensed that he was out to become world famous by crushing her. He pointed a bony finger at her and said, 'Now, Mrs. Roosevelt, you didn't know Dr. Hammer at all well, did you?'

"Mrs. Roosevelt replied, in her high-pitched voice, 'On the contrary, not only did I know Dr. Hammer very well in a business way but I knew him much better, socially. He was many times to the White House for dinner . . . and the President and I were to his home for dinner. Not only do I admire him for his great service to our country in the late war; my husband, the President, esteemed him greatly.' O'Toole opened his jaws, but he couldn't come up with another question. He shook his finger at

Mrs. Roosevelt in a frustrated manner, while she just stared at him in her cheerful, unflappable way. Finally he sat down. And during the rest of the trial, every time he would look at the judge, the judge would start to chuckle.

"We had two other character witnesses, Beardsley Ruml and David Wilentz, the former New Jersey attorney general and prosecutor of Bruno Hauptmann in the Lindbergh kidnapping case. They were both fine. We had some fun in court while Ruml was in the chair. He was a stern man who had his own views on how he would answer questions. He said to me, 'If you think I'm going on the stand and recite my biography, you have another think coming.' So I read up on him, and when I put him on, the questioning went something like this:

" 'Your name is Beardsley Ruml?'

" 'Yes.'

" 'You're the chairman of the board of Macy's?'

" 'Yes.'

" 'You're a Trustee of the Rockefeller Foundation?'

" 'Yes.'

" 'You're the former head of the Department of Sociology at the University of Chicago?'

" 'Yes.'

" 'You're a trustee of Cornell University?'

" 'Yes.'

"At this juncture, O'Toole jumped up and said, 'Your Honor, I object!' The judge said, 'You object, Mr. O'Toole? On what grounds?'

" 'Mr. Groman is leading the witness!' O'Toole shouted.

"The judge said, 'He's leading the witness through his own biography, Mr. O'Toole. Motion dismissed.'

"But looking back," Groman said much later, "it was Mrs. Roosevelt who won our case."

Hammer had met Arthur Groman under grave circumstances in 1953, indirectly through Jimmy Roosevelt. Within minutes after learning from his first wife, the baroness, that their son Julian had been arrested for killing a young Korean war veteran, Hammer reached his friend Congressman Roosevelt by phone and asked him to recommend the best obtainable California lawyer to represent the son. Roosevelt suggested Mendel Silberberg, a revered member of the bar and senior partner of Mitchell, Silberberg and Knupp, attorneys for Columbia Pictures, Edward G. Robinson, and others in the movie colony. Hammer picked up Maurice Wormser, his attorney since his father's trial, and the two flew to Los Angeles, arriving just in time to be greeted by provocative headlines about the shooting. They were painfully reminiscent of stories of long ago, in that a quick glance at the wording of the heads would indicate to the casual observer that millionaire's son kills poor G.I. The two travelers from the East bought the papers and soon discovered the source of the pre-arraignment commotion: flamboyant Jerry Geisler had been retained by Julian's mother and, typically, had opened his defense campaign by calling a press conference.

Silberberg said his firm did not handle criminal cases but, as a favor to Jimmy Roosevelt and after hearing Armand's plea of his son's innocence of the murder charge, assigned his junior partner Arthur Groman to the case.

Wormser, Groman, and Hammer, the amateur advocate, fashioned their own defense without consultation with Geisler. These facts were soon revealed: Julian had met the victim while both were in boot camp. Julian was assigned to Stateside duty; his friend—a former Golden Gloves fighter—went overseas. When he returned from Korea, the friendship was renewed at a Los Angeles bar. Julian invited him home to meet Mrs. Hammer, who was expecting a child. While there, the young Korean War veteran drank a lot and attempted to rape the young wife. Julian, trying to protect his wife, was badly beaten by the fighter. In final desperation he stumbled into his bedroom, came back with a pistol, and shot the man dead. An autopsy report, ordered by Wormser and Groman, showed an extremely high level of alcohol in the dead man's blood. The wife corroborated her husband's account. Groman's motion before Judge Coleman was compelling enough to move the jurist to dismiss the case without going to trial.

Dr. Hammer was understandably impressed by Groman. He has retained him a number of times since that case, made him a director of Occidental, and rates him equal with Nizer (and himself) in both the preparation and presentation of his court cases.

Nizer's most momentous court case with Hammer was the Wall Street brokerage house, Allen and Company, claim. It involved so much money, $100 million, that if Oxy lost, it could have as profound an effect on the doctor's already sensitive stock as a simultaneous court case in which IBM was ordered to pay more than $300 million to Xerox for certain infringements. When news of that verdict reached the floor of the New York Stock Exchange, IBM swooned twenty-six points.

The Allens claimed that Occidental's fantastic success in Libya began in the summer of 1964 when two colorful characters met in Paris for the first time. One of them called himself General de Rovin; the other, Ferdinand Galic. The court documents reveal that de Rovin, then sixty-three years old, was a swindler in Paris, Berlin, Vienna, and elsewhere in the period prior to World War II; that he had dealings with the Nazis during the war for which a French court later sentenced him to death in absentia; that in the postwar period he traveled about South America and Canada passing bad checks, and returned to France from Argentina under the phony name of de Rovin; that he was employed by a French firm and promptly squandered its assets; that in February 1970 he was sentenced in absentia to a year in jail by a French court after a conviction of violation of foreign controls.

"Galic, a Czech married to an American and a well-known figure in Paris society, allegedly had no knowledge of General de Rovin's shady past when they first met," Nizer recalls. "Hammer doubts this and lumps the two of them together. De Rovin had a proposition: If Galic could find an oil company willing to put up millions, he had the means, through a highly placed Libyan, of obtaining lucrative concessions in that country.

"Galic at once telephoned Charles Allen, multimillionaire founder and general partner in Allen and Company, whose present wife Galic had befriended in Paris while Allen was getting a divorce from his former wife. According to Galic's deposition at a later date, Allen asked for time to 'look around.'

"In September 1964, Dr. Armand Hammer, Herbert Allen, Sr. [Charles Allen's brother], Galic, and de Rovin met in Claridge's in London with a Libyan businessman named Taher Ogbi. It soon became clear that Ogbi, a small-time businessman, was the highly placed Libyan whom de Rovin had been talking about. Subsequently it was claimed that as a result of this meeting, certain agreements were made between Occidental and Galic, de Rovin, and Ogbi in regard to Libyan oil concessions. A separate agreement was said to have been made with Allen and Company.

"Later, Allen and Company discovered that General de Rovin was not all he claimed to be, and they felt it their duty to inform Dr. Hammer and Occidental of the checkered nature of their go-between's past. The deadline for submitting bids for the new Libyan concessions was July 29,

1965. Two weeks before this date, acting on the information Allen had sent and which had been found to be even worse than Allen reported, Occidental canceled the agreement with Ogbi and sent telegrams to de Rovin and Galic telling them that the agreement Dr. Hammer had signed with them in London was canceled forthwith. At the same time, a telegram reached Allen and Company telling them that their agreement of December 1964 with Dr. Hammer was also canceled."

The case in all its ramifications stretched from September 1967 to September 1974. Essentially, Allen claimed that Dr. Hammer had promised to pay Allen 25 percent of Oxy's Libyan oil earnings for having arranged to swing those rich concessions Oxy's way. Nizer's courtroom counterattack was that Hammer won Oxy's drilling rights by promising 5 percent of the profits for agricultural development and clinched the deal when he wrought the miracle of the Kufra waters.

Near the end of the long embroilment with the Allens, Hammer told a friend, "More than the hundred million dollars is involved in this one. If we lose, there's sure to be a whispering campaign that I can't be trusted to keep my word. My reputation in Wall Street, my image, hinges on this outcome. Over the years I've learned one sure thing about investment bankers. They compete against one another right up to the hilt, but when it comes to a case where an outsider is fighting one of them, they all stick together. Allen claims I welshed, which I didn't. But if we lose, the Street will think I did.

"We're going to win this case. They've made all kinds of overtures to settle. I've turned them down. I think it's more important for me to be vindicated than to settle for, let's say, a few million dollars. Most people would say I'm foolish; that the lawyers will cost me half a million. But I'm staying in there to win, and win decisively."

The dramatic case, meat for an old Humphrey Bogart movie, was argued for five weeks before Judge Edward Weinfeld in the U.S. District Court, Southern District of New York, during the late summer and fall of 1973. The judge took over nine months to render his decision, so voluminous was the record, which covered three thousand pages, with briefs and exhibits a foot high. Dr. Hammer was examined endlessly before trial and his deposition ran for hundreds and hundreds of pages. So were both Allens examined at great length. They, however, made a total of ninety-nine changes of their testimony before signing it, whereas Dr. Hammer made none in his. The result was that when Nizer cross-examined Herbert and Charles Allen for almost two weeks, he confronted them with their own changes in their own sworn testimony, whereas Dr. Hammer was impervious.

The judge found that there was no valid agreement between the parties since Herbert Allen had insisted that costs should be mutually agreed upon, which was intended as an escape clause for the Allens. Since this was an essential term upon which the parties never reached an agreement, the judge found the contract to be so indefinite as to be unenforceable.

The judge goes on to say that even if there was an enforceable agreement, Hammer was justified in canceling it when he learned that the Galic group, including the international crook and swindler "General de Rovin," recruited by the Allens, had misrepresented their ability to turn up the Libya concessions. The judge found that the Allens accepted the termination but eighteen months later, "the day the public press carried the news of a large oil discovery by Occidental in the Libyan concession," Herbert Allen first inquired as to the status of the "concession granted to Occidental through the intervention of Galic." Prior to this time, the Allens were part of an underwriting group in a $61,186,300 debenture issue of Occidental, and stated in answer to an S.E.C. questionnaire that they had no material relationship with Occidental.

In summary Judge Weinfeld wrote, "The Allens sought the best of two worlds. If oil was struck it could claim a twenty-five percent profit in the joint venture. If it turned out to be a dry hole, it could disavow liability for twenty-five percent of the loss."

The judge also found that Galic did not render any services at all. In a letter to de Rovin two days after the concessions were granted to Occidental, Galic asked if de Rovin could learn what blocks had been granted to it.

Referring to a letter allegedly written by the then Libyan Petroleum Minister Fiad Kabazi to Galic four days before the announcement of the granting of the concessions, stating that he was recommending that the concessions be granted to Occidental because the Allens had provided the necessary financing, Judge Weinfeld found that this letter was spurious and back-dated. He stated that the evidence warranted the finding that the letter was deliberately contrived. The Allens announced they would appeal this decision, but Nizer and Groman are confident of the outcome, in view of the forty-six-page opinion and the findings of fact as well as law.

As for the doctor, who had presented a vital exhibit into the courtroom

—a documentary, narrated by Lowell Thomas, dramatically depicting his company's discovery of pure water near Kufra and the wonders it had wrought in Libya—he had a brisk word or two in the wake of Judge Weinfeld's verdict.

"After legal proceedings of many years and a trial of months, the decision in favor of Occidental is gratifying, not only because it fully preserves our company's assets but also because it vindicates the integrity of our dealings," he said. "That is the reason I refused any settlement in this matter."

The doctor had been saved $100 million (and change) with which to work wonders in other lands.

Another of Hammer's astronomical court triumphs involved a breach of patent suit brought by Armour and Company. Armour claimed infringement of its patent on superphosphoric acid. The case was in the United States District Court, Central District of California, from 1965 to 1970, such was its complexity. Occidental was represented by O'Melveny and Myers, a leading Los Angeles law firm whose specialist in the case was Philip Westbrook. Louis Nizer's firm was co-counsel. The case was won by Westbrook and Nizer in an extraordinary way: Not only were they able to quash Armour claims against Oxy, but they also proved that Armour had obtained its patent by fraud.

"It was a great day," Hammer says with undiminished relish. "If we had lost that one, well, I doubt if we would ever have been able to make that twenty-billion-dollar fertilizer deal with the Russians. Its core is superphosphoric acid 'made under our patented process.' "

There were other eminent establishments to be challenged. As he neared seventy-six, still possessed of his marbles and his beans, the doctor faced up to a nagging battle with the Securities and Exchange Commission that had been going on for several years. When the matter first surfaced in 1970, Occidental and Hammer were accused of creating inflated profits in certain real estate and coal transactions. Hammer was charged individually with putting out deceptive press releases. Arthur Anderson and Company, Occidental's auditors, saw nothing improper in the coal and real estate transactions, having certified the correctness of the company's financial statement for the period involved with a clean certificate. Occidental's financial and accounting staff, headed by Dorman

Commons, financial vice-president; Charles Lee, treasurer; and Jim Murdy, controller (all C.P.A.s), had approved the transactions. Hammer's in-house counsel did not find the charge concerning the press releases to be substantiated and recommended that Hammer fight the S.E.C. in the courts. Arthur Anderson and Company's testimony, they felt, would demolish the flimsy case of the inept S.E.C. accountants. Hammer engaged the distinguished counsel John J. McCloy, former board chairman of Chase Manhattan and president of the World Bank, to fight the charges. McCloy felt it would be wiser to yield to an S.E.C. consent decree which merely stated that Occidental and Hammer agreed not to violate security laws in the future, without admitting to any of the S.E.C. charges that they had violated them in the past. "You can't fight City Hall," McCloy reminded his angry client. Hammer followed his advice and took the usual beating in the press. He assumed he had bought his peace with the S.E.C. However, when a year later the S.E.C. brought new charges involving tanker charters and improper registration disclosure, again approved by Arthur Anderson and Company and members of Occidental's staff, Hammer was on his feet and swinging. The S.E.C.'s case, as presented in the *New York Times*, read bleakly; excerpts:

> . . . The SEC alleged that the defendants had made false statements and failed to disclose important facts about the size of Occidental's chartered tanker fleet and the financial risks involved in the fleet's operation.
>
> In its complaint, the SEC mentioned specifically a $125,000,000 offering of the company's convertible debentures in 1971, and a subsequent secondary offering of 1,550,000 shares of common stock the same year.
>
> At the time of the securities offerings, the SEC said, Occidental failed to disclose that the size of its tanker fleet had jumped sharply in 1970 and early 1971, and the company could have had three times the tanker tonnage it needed.
>
> Dr. Hammer is known in the oil industry as a controversial leader in the development of trade with the Soviet Union. He has been criticized in the past for issuing dramatic news releases and has been accused of exaggerating the scope of some of his international deals. . . . The agency asked for a court order enjoining Dr. Hammer and the company from future violations of the antifraud laws.

This time Hammer engaged Sam Harris of the prominent firm of Fried, Frank, Harris, Schriver and Jacobsen. Stanley Sporkin, the capable and incorruptible head of the enforcement division of the S.E.C., was said to regard Harris, formerly with the S.E.C., as one of the outstanding S.E.C. lawyers in the country. Harris spent over a year battling with the staff of the S.E.C. He was convinced that the S.E.C.'s position was untenable. Differing from John McCloy's advice in the previous case, he urged Hammer to fight the S.E.C.'s charges in court. "I'll stake my reputation on the fact that you will win your case," Harris assured the doctor.

Remembering McCloy's earthy advice (and realizing the effect a fight would have on the S.E.C.'s required approval of a pending $125-million debenture offering, urgently needed), Hammer overruled Harris and for the second time agreed to a consent decree.

In response to an inquiry from the *Times*, Hammer stated: "In consenting to the injunction, neither Occidental nor I concede that we have violated any statute, rule, or regulation administered by the S.E.C., or any other rule of law or good business practice."

He was consenting to the injunction, Hammer said, to avoid "unnecessary, expensive, and burdensome litigation." He added: "The matters alleged in the complaint do not in any way relate to the accuracy of Occidental's current financial statements. . . . Occidental and I do not consider that the complaint and consent will have any material adverse effect on the conduct of the company's business. Occidental and I in the past have complied and will continue in the future to comply with all securities laws and other laws."

Hammer gave vent to his real indignation in a letter to a friend. He contended that he was badgered unduly by certain members of the S.E.C. staff, though one of the staff interrogators told Hammer's attorney Arthur Groman that there was great respect on the part of some of his fellow staff members for the officials of Occidental Petroleum, "particularly, Dr. Hammer."

The doctor's letter continued:

> . . . On two occasions since the SEC investigation started, Occidental has found evidence that its phones were bugged. This was reported to the police and the FBI, who conducted an investigation, but have been unable to find the culprit.
>
> The latest outrage is the fact that on the evening of the annual meeting, May 16, 1973, the public relations office of Occidental in Los Angeles was burglarized. The locked door was jimmied, and the tapes of the annual meeting were stolen before they had been transcribed. This, too, has been reported to the police, but no one has been apprehended to date.

(Occidental offered a $50,000 reward for information leading to the arrest and conviction of the person guilty of the bugging and burglary.) Hammer does not mean to infer that the S.E.C. had anything to do with these illegal activities. On the contrary, he has reason to believe that this is the work of a disgruntled former Oxy employee who notified the S.E.C. about his complaint.

With that off his barrel chest, Armand Hammer turned confidently toward the fourth quarter of his century.

Chapter 23

The Doctor Meets the Press

Hammer has an able public relations staff headed by Carl Blumay, formerly with the Los Angeles *Times,* who had been with him since he entered the Occidental picture. But in a pinch, the doctor becomes his own PR man. He is not easily intimidated by bad notices. There was, for example, his counterattack on the distinguished art critic of the formidable Washington *Post* and his contest with a top reporter assigned to the Los Angeles bureau of the *New York Times.*

On March 28, 1970, *Post* critic Paul Richard lowered a heavy boom on the doctor's pride and joy, his art collection, then being shown at the Smithsonian. The head on the elegant blast read: "AN EXHIBITION OF LOSERS BY MAJOR MASTERS."*

> The night the Armand Hammer Collection opened at the Smithsonian Institution, three women, all in evening gowns, stood between the Rubens portrait and the Rembrandt, scornfully condemning the pictures on display.
>
> Their derisive comments, and those of other guests, sent hints of fraud and forgery drifting through the room.
>
> Until then the evening had been glittering. Dinner had been served amid giant diamonds, sapphires and rubies in the Smithsonian's hall of gems, and then Dr. Armand Hammer—oilman and billionaire and omnivorous collector—had given every dinner guest a polished hunk of jade, but now the women sneered and snickered at the paintings on the walls.
>
> "Never have I seen," said one, "a public exhibition with quite so many fakes."

*See excerpts in Appendix E.

Hammer hit the ceiling. He reached for his favorite weapon, an invention of Alexander Graham Bell's, and dialed Kay Graham, the delightful owner of the *Post, Newsweek,* and TV and radio stations. She had the first word. "I expected your call, Armand," she said with laughter. "I know what you're going to say, so why don't you write us a piece in reply? We'll give it the same prominence."

The man with so many other things on his mind accepted the challenge immediately and wrote what may have been the longest and perhaps most erudite *pro bono publico* letter ever sent to an editor. Hammer wrote it himself, disdaining any assistance from his resident speechwriters. The Richard article began on page one of the *Post*'s Style Section. So did Hammer's by-lined retort, but Hammer's words spilled all over a second page and most of a third. He estimates that his original unexpurgated reply ran to 15,000 words. (See Appendix E.)

Still smarting from some of Richard's statements, Hammer decided to expand his collection. Through a series of expensive acquisitions over the next few years, he added some of the world's great masterpieces, replacing lesser works by the same great masters. All selections were left entirely to the judgment of internationally renowned art authority John Walker, director emeritus of the National Gallery in Washington.

Hammer's instructions to Walker were simple: "I want only works of art in the collection worthy of hanging in the National Gallery or the Metropolitan Museum."

How well Walker carried out his assignment is shown by Kenneth Donahue's introduction to the new catalog for the exhibition that opened December 20, 1971, at the Frances and Armand Hammer Wing of the Los Angeles County Museum:

> Dr. Armand Hammer is a man for whom the impossible is natural and from whom the unexpected is expected. Yet the development of his collection from the time of its first public exhibition only two years ago is still astonishing. At that time the collection numbered seventy-nine works, most of them European paintings and drawings from Corot to Chagall. Today the collection is almost double that number. In 1969 there were no drawings earlier than the Boudin of 1869. Today the old master drawings in the collection, including works of the rarest masters, Raphael and Dürer, would do honor to a veteran connoisseur of drawings. Two years ago the collection included only one American painting, the Sargent portrait of Mrs. Edward Livingston Davis and her son; today there is a distinguished

group of Americans from Gilbert Stuart to Andrew Wyeth. In the field of concentration of the collection, the nineteenth and early twentieth century, master works of Moreau, Pissarro, Monet, Degas, Renoir, van Gogh, and Cézanne have been added.

From this augmented collection, John Walker, Director Emeritus of the National Gallery of Art in Washington, has selected for exhibition at the Royal Academy in London, the National Gallery of Ireland, and the Los Angeles County Museum of Art those works which he believes best represent Dr. Hammer's tastes and intention. Dr. Hammer's objective in collecting is to bring together works of art which he feels have a special aesthetic significance and meaning to the American people today and to share them with the people. The sincerity of his intention is demonstrated by the fact that during the past two years Dr. Hammer's collection has been shown in whole or in part in Memphis, Washington, Kansas City, Columbus, New Orleans, Little Rock, Oklahoma City, San Francisco, and San Diego, that is, not only in the large metropolitan museums which might enhance the prestige of the collection but also in the smaller institutions whose visitors might not frequently have the chance to see paintings and drawings by the masters represented in it.

Our deepest gratitude, of course, is owed Dr. and Mrs. Hammer for allowing us to present their collection to the people of Los Angeles and to the many young visitors from Southern California and across the country we expect here during the holiday season.

To climax the opening at Los Angeles, Hammer announced that he had willed his entire collection of paintings to the Los Angeles County Museum and his drawings to the National Gallery in Washington.

The following story in the *New York Times*, by Everett R. Holles, made the front page of the Business and Finance Section on Sunday, May 20, 1973. Hammer was alerted by a phone call from a New York operative who spotted it in the late Saturday-night edition. It was headed: "HAMMER'S KREMLIN CONNECTION."

For Armand Hammer, 74-year-old head of the Occidental Petroleum Corporation, the Soviet Union has been a capitalist's paradise for a half century, rich in profits for a shrewd trader with the right connections in the Kremlin. . . .

Over the years, he has taken several fortunes out of the Soviet Union and parlayed them into personal wealth reckoned at $125-million or more, including one of the world's great art collections, and control of Occidental,

which he rescued from the brink of bankruptcy in 1957 and built into a
$2.6-billion conglomerate doing business in 28 countries.

Last month in Moscow, with an extravagant burst of publicity but a
paucity of hard facts, the Russians announced the newest and by far the
largest of their many deals with Dr. Hammer. . . .

One Occidental official, accustomed to being caught off guard by Dr.
Hammer's bold exercise of his financial and executive control of the com-
pany, spoke cynically of the deal, not as an Occidental undertaking but as
"Dr. Hammer's latest fling."

"All I know is what I read in the papers," he said. "I don't know where
all the money is coming from, but perhaps that's an insignificant detail."

There have been estimates that the fertilizer complex alone might cost
anywhere from $100-million to $400-million. Occidental reported $82-
million in cash on hand at the end of 1972 plus unused credits of around
$175-million and $253-million in working capital, against debts of nearly
a billion dollars.

The company's indebtedness last year put a stop to further payments of
cash dividends to Oxy's 303,000 common stockholders, and caused a bail-
out by holders of about a million shares.

Wall Street specialists and Occidental's competitors, many of whom
regard Dr. Hammer as prone to careless optimism in publicizing Occidental's ventures, have been less than enthusiastic over his latest Russian deal.

"He has a long-standing and well-documented habit of counting his
chickens before they're hatched," said a West Coast oil executive.

He recalled that, as far back as 1964, Dr. Hammer was talking expan-
sively about a big deal to build fertilizer plants in the Soviet Union and that
plans were drawn up for a big complex on the Kamchatka peninsula. But
two years of negotiations came to nothing.

Others suggest that Dr. Hammer may have become involved, in this
latest "historic agreement," in a Soviet propaganda ploy aimed at paving
the way for the visit of Leonid I. Brezhnev, Soviet Communist party chief,
to Washington next month.

This fact may account for Dr. Hammer's uncharacteristic reticence to
talk about the deal, they add.

To some observers, last month's announcement appears to be a "replay"
of even more elaborate plans announced by Dr. Hammer last July, which
the Russians have now seized upon as a means of combatting opposition
in Congress toward the Nixon-Brezhnev detente and the granting to the
Soviet Union of more liberal credits and a most favored nation tariff status.

Standard & Poor's, in an April 26 report on the latest announcement,
cautioned investors that the deal is "still awaiting clarification" and that,

in any event, it could not be expected to add much more than 30 cents a share to Occidental's business.

The report added that Occidental, despite improved earnings in 1972 and even more profitable first quarter of 1973, remains a high speculative gamble to be undertaken only by "a hardened risk-taker able to live with its volatility."

Last July, when Dr. Hammer announced a $3-billion, five-year technical assistance pact with the Soviets—broader in scope than the new announcement—the stock market excitedly bid Oxy's stock up more than 50 per cent from a low of 11-¾, despite Department of Commerce warnings against over-optimism. The splurge brought more than $200-million in profits on sales of 5.7 million Oxy shares.

On that earlier occasion the deal was to include not only a chemical fertilizer complex and pipelines, but also joint oil and gas exploration, metal-treating plants, processing of solid wastes and rather grandiose plans for building hotels and a large trade center in Moscow. Nothing has been heard recently of those more far-reaching projects.

As a result, the latest Occidental-Soviet announcement caused hardly a ripple on the stock exchanges, where Oxy rose barely a point, then promptly fell back to 11-½, and later to 10-½, very near its 1973 low.

Dr. Hammer offers a curious amalgam of Yankee trader, circus barker, big-time entrepreneur and cultured devotee of the arts, a man whose modesty concerning his many philanthropies is in striking contrast to the bravura style of his business dealings.

He is convinced that he knows more about doing business with the Russians than any other American and has described himself as "something of a hero" in the Soviet Union.

He recently informed stockholders, in the company's annual report, that Occidental's "historic arrangements" with the Soviet Union were possible because of his ability to deal "directly and personally with the Soviet Government's top leaders."

He negotiates with them in their own language, using what a Russian diplomat tactfully described as "fluent but not entirely flawless Russian" acquired during his sojourn there from 1921 to 1930.

When reminded that he has sometimes been described as a wheeler-dealer inclined to dramatize his business ventures, he replies good-naturedly:

"I am first and foremost a catalyst. I bring people and situations together. That's the big thing, bringing the deal together."

The doctor, like Queen Victoria, was not amused. He phoned Holles
—both were in Los Angeles—and the reporter complained that he had
been unable to interview Hammer. He had to pick up his information
where he could from other sources. Hammer's reticence was explainable
because of the delicate negotiations that had been going on at that time
over the $400 million loan between Eximbank, Bank of America, and
the Soviet government. "It's backed up on the presses and too late for
any changes," Holles said. Hammer then put in a call to *Times* publisher Arthur Ochs Sulzberger, whose deceased father, Arthur Hays
Sulzberger, former publisher of the *Times*, had been Hammer's long-
time friend. Whatever was said, a remarkable change of mood vis-à-vis
Hammer was presented in Monday's paper. Holles, having been invited
to Hammer's home for an interview, wrote under a front-page two-
column head (U.S. COMPANIES AND SOVIET DISCUSS A VAST GAS LINE) as
follows:

> Dr. Armand Hammer, chairman of the Occidental Petroleum Corpora-
> tion, is negotiating a "massive" new pipeline deal with the Soviet Union
> that, he says, could be twice as big as the estimated $7-billion or $8-
> billion transaction in chemical fertilizers that he signed in Moscow last
> month.
> In his first interview since the fertilizer contract was signed, the 74-year-
> old international entrepreneur said that the pipeline project would be a
> joint venture of Occidental and the El Paso Natural Gas Company, and
> would involve construction of a 2,000-mile line from western Siberia to the
> port of Olga to supply natural gas to the West Coast of the United States.

The *Times* man then went into considerable detail on the Hammer–
Soviet Union deal and spelled out the ways and means to lend muscle to
Hammer's grandiose dreams.

> "I am confident that our fertilizer agreement will go forward as planned
> and will be fully in operation by 1978 or sooner," he quoted Hammer as
> saying.
> He said a late development, following the April 12 signing in Moscow,
> indicated that the Soviets may want to begin the exchange of potash, urea,
> ammonia and super phosphates in 1975 rather than 1978, thereby adding
> perhaps a million extra tons and another $200-million or more to the
> over-all deal.
> Dr. Hammer has been in almost daily conferences seeking to help the

Soviet Union obtain American financing for construction of the ten plants and two pipelines to carry the agricultural chemicals to ports on the Black Sea and the Baltic.

The front-page story—which appeared on his seventy-fifth birthday—was illustrated with a one-column cut of Dr. Hammer. Straight. Not a caricature.

Hammer's call to Sulzberger also must have sounded a buzzer in the Moscow bureau of the *Times*. Underneath the somewhat conciliatory Holles piece there appeared the following:

RUSSIANS EAGER FOR ACCORD
By Theodore Shabad
SPECIAL TO THE NEW YORK TIMES

Moscow, May 20—In 1922, after a meeting with Dr. Armand Hammer, a young American physician eager to do business with the Soviet state, Lenin told other members of the ruling Politburo:

"Here we have a small opening into the American business community and we must make use of that opening in every possible way."

The remark was cited here the other day in Pravda, the authoritative Communist party daily, to justify the new Soviet "trade offensive" toward the United States and, in particular, the very special relationship that has been developing between the Soviet Government and Dr. Hammer, the chairman of the Occidental Petroleum Corporation, a Los Angeles based conglomerate.

The doctor takes understandable pleasure in confounding his media critics, especially those in the financial press who tend to imply that he overstates Oxy's prospects. A week after his September 12, 1973, dinner report to the New York Society of Security Analysts, he called a news conference at the Waldorf which at the time seemed like a tart reply to those who had not believed that he could swing his dreamed-of international trade center in beautiful downtown Moscow.

The *Times*, which had expressed some doubt about that project, gave full and generous coverage to the impressive signing of the agreement:

Dr. Hammer said that the proposal for a trade center originated during the Moscow summit meeting. The concept was further developed as a result of conferences and an exchange of letters. "Our governments jointly recognized the need for this trade center both as a symbol of good will and as an important cornerstone in building trade relations," he added.

Dr. Hammer, in reply to a question, said that to "deny to the Soviet Union the most-favored-nation status in trade would be contradictory" to emerging American policy.

When Mr. Borisov was asked whether Occidental had a "most favored company" status in the Soviet Union in light of Dr. Hammer's several actual and pending deals in that country, he replied by praising Dr. Hammer as an instrument for good will.

Mr. Borisov's words were sweet music to the doctor's ears. The doctor looked across the Basildon Suite, cluttered with reporters, cameras, and Klieg lights, caught the bartenders' eyes, and the champagne began to flow. He had struck another and different kind of well.

And given his critics pause. . . .

═══════════════════════════════════

Chapter 24

Endless Search, Triumphs, and Disasters

═══════════════════════════════════

The crust of Mother Earth and the zeal of Armand Hammer to puncture it for profit have been at war for years. The doctor won a relatively easy victory in Libya, all things considered. But since that breathtaking strike, still the envy of the petroleum giants, Hammer's people have had to scratch for every barrel of crude. Mother yields her remaining juices with dismaying frugality.

Oxy still pumps oceans of crude in Libya, nationalization or not. But its position there rests on the quicksands of Colonel El-Gathafi's iron whims. Thus it has behooved Oxy to look around the world for less traumatic places from which to extract its oil.

Peru, for example.

That Oxy is in Peru and on good terms with the military junta is, in the first place, symptomatic of Hammer's drive. He found it hard to abide the profit-making hits that had been scored by Texaco and Gulf in Ecuador. Also more or less unbearable, when Peru agreed that his geologists could start searching, was a law prohibiting any foreign activities within fifty miles of the Ecuadorean border.

"The Peruvian Government agreed to have the law waived in our behalf," he says, as if it was simpler than fixing an overtime parking ticket. "So we moved in fifty miles closer to Texaco and Gulf. We've had five strikes in five tries. You watch, the Amazon Basin oil will be one of the biggest bonanzas since the opening of the first Middle East fields. In the multibillion range."

The doctor dismisses with a wave of the hand the engineering task Petroperu, the Peruvian national oil company, has agreed to undertake.

Bechtel has already done the preliminary engineering.

"Six hundred miles across the Andes?" he says with a shrug. "That won't be too tough. The Andes where they will cross them are lower than Texaco's and Gulf's; the oil will be easier to get out. There's a military road that runs parallel with the position of the pipe for miles and miles. And they can always build pumping stations to help the oil go upgrade."

A more realistic view, perhaps, is contained in an article by Greg La Brache in the 1973 summer edition of *Oxy Today,* company house organ. It minced no words about the excruciating difficulties of kneading a drop of crude out of Oxy's Peruvian concession. The despotic conquistador Francisco Pizarro found profits much easier to come by in Peru nearly five hundred years earlier.

La Brache reported:

The Amazon.

Dawn slashes a broad, fiery brushstroke across the eastern horizon. Puff clouds of steamy mist rise in scattered patches over the thick tangle of green jungle.

The newborn equatorial sun turns on its relentless energy for another merciless day of searing heat and suffocating humidity.

The Amazon River—draining the South American continent from thousands of streams and rivers lacing the vast jungles—twists and coils like some giant tan reptile as it writhes toward the Atlantic Ocean where its force spews millions of gallons of muddy fresh water more than 150 miles out to sea.

My journey takes me 250 miles up into the headwaters of the Amazon, up the narrow, corkscrew tributary rivers that feed the mighty Amazon— the world's most awesome river, the Father of Waters.

Up into the huge Upper Amazon Basin into some of the most primitive, isolated and dangerous territory on earth. Up into what explorers have called the "Green Hell."

In this area, in its millions of square miles of unexplored jungle, man is the intruder, the interloper who must use his every sense, his total strength and intelligence just to survive.

This jungle offers a formidable array of obstacles for the white man who is adventurous—or foolish—enough to challenge it.

There are over 30 varieties of deadly poisonous snakes, including the fer-de-lance and the feared bushmaster—called "shushupe" by the natives and reaching a length of 12 feet.

In the constrictor family, there is the world's biggest snake, the anaconda

217

—rumored to reach a length of 60 feet and easily capable of swallowing a grown man whole.

There are ants and flying beetles whose bite can blind a man, vampire bats and leeches to suck his blood, diseases to rot his flesh, trees with poisonous sap that burns the skin like acid, savage piranha fish that can strip a 150-pound wild boar to a skeleton in minutes, clouds of insects whose bite and sting have driven men insane, and in the unexplored areas, the Jívaro headshrinkers and fierce Auca Indian tribes living by Stone Age codes of survival.

In the heart of this hostile reach, in Peru's Oriente Province, men—a special breed of men—have come to extract the jungle's hidden treasures.

Oro negro—black gold. That magic word—oil.

On a 2.9–million acre tract of land along Peru's border with Ecuador, Occidental oil men—in partnership with the Peruvian government—are drilling for and finding oil.

In one of the most intensive and aggressive exploration programs in petroleum history, Oxy has drilled fifteen wells in the jungle and come up with six field discoveries—not one dry hole.

Even more difficult, if possible, is the probing of the bottom of the North Sea, where Oxy is the major company (36.5 percent) in a consortium whose other members are Getty Oil International (England) Ltd., Allied Chemical (Great Britain) Ltd., and newspaper tycoon Lord Thomson's Scottish Petroleum Ltd.

Ocean Victory, flagship of the group's costly sea venture, is a monstrous self-propelled floating rig that resembles one of the denizens of the deep so feared by pre-Columbian voyagers. Its six huge legs are imbedded in twin submerged pontoon hulls. Measured from the keels of the pontoons to the crest of the rig, the thing stands twice as tall as Niagara Falls, or as high as a twenty-nine-story building. Twelve huge anchors keep the vessel stable while drilling in the face of one-hundred-knot winds and wintry waves as high as seventy feet.

It costs $40,000 a day to operate. But as of now it has had two promising strikes about 115 miles east of Aberdeen. The first, named the Piper field, should yield 642 million barrels of crude, using a 40 percent recovery factor, according to the independent engineering consulting firm of De Golyer and MacNaughton. Oxy's engineers are certain the field will give up 800 million barrels. Whatever, *Ocean Victory* inched onward through the turbulent grave of countless sailors of old, anchored, and bit down into the black gold of the Claymore field.

Enough oil is now known to exist beneath the North Sea to supply 70 percent of the energy needs of the United Kingdom by 1980.

The pipeline needed to bring the North Sea oil to land—probably Flotta Island in the Orkneys—will be an engineering feat roughly comparable to the oft-frustrated tunnel under the English Channel. But once in place it will need little or no tending. Back at *Ocean Victory*, however, the relentless search will continue to call for extraordinary human labor on the part of roustabouts, roughnecks, drillers, mud loggers, derrickmen, engineers, and divers. The hostility of the environment may be measured by the fact that divers, regularly called upon to inspect the underpinning of the oil-sucking monstrosity, can withstand the freezing water for a maximum of forty minutes. The diver, once exhumed from the deep, must spend the next seven days and nights in a decompression tank to avoid death from the bends.

Through much of the year, crewmen whose duties keep them on deck are subjected to the rawest side of nature. They are bombarded by sleet pellets whipped by high winds. They work twelve-hour shifts, seven days a week, and their link to land is the big Sikorsky shuttle helicopter that brings them mail and periodically takes them back to their homes in Scotland, sometimes with a finger or an arm missing.

But the drilling, like The Show, must go on. And on.

Five years ago—despite the pressure on the corporate treasury—Hammer authorized Garrett Research Laboratories to embark on a project to develop oil from huge shale rock deposits in the Piceance Basin of Colorado.

Countless millennia before man walked upright, a portion of what we know as the Rocky Mountains was the bottom of an enormous lake. Minute organic life, protozoa, bacteria, pollen, great and small fishes and fearsome animal life sank in the silt of the lake, and with earthquakes and tremors were packed and eventually escalated into towering piles of hard rock.

Compressed within the rock was oil. Dr. Hammer got wind of it some years after the Eocene Age. So did others in the world as early as the fourteenth century, when similar deposits, named "ichthyol," a fish-laden and inflammable rock, was used for lighting, cooking, and warmth in middle Europe.

Dr. Hammer is taking dead aim on a bit of the frozen oil assets of a

219

swatch of the Colorado Rockies, fifty miles northeast of Grand Junction.

Through the lean years of financial reorganization, Hammer kept the multimillion-dollar project funded. Other companies were also aware of the potential value of oil shale and concentrated on processes that involved strip mining the rock and converting it to oil in huge above-ground retorts.

Hammer chose the other route—internal or, as it was scientifically termed, *in situ* mining.

In its basic form, this called for tunneling inside shale-oil-rich mountains, building huge internal chambers, blasting the rocks into pieces, and setting them afire, thus separating the oil from the rock without disturbing the mountain or the surrounding countryside.

Almost simultaneously with President Nixon's announcement of Project Independence—an America independent of foreign energy supplies by 1980—Garrett Laboratories reported to Hammer that the five-year experiment had resulted in success on their leased site in Colorado.

Oil was being produced from a small *in situ* operation in the amount of twenty to thirty barrels a day. Hammer immediately ordered the test plant to be developed into a much larger pilot project, capable of producing 30,000 barrels of oil a day by 1977.

He also commissioned the Stanford Research Institute to provide its own evaluation of the process. Stanford reported that their estimates showed that the oil could be produced on site for as little as $1.18 (direct cost) a barrel. Added onto this figure, of course, would be land costs, transportation, refining, and all the other normal costs of such an operation. But even at that, oil could be produced at a total cost of approximately $5 per barrel from medium quality shale and as low as $3 per barrel from high quality shale—and this at a time when world oil prices were approaching $12 a barrel.

Hammer could have kept his development a secret. Instead, he immediately flew to Washington to consult with Secretary of the Treasury William Simon, Secretary of the Interior Rogers Morton, and Atomic Energy Commission Chairman Dixy Lee Ray.

Hammer's proposal was simple:

The basic technological breakthrough had been accomplished. Oxy could keep it to itself and gradually develop its patents and pilot plant and then go into commercial operation.

But if the United States government was looking for something that would give it the chance at a quantum jump toward independence, then oil shale might be the answer, and Hammer was willing to help form a Manhattan Project to get it done.

In his nationally syndicated column of January 15, 1974, Jack Anderson reported:

> With unconcealed excitement, the Federal Energy Office is investigating a revolutionary technique for extracting oil from shale at a cheap $1.18 a barrel without ecological damage.
>
> Energy director William Simon is talking privately about an all-out Government effort on the scale of the Manhattan Project which developed the atomic bomb to bleed the mountains of Colorado, Utah and Wyoming of critically needed oil.
>
> An estimated 1.8 trillion barrels of oil, nearly three times the world's present proven reserves, are locked in the shale formations of the Rockies. The problem is separating the oil from the rock.
>
> But now Occidental Petroleum has developed a way to extract the oil inside the mountains without massive strip mining and monstrous shale dumps. Even more promising, the Occidental process would reduce the [direct] cost from around $5 to $1.18 a barrel.
>
> The cost estimates were made by an independent Stanford Research Institute group which studied Occidental's pilot project in Colorado. The final cost of delivering the oil to suppliers would run between $2 and $3 a barrel. [Since then, with inflation, the cost would be more likely double these figures.]
>
> Occidental's enterprising chairman, Dr. Armand Hammer, showed a movie of the process the other day to Simon and his staff.
>
> The energy chief came away from the briefing highly impressed. A crash program could relieve the U.S. oil shortage in three years.

Anderson's source had been from within the government, and his column provoked a lot of sudden action among other factions of the oil industry, who were not enamored of the concept of cheaper oil from an *in situ* process which they did not possess.

Hammer's offer to the government to share the process and rapidly develop it under a Manhattan Project was overwhelmed in a tidal wave of intricate Washington movements and shifted to the back burner at the Federal Energy Office.

Undaunted, Oxy under Hammer's leadership pressed on with his project, funding it with an additional $20 million of capital to complete the

221

first commercial-size chamber, which would be capable of producing 500 barrels of oil per day by the summer of 1975.

As other companies stressed the benefits of aboveground mining of oil shale—and invested millions in spirited bidding for two federal tracts offered in Colorado—Occidental continued its low-profile, low-budget operation on its leased privately owned site.

Throughout the year its engineers enjoyed increasing success with their experiments with increasingly larger chambers to the point where, if the 500-barrel-per-day chamber proved to be successful, full-scale production of a 30 to 50,000-barrel-a-day plant could be foreseen in 1977 at an investment cost of about $100 to $200 million.

Large numbers of technical experts, from both the government and the private sector, including the famous nuclear expert, Dr. Edward Teller, visited the site as the work went on. Their investigation invariably led them to support the unusual concept. Scientific opinion was best summed up by Dr. Glenn T. Seaborg, former chairman of the Atomic Energy Commission (1961–1971) and a 1951 Nobel Prize winner in chemistry. An acknowledged expert in the field of natural resource energy, he wrote to Dr. Hammer on February 4, 1974, as director of the Nuclear Chemistry Division of the University of California's Lawrence Berkeley Laboratory:

> My analysis of this information leads me to the conclusion that your *in situ* (underground) oil shale recovery process is technically and economically feasible and is capable of recovering raw shale oil at a cost that is attractive and substantially below that of other (conventional) extraction methods known to me.
>
> I am especially impressed by the capability of your process to produce its product with no shale ash disposal above ground, in contrast to the other methods—a tremendous asset in minimizing adverse environmental impact.
>
> I believe that your process shows enough promise to merit the federal government involvement necessary to place it into operation on the massive scale which is needed if the process is to make the large contribution to our nation's future energy supply of which it apparently is capable.

Concurrently, the aboveground oil shale methods appeared to have foundered when on October 4, 1974, the Colony Development Group—Atlantic Richfield Company, Shell Oil Company, The Oil Shale Corporation, and Ashland Oil, Inc.—announced that they were suspending plans to start construction of a 50,000-barrel-a-day plant scheduled for completion in the spring of 1975. They were having environmental difficulties, as foreseen by Hammer. The capital costs of their more experimental process had escalated to the astronomical figure of $800 million.

Hammer had clearly won a major victory in a technological gamble. The Occidental *in situ* process Hammer believes could produce oil more cheaply than imported oil and in quantity sufficient in the years to come to play a major role in the national pursuit of energy independence.

"It's the largest potential source of petroleum known in the world today," Hammer swears. "More than two and one-half times the proven oil reserves of the world, at least forty-seven times the U.S. reserves. Assuming even a fifty percent recovery, this would equal a one-hundred-and-forty-year supply of oil for the U.S. at the 1973 rate of petroleum use. . . ."

For a man who was ready to hole up in 1956, content with his fat fortune and books of clippings about his triumphs in business and the arts, Hammer had a busy year—seventeen years later. In 1973 he logged about 300,000 miles, including one round-the-globe business trip that included stops at Honolulu, Kwajalein, Tokyo, Nagoya, Khaborovsk, Novosibirsk, Moscow, Paris, Zurich, London, Bangor, and home to Los Angeles by way of New York. That one knocked fifty-eight days off Phileas Fogg's record.

Highlight of the latter search for new business was the visit to Japan, his first. American businessmen have been a dime a dozen in Nippon since V-J Day, but Hammer's reputation for getting things done had preceded him. He was greeted with a deference usually reserved for ranking diplomats. Premier Tanaka received him with warmth and the top tycoons of the explosive Japanese economy entertained him and his party lavishly. At Mishima, near Tokyo, the doctor accepted a relatively rare invitation, a hot bath in a spa's solid-gold bathtub. The symbolism was not lost on host or guest. The Japan trip was a golden excursion, a blooming of five deals and partnerships which will enrich the parties concerned into the distant future.

The Japanese agreed to become Oxy's partner, together with El Paso Natural Gas Company, in the titanic and astronomically costly task of moving Siberia's liquefied gas out of the U.S.S.R. Japan would receive half of it, a hoped-for billion cubic feet a day, assume half the cost of building twenty tankers, and assist El Paso and Oxy (and the Soviets) in a $3 billion program to develop and prove out the incredible field. Ten trillion cubic feet of gas is now known to be there; two or three times that much is expected to be tapped as the earth is probed by new wells.

The Japanese have also offered Petroperu, the Peruvian national oil company, to take the matter of financing the 600-mile pipeline across the Andes in Peru off Oxy's shoulders, with the understanding that they will get the right to buy a share of the oil Petroperu has found in Peru at world market prices. That would represent a saving in outlay for Oxy of some $300 million. Peruvian crude is the cleanest found since the Libyan strikes, very low sulphur quotient, as pollution-free as oil can get. Japanese industries and public utility plants prefer to dispense with refinery costs and burn crude directly, unthinkable in the United States. Japan is buying considerable quantities of Oxy's Libyan oil, which is uniquely suitable for this purpose.

The doctor has lost oil as well as found it—lost it in places that even his most inquisitive and demanding stockholders might never have heard of.

Hammer's war against the British-protected Trucial States may not be remembered with those of 1776 and 1812, but the Sunday *Times* of London took notice of it on May 31, 1970:

A Royal Navy frigate accompanied by RAF planes is circling this weekend in the waters off the tiny Trucial Sheikdom of Umm al-Qaywayn as Dr. Armand Hammer, head of the California-based Occidental Oil Co., makes up his mind whether or not to send in a drilling barge tomorrow to open up Occidental's promising but now highly controversial off-shore concession.

The Umm al-Qaywayn row, which started as an argument between two U.S. oil companies, Occidental and the much smaller Buttes Gas & Oil of San Francisco, has now escalated to a point where it involves the British Foreign Office, the Iranian Government, a platoon of international lawyers and virtually every State and oil company in the Persian Gulf. Occidental was asked to hold off until June 1 in the hope that the dispute could be settled, but this time limit has now run out.

The Foreign Office states officially this week-end that it is "actively trying to contribute to a solution." Yesterday the police chief of Sharjah served notice on Occidental that any drilling operations will be treated as an act of trespass. No information was available in London as to the precise function of the frigate and the planes reported off Qaywayn.

Late yesterday Dr. Hammer offered to put all royalties into trust for whichever party finally wins. This offer has gone to Iran, Sharjah and Qaywayn.

The doctor assures all the above countries and cast of exotic characters, including the Arabian knights, that they haven't heard the last of him. And they haven't. He is suing Buttes and their partners in the U.S. courts and in the British courts and expects to win in both places.

Water does not mix with oil, some Stone Age wizard observed. But oil and politics meld immediately upon confrontation, the doctor has had good reason to note over the years. For example, he will unquestionably go to his grave sometime around the tricentennial of the country firmly convinced that he was given a bad deal by politicians in general, the late Representative Hale Boggs (Democrat, Louisiana) in particular, and lobbyists from the major companies. Boggs was killed in a plane crash in Alaska in 1972. Hammer's complaint dates back to his attempt in 1968 to build a refinery at Machiasport, Maine, to break his relatively cheap Libyan oil into its various components—at savings to that part of the Eastern seaboard.

Permission for this sort of enterprise comes under the direction of the Secretary of Commerce's Foreign Trade Zones Board.

To his surprise, at that time, Hammer was turned down, even though his spokesmen argued that such a new refinery, using cheaper oil, would comply with the Zones Board's requirement that it would provide cheaper petroleum products for the state.

"Looking back on it," Hammer philosophizes, "Oxy was not permitted to build the refinery because the major companies would suffer financially as they tried to compete.

"The chance that Maine might win this refinery prompted Mr. Boggs to take extraordinary countermeasures. On learning that Oxy would like to contribute legally to his 1968 reelection campaign, as did so many others, Mr. Boggs arranged a meeting with our representatives at his office in Washington. He also invited a photographer. He asked our people to tell him more about the Machiasport proposal, then interpreted the response, and the offer to contribute to his campaign, as an offer to bribe him to support our application in Maine. But, curiously, he didn't mention it to the press for another ten days, timing the disclosure to coincide with testimony to a committee of trade zone examiners in Portland.

"We lost out, of course. Secretary of the Interior Udall was sympathetic to us, but ineffectual. President Johnson was a lame duck. Besides, I realized that my friend Lyndon would soon be back in Texas, where even an ex-President wouldn't be welcome at the Petroleum Club if he allowed me to get that refinery in Maine."

What Dr. Hammer calls "fanatical ecologists" have thwarted him in California as well as in Maine. Oxy owns a section of land along the Pacific Palisades—not too far from the doctor's Los Angeles home—but has been prevented by assorted court orders and environmental groups from tapping the oil it feels certain lurks below.

By comparison, the Los Angeles impasse makes Oxy's Libyan acquisition appear routine. The odd cast of characters involved include St. Patrick, retired Cardinal McIntyre, ex-Mayor Sam Yorty (who once had dreams of the presidency), the Irish-Israeli Society of Los Angeles, and a 450-year-old shrine in Clonmel County, Tipperary.

Put them all together and they spell h-e-a-d-a-c-h-e.

It started when the city fathers asked Hammer if he would give up some Oxy land along the beach—the city wanted it for a park—in exchange for a plot of land on higher ground inshore. The deed, unanimously approved by the City Council, specified that Oxy could use its new property only for oil digging. Mayor Yorty, who had held stock in Oxy, was an enthusiastic supporter of the exchange.

But the very councilman who had suggested the exchange in the first place had a change of heart. He was given the support of pressure groups and an articulate minority of property owners, who were told that if Oxy struck oil in their general neighborhood it might cause earthquakes, mudslides, and other disasters.

Their attack in the press intimated also that there must have been a conspiracy between Yorty and Hammer, dating back to a gift of $10,000 Hammer made to Cardinal McIntyre to complete the restoration of the shrine in Ireland, insufficient funds having been raised for that purpose by the Irish-Israeli Society. The shrine was said to be built over a well that St. Patrick had visited and blessed in the fourth century.

Anyway, Yorty's mother was born in Clonmel, and Frances Hammer's mother had been born nearby. So the St. Patrick's Aid Society of Clonmel invited the Hammers and the Yortys to attend the unveiling of the refurbished place of prayer. The foursome traveled in Oxy's jet.

The "no oil" group, as they call themselves, were elated when a broker's customer's man announced to the press that he had sold Yorty several hundred thousand dollars' worth of Oxy stock, which he said he had carried to the Bahamas in a suitcase. He added that Yorty had paid for the shares in cash. Yorty sued for libel and got a letter of apology from the brokerage house, and the customer's man was judged to be mentally deranged.

The doctor feels that the media in Los Angeles has tended to stress the charges made and warnings issued by the "no oil" brigade, but is reluctant to air his own views and the findings of the court which the "no oil" group is appealing. These include, in addition to the go-ahead language of the original deed of transfer, a geological study suggesting that there have been no landslides on Oxy's new property, purchased for an alternate drill site, for millions of years. Hammer has emphasized the need for this oil, and his experts have deduced that the city of Los Angeles alone could have saved $20 million during the 1973–1974 crisis if they had been able to use the oil beneath their land instead of buying it abroad.

Seventy-five percent of the owners of adjacent real estate have leased their mineral rights to Oxy.

But the oil remains in the ground, the worst possible place for it, in the doctor's estimation and that of Oxy's shareholders.

Chapter 25

$20 Billion—A Nice Round Figure

Few men achieve their finest hour at nearly seventy-six. But in the sincerest judgment of one of his more competent aides, former Boston newsman Bill McSweeny, the doctor reached that magic sixty minutes on Friday, April 26, 1974.

What Hammer did that day as a witness before the Senate Banking Committee's Subcommittee on International Finance, and what he had contrived to do before taking the stand, offered abundant proof that he was in as complete possession of all his marbles as he had been the day he sat down with Lenin in 1921.

The $20 billion barter fertilizer deal could become a reality if a loan, microscopically smaller, was made by the U.S. Export-Import Bank to the Soviet Union, a modest but log-jam-breaking $180 million.

Now it was feared that the Eximbank loan—the trigger mechanism that made it all possible—might be in jeopardy.

Senator Adlai Stevenson III, the Illinois Democrat who chaired the sub-committee, agreed that Richard Stone, secretary of state of Florida and a Democratic senatorial candidate, would be the lead-off witness.

Then Secretary of State Stone, who won election to the U.S. Senate the following November, had an excellent campaign issue, aimed not just at the fertilizer loan but at the whole wide-ranging issue of the role of the Eximbank in détente.

Mr. Stone and the doctor obviously could have gone at it hammer and tongs, since each was dedicated in support of his position, but the good doctor recognized that a collision course would never resolve the immediate issue.

"I understood Mr. Stone's position," Hammer recalled. "I hoped that at a later date we could have a better understanding of each other, and I certainly had no intention of injuring his political campaign. So I only asked that I be permitted to speak second. I think it worked out very well. Both sides had their say. As a matter of fact I met Mr. Stone for the first time in the hallway after the hearing and we had a pleasant chat, and I think he did a very good job of expressing some very strong opinions he shared with some of the voters in Florida. The important thing was that we both got the job done. He was elected a Senator and the fertilizer loan was approved."

So the battle was joined in a dialogue closely observed by the White House, the Senate, and the press in the overcrowded hearing room.

Hammer had been invited to testify as the lead-off witness. The hearings—forerunner of what finally became the wide-ranging dispute between President Ford and Senator Jackson linking the trade bill and most-favored-nation status for the Soviet Union to the granting of exit visas to Russian Jews—were convened to illuminate the U.S. Export-Import Bank's role in Russian loans and, specifically, the highly complex fertilizer transaction that Hammer had put together with the written approval of the executive departments of both the United States and the U.S.S.R.

That the feritilizer loan should be in question was an unusual aspect of the Washington climate that year.

As has been detailed elsewhere, Occidental's role had been carefully checked, double-checked, and cleared over a period of two years.

In the past two years Hammer had made some twenty trips to Moscow and an equal number to Washington. His contact points stretched across the width and breadth of the leadership of both countries—President Nixon, Secretary of Commerce Frederick Dent, Secretary of the Treasury William Simon, and chairman of the Export-Import Bank William J. Casey on the U.S. side; General Secretary Brezhnev, Minister of the Chemical Industry Kostandov, Minister of Foreign Trade N. S. Patolichev, Deputy Trade Ministers Alkhimov and Komarov, and the chairman of the Bank of Foreign Trade Y. A. Ivanov on the U.S.S.R. side.

Stone come on strong. He covered the gamut from waste of the taxpayers' money to the accusation that we are draining Floriada of priceless natural resources to the threat that we are giving an enemy, Russia, a weapon against us.

Hammer descended to the nitty-gritty of the "bottom line." He said:

"Eximbank has granted a preliminary commitment for credit of one hundred eighty million dollars to the Foreign Trade Bank of the Soviet Union. Additionally, ten private American banks, led by the Bank of America, will provide an additional hundred eighty million dollars. The Soviets themselves will put in forty million in cash. The private bank consortium is committing its one hundred eighty million dollars without any participation or guarantees from the Export-Import Bank, relying on the full faith and credit of the Soviet Union to repay the debt. In addition to the moneys I have described, Occidental Petroleum will privately finance its role in the expansion of the Florida plant, which we calculate to be an investment of about three hundred forty million dollars. Lastly, the Soviet Union will receive an additional four hundred million dollars in Western Europe, and will spend the ruble equivalent of more than an additional billion dollars internally.

"Thus, the construction elements necessary to create facilities to serve the fertilizer exchange amount to over two billion dollars. Of this, only one hundred eighty million will come from the Export-Import Bank, and is only valid if used to purchase equipment made in America and supplied by American companies. Occidental is not a participant in the loan between the Eximbank and the Soviet Bank of Foreign Trade. Occidental's participation is strictly through private financing arranged by it, and not a single dollar of the taxpayers' money will be involved in our plant construction.

"It is pure nonsense to speak of especial favor and playing loose with taxpayers' dollars. Credit is a basic tool in any large international business transaction. If everything had to be done on a cash-and-carry basis the wheels of industry would grind to a halt. So, if we are to do business with the U.S.S.R., credit arrangements should be expected as the normal part of any transaction. Every industrial nation engaged in export has set up the equivalent of our own Eximbank. The United Kingdom has its ECDG, France its COFACE, in Italy EMY, in West Germany HERMES, and in Japan the Export-Import Bank of Japan. . . . If we are to get our share of this export market, our Eximbank rate of interest must be competitive so that we, too, may reap the benefit of increased balance of trade and, above all, more jobs for our unemployed.

". . . The Soviets have an abundance of natural gas. They also have a number of ammonia and urea plants already functioning, some built by western European or Japanese companies using American equipment and licenses and some built by the Soviets themselves. But now, because General Secretary Brezhnev and the leadership have determined to expand their agricultural production, they have a need for more phosphates which are more readily accessible to the areas where their agriculture exists. We offered to supply this phosphate in a highly concentrated form to save costs of transport. This can be done by converting phosphate rock from our Florida mines to superphosphoric acid. By this process, we can deliver in one ship as much phosphatic material as would otherwise require four ships, three of phosphate rock and one of sulphur. Shipments will start in 1978 and will be produced from new mines which Occidental did not intend to open in the remainder of this century.

"Thus, we will not be depriving the domestic market. . . . Once the ships unload the SPA, as we call it, they will then reload with the ammonia coming down the pipeline from Kuybyshev, and make a return voyage to Jacksonville and to New Orleans to deliver this much-needed fertilizer ingredient to the American market.

"In the matter of energy requirements, if we were to use our own domestic natural gas to make ammonia and urea in the same quantities to be imported, we would expend over fifty times as much energy as will be required to mine, dry, and convert the phosphate rock into the twenty million export tons of SPA which we will export over twenty years. One of the points raised by a previous speaker referred to the use of electrical energy. Considering the energy exchange on a BTU basis, in this deal the United States will profit fifty to one. And that's a conservative figure. It is equivalent to the energy needed to heat one million, one hundred thousand American homes each year, equivalent to saving the United States twenty-five million barrels of oil per year for twenty years. The Fertilizer Institute estimates that the United States between now and 1980 must find an additional eighty million tons of ammonia. Our exchange will help to relieve this deficit."

The doctor scoffed at the proposal that national security might be impaired by his astronomical deal.

"This is, of course, not true. Certainly, it is possible to convert superphosphoric acid into phosphorous, but it requires a lengthy and expensive process. It would be the height of economic absurdity for the Soviets to do this, since they would be taking an expensive fertilizer component, for which they were paying a high price, and reducing it back to basics, then

231

extracting chemicals which they already have in large supply in their own country.

"Let me say right here that the amount of gas, poison gas, that could be made out of this phosphate would require the use of only eighteen tons of phosphate rock. In other words, with eighteen tons of phosphate rock you could produce twelve tons of an ingredient which, in turn, would produce two and a half tons of a substance which is called elementary phosphorous. This, in turn, could destroy the whole population of the United States. Now, the Russians have over two billion tons of phosphate rock of their own. A previous speaker here today asked, 'Why don't they use it?' Well, it is located in areas which are not convenient to the agricultural belts. They will save a great deal by buying phosphates from our country. That is good business. But if they were going to import this phosphate of ours in order to use it for military purposes, don't you think it would occur to them, if they planned to destroy the whole population of the United States, that they'd look around for only eighteen tons of their own phosphate rock?"

As for his opponents' complaints that the United States is running out of a precious mineral needed to make U.S. farms burgeon and deserts bloom, Dr. Hammer marshaled another battalion of statistics, as if that was all he had been cramming on for months:

"As projected by the United States Department of Commerce, the phosphate reserves in Florida, now minable at a cost of seven-seventy-five per ton, amounted to four and one-half billion tons. The annual consumption of phosphate rock in the United States is forty-three million tons, and in Florida it is thirty-three million tons. Just imagine, divide thirty-three million tons into four and one-half billion tons, and you have enough reserves here for over one hundred thirty-five years. In order to deliver our SPA, we will have to mine eighty million tons over twenty years. That is four million tons a year. This has absolutely no significant impact on our national reserves. It will amount over those twenty years to less than one point seven percent of the Florida reserves and less than half of one percent of the United States reserves. I hardly think this can be construed, as some have suggested, as jeopardizing the future of American agriculture —but I can tell you that American agriculture, which is still the breadbasket of the world, is going to be in serious trouble if we don't use such transactions as this deal to bring in ammonia and urea.

". . . Well, I didn't come here to continue a long table of figures. . . . Since last January, the Soviets have been paying a commitment fee —a very substantial commitment fee—to the consortium of banks led by the Bank of America. At the same time, they are prevented from utilizing this credit because it is contingent on the final commitment of the Eximbank for the other half. In line with this, I noted that Secretary of Commerce Dent, who has recently been in Russia, told the press, 'If we cannot deliver on our promise in the trade and economic field, it will indicate to them an absence of real national sentiment to improve our political relations.'

"Meanwhile, because of the inflation, American suppliers are already losing parts of the potential business. The Soviets have recently told us that the costs for their ammonia and urea plants as well as for other equipment have escalated so much that they will buy only four of the eight ammonia plants in the United States and the remaining four plants in France. The Baltic and Black Sea Terminals, storage tanks, and railroad tank cars have also escalated so much that their four-hundred-million-dollar credit in the United States after the purchase of the four ammonia plants will be expended on these alone. I hope the Eximbank credit will come in time so that we can utilize this credit in this country. The Russians have sought additional credit from West Germany recently, and they inform us it is their intention now to buy the pipe in that country. Further, as time has gone on, the highly competitive banks of western Europe—both private and those which correspond to our Eximbank— have indicated to the Soviets that they will be most happy to undertake the financing, provided, of course, all the equipment is bought in those countries which will lend the money. The Soviets have recently been offered a deal by Morocco for phosphates, and they have signed a preliminary agreement under which they could obtain several times the quantity of phosphates we are offering them from Florida. . . . It would be a very sad day for U.S.-U.S.S.R. relations if this fertilizer deal of ours does not go forward because of the delays we are experiencing in getting finalization of the Eximbank commitment.

". . . I feel deep in my heart that for the very first time we have achieved a point in the relationship between our country and the Soviet Union from which we can move forward into solid bonds of detente through trade. Then we will be close to leaving this a better world than we found

233

it. The alternatives are far too awful to contemplate—fear, famine, pestilence, small wars, more Vietnams, cold wars, even the potential of nuclear war.

"I do not say that we should not use great care in very pragmatically assessing the issues before us. But my readings of history have convinced me that wars begin when communication fails. Trade is the most important element of modern communication. I believe that if we approach this magic moment in the history of time with determination to seek and cultivate détente, we may have at last achieved an era when we can inhabit this constantly shrinking planet together in some form of mutually beneficial trade that could lead to prosperity and détente for all mankind. I thank you."

The Senators—Stevenson, Sparkman, and Alan Cranston—thanked Dr. Hammer in turn. They said in their separate ways that they had never heard anything like his laser-beam expertise. Eximbank sprang the $180 million to the Soviet bank, which in turn forwarded it to such U.S. companies as Chemico and Occidental, which in turn parceled bits of it out to about fifty subcontractors—and life was pumped into the "$20 Billion Deal."

Armand Hammer had come a long way from the Lower East Side . . . the poor asbestos mine . . . "Gimbels basement" . . . potato alcohol . . . Prince Eric's $5,000 spermatozoa . . . retirement . . . and the $50,000 he and his wife bet on worthless little Occidental.

Chapter 26

The Aborted Coup

Two self-made, strong-willed men faced each other across a hardwood custom-made desk that had suddenly taken on the guise of a green-topped gambling table. The place: the *sanctum sanctorum* of Occidental's world headquarters, Los Angeles. The date: November 14, 1974. The players: Dr. Hammer and a fellow tycoon who was about to send him into a righteous rage, John H. Swearingen, board chairman of the Standard Oil Company (Indiana). The stakes: astronomical.

Swearingen, twenty years Hammer's junior, coolly laid his proposition on the line. He would give $1 billion in Indiana's perennially productive stock for the 55 million shares of Oxy common and later take care of the 15 million outstanding preferred shares.

He would offer the holders of the 55 million shares $17 a share. That was $3 more than it was being traded for that day on the New York Stock Exchange, $8 better than its stagnant position of several months earlier.

There would be more to the deal than a simple acquisition of $1,300,500,000 worth of Oxy common and converted preferred, Swearingen explained. Key Occidental personnel, perhaps even Hammer, would be retained in the expanded company. Oxy's explorations for more oil in the North Sea and elsewhere would be encouraged, and there would be fresh capital available for Oxy's promising shale-oil experiments in Colorado.

Besides, the chairman of the nation's sixth largest petroleum producer told the chairman of the country's eleventh biggest, their combined companies would move into the first ten largest industrial companies in the U.S., with 1974 sales of nearly $17 billion.

(Swearingen had the good taste not to mention that if Hammer accepted and helped push the deal to total fruition, he, Oxy's largest stockholder with approximately 1,200,000 shares of common, would realize a nice profit of about $21 million for nodding his head.)

There are several versions of what transpired immediately after the offer was made.

Swearingen later said, "I had the distinct impression that Dr. Hammer was willing to explore a consolidation with Standard." Hammer's recollections sharply differ. "Once I realized they were trying to raid us I decided to play along, draw them out and see just what they had in mind."

Swearingen had hardly reached the elevator at the end of the hall before Hammer was barking to the unflappable Dorothy Prell to get all of his officers, advisers, and lawyers on the phone, preferably simultaneously. His choler pressed harder and harder against his tab collar as he told them of his unnerving experience. Swearingen had threatened him, he said; had more or less *told* him Indiana Standard was taking over, not *asked* him to sell.

There were harsher words to come. Two hours after the meeting, Swearingen phoned Hammer to alert him that—in accordance with S.E.C "disclosure" rules—he felt compelled to issue a press release to the effect that they had held "talks" about a merger. Hammer bristled and replied, "I can't stop you from saying anything to the press you might wish to. But I'll put out a denial. You can bet on that!"

Swearingen released his handout the following morning. Hammer's angry refutation followed shortly thereafter, plus his announcement that he would take the matter to the courts and the Congress.

Then the Doctor resumed his routinely kaleidoscopic life. He and Frances flew to Cody, Wyoming, where he spoke to the directors of the Buffalo Bill Historical Museum about a loan of some of their paintings by Western artists such as Remington and Russell. He had previously requested his friend, Peter Kriendler, of New York, a trustee of the museum, to help him obtain the group for exhibition in the Soviet Union, where Brezhnev heads a multitude of American cowboy-and-Indian buffs.*

That much attended to, he jetted to New York, four hours late, to

*This is part of another U.S.-U.S.S.R. historic cultural event, even greater than the U.S.S.R. French Impressionist success. It will be a six-month tour of U.S. cities of Old Masters that have not left the walls of the Hermitage since the time of Catherine the Great. In exchange for this, there will be an equal number of Old Masters loaned for tour of the U.S.S.R. from the National Gallery, Los Angeles County Art Museum, Knoedler's, and others.

deliver some of the family photographs which illustrate this book. The Harper & Row offices had closed for the night, but a note had been left for him to join the book's editor, Amy Bonoff, and the writer at "21." I had ordered a bottle of Pouilly-Fuissé and some of the imported cheeses he devours at the drop of a hat. He arrived somewhat out of breath, accompanied by his wife and his New York secretary, Rosemary Noël-Clarke, and reached for a table phone instead of the wine or cheese. For the next twenty minutes he called his lawyers in New York, Washington, and Los Angeles, denounced Swearingen, discussed with them the best city in which to try his suit, made an overseas call, spoke to his pilot at the Newark airport, called a waiter and ordered a Napoleon to go.

The flaky cream-laced delicacy arrived, neatly boxed. Hammer picked it up, took a sip of the wine, stood up and said, "We'll have it for dessert on the plane." And off he and Frances sped to Newark, where the Oxy jet would resume its briefly interrupted flight to Paris for further negotiations with Russian and Japanese officials on the proposed multibillion-dollar liquefied natural-gas deal.

Two weeks later he was back on his familiar perch on Capitol Hill—a witness chair. He may have needed to glance at the name of this particular Congressional panel—"The Special Subcommittee on Integrated Oil Operations of the Committee on Interior and Insular Affairs." But he needed no prompting to begin his appearance by saying cheerfully, "Good morning. My name is Armand Hammer. I am chairman of the board and chief executive officer of Occidental Petroleum." How many times in his life had he prefaced his testimony with that salutation?

But this time was not like any of his previous experiences, he told Senators Floyd K. Haskell (Democrat, Colorado), Gaylord Nelson (Democrat, Wyoming), Dewey Bartlett (Republican, Oklahoma), and Howard Metzenbaum (Democrat, Ohio).

"I believe these hearings are of greater national importance than any in which I have previously participated," he said with the resolution of a musket-bearing pioneer protecting his plot of prairie land.

"The freedom and independence of Occidental Petroleum is at stake," he went on, warming up. "This is a matter of vital importance to our three hundred thousand shareholders, to our thirty-two thousand employees, and to the many companies, large and small, with whom we deal in the free marketplace.

"If Occidental falls into the hands of one of the major oil companies, then the American people will have lost the largest independent energy company and, with it, a strong champion of competition in the world of oil, coal, chemicals, fertilizers, and international trade.

"What Standard is embarked on is conquest, plain and simple, conquest insidious to its anticompetitive consequences and overwhelming in its economic implications, a conquest which is an unprecedented challenge to the antitrust policies of the United States. If Standard succeeds, it will accomplish the largest corporate seizure ever consummated in the United States—and a message will reverberate through every competitive zone of American business: Free enterprise and independence are dead!

"If Standard can so arrogantly pull this off, then how can any businessman consider himself safe? Standard apparently believes they can accomplish their monopolistic drive because no power can stop them. I say this time they can be stopped. I say that Occidental's management and shareholders will stop them. I say that our government will stop them, not because it defends Occidental but because I believe the laws of our land are designed to halt rapacious takeovers!"

Swearingen, a graying South Carolinian who looked more like a Senator than the real ones in the room, looked pained. His remarks in response to Hammer's charges suggested chagrin rather than discordant rebuttal. He said he found it difficult to understand Hammer's or anybody else's fear of bigness. He had said on another occasion that integration of oil operations, from exploration through to pumping gas at the corner station, would be good for the country. Those who opposed his view, he added, displayed "economic know-nothingism on a par with Chairman Mao's injunction to the Chinese to make steel in backyard furnaces."

He told the subcommittee that he was astounded by the angry intransigence of a company whose financial picture did not compare well with Indiana Standard's. "Capital expenditures of Occidental dropped from $344 million in 1969 to $199 million last year in comparison to Standard's increase in the same period from $700 million to $901 million. We are of the opinion that Standard's management and financial resources can bring about a more rapid and efficient utilization of Occidental's energy resources."

That hurt the feelings of the man who had built Oxy from a faceless $34,000 company with three employees and a few fading wells to a complex which Hammer had described to the Senators as approaching

"$6 billion in revenues and an after-tax profit this year [1974] of almost $300 million."

Swearingen had his last word:

"We believe that a possible Standard–Occidental consolidation would have substantial advantages without any discernible adverse effect on the public interest."

Swearingen's opinion was apparently not shared by many Senators, nor by the Federal Trade Commission, which immediately prepared for lengthy hearings and possible antitrust action.

But as suddenly as it began it ended.

In a terse announcement following a board-of-directors meeting in Chicago, Indiana Standard called it quits. As *Forbes* magazine predicted: "Hammer in the first round by a knockout."

United Press International carried it this way:

STANDARD OF INDIANA DROPS OCCIDENTAL BID. Chicago (UPI)—Standard Oil Co. of Indiana announced its directors decided to call off the attempt to acquire control of Occidental Petroleum Corp.

Occidental's chairman, Dr. Armand Hammer, has been vigorously resisting the Indiana Standard merger proposal, saying the Indiana company's offer was not adequate and that a merger between the two companies would violate antitrust laws.

Occidental also filed suit in federal court in Los Angeles to bar any takeover bid by Indiana Standard.

Chairman John E. Swearingen of Indiana Standard made no bones of the fact that he was interested in getting control of Occidental's Island Creek Coal Co. and to benefit by the big fertilizer deal Dr. Hammer negotiated with the Soviet Union in 1973.

The *Wall Street Journal,* in a longer story, also reported that, on this very day when Indiana Standard's directors had voted against continuing the fight, the doctor had impressed the New York Oil Analysts group in a luncheon speech, stating that Oxy's oil earnings had surged and the company was in better shape than it had been in years.

So was the good doctor.

Until something else traumatic occurs, as it is prone to do in the remarkable life of Armand Hammer, he is at peace with the world of giants into which he ventured a generation ago when he had every intention of retiring. He has defeated a Goliath's best efforts to dethrone him.

The next colossus that tries to put him in golden bondage will have to offer more than Swearingen did—perhaps $100 a share. Perhaps best of all, in Hammer's eyes, is that Wall Street, the S.E.C, and other establishments that have frowned at times on his colorful stewardship of Occidental now at long last show a grudging admiration for the most versatile tycoon of our times.

Epilogue

It is not easy or sensible to close a book about Armand Hammer. There were several times during the preparation of this biography when the author felt that all the salient facets of Hammer's many lives had been sufficiently buffed and it was best, then and there, to bring matters to a close. But on each occasion, the doctor bounded back with some new enterprise, some special vision or battle that demanded inclusion in the events and diagnoses of his immense interests.

For example, the press has carried a story recently that Hammer and the I.R.S. are opponents in a quarrelsome suit over whether he has paid sufficient taxes on gifts to museums from his art collection. This dispute revolved about the varying opinions of different experts over the value of the paintings but has now been resolved by a compromise and is awaiting final approval. Even more attention has been given recently to an investigation of an alleged charge of an illegal political contribution to President Nixon's 1972 campaign. It concerns a personal cash contribution given by Hammer to the ex-Governor of Montana, Tim Babcock, formerly an executive vice-president of Occidental International Corporation, to be delivered to Maurice Stans for the Committee to Re-Elect the President. Hammer says he gave the money to Babcock before April 7, when a new law went into effect, in order that it could be anonymous, "as I've always made my political contributions going back to the days of President Roosevelt." Babcock did not deliver the money until some months later, Hammer states. So the doctor faces the possibility of a charge of making a contribution in the name of another, which is forbidden by the new law.

Based on Hammer's past record, he will fight this and anything else that comes along. He's indefatigable.

At three score and sixteen, Hammer remains unique in a disarming number of fields of endeavor ranging from Lenin to Leonid, Roosevelt to Ford, one-horse shay to 12,000 pound thrust jet, shah to sheikh, Lower East Side to Lagos, not to mention Memphis to Mobile to Modigliani. This man, who tried to retire many years ago, has no scheduled termination point for his vigorous activities. His days and nights are almost monastically dedicated to improving the strength of the corporations he heads, expanding their yields, escalating the value of the stock. There can be no rest for him. As he once remarked to Arthur Groman, "I guess I must be a pretty tough old bird." Audubon never saw a tougher one.

No ploy by friend or foe seems likely to dethrone the doctor or stay his hand from the swift completion of his appointed corporate rounds. He is Oxy; Oxy is he. The middle 1970s are tailor-made for him because they present relentless foreign and domestic challenges of the kind that he has aggressively overcome for decades. Every sign indicates he will be around and kicking and working and dreaming until countries throughout the world have enough cheap fertilizers to raise all the food needed to feed their people and oil once more flows unabashedly, and until coal, shale, waste, and sun and tides divest themselves of their torrents of energy.

. . . And then he can spare a few days to write his autobiography.

References to Armand Hammer in Papers and Correspondence of V. I. Lenin

THE INSTITUTE OF MARX-LENIN OF THE
CENTRAL COMMITTEE OF THE COMMUNIST
PARTY OF THE SOVIET UNION

VOLUMES 45, 53, 54, AND 37

NOVEMBER 1920–MARCH 1923

MOSCOW 1967

THE INSTITUTE OF MARX-LENIN OF THE
CENTRAL COMMITTEE OF THE COMMUNIST
PARTY OF THE SOVIET UNION

VOLUME 45

LETTERS

439

TO THE MEMBERS OF THE CENTRAL COMMITTEE
OF THE RUSSIAN COMMUNIST PARTY (B)

For the information of all members of the Central Committee

Reinstein informed me yesterday that the American millionaire Hammer, of Russian birth (who sits in prison, accused of illegally performing an abortion, but in reality because of communism), is giving a million poods of bread to the Ural workers on very profitable terms (5 percent) and is accepting in return Ural valuables on commission for sale in America.

In Russia is the son (and partner) of this Hammer, a physician, who brought Semashko a gift of surgical instruments of $60,000. This son was in the Urals with Martens and decided to help rehabilitate the Ural industry.

An official report will be made immediately by Martens. 14/X

LENIN

(Handwritten October 14, 1921)

PAGE 274

441

TO L. K. MARTENS

15X

COMRADE MARTENS!

Is it not possible to interest Hammer (about whom Reinstein spoke to me) so that he would assume financing the Rutgers group for the saving of the Urals, by joining that group? In addition we could add four American businessmen.

Answer me about this as soon as possible.

Secondly, is it possible to interest Hammer in the plan for electrifying the Urals so that Hammer would not only supply bread, but also electrical equipment (as a loan, of course).

The Rutgers plan needs to be improved (maybe it is possible to do this through Hammer), and not simply be discarded.

With Communist greetings,
LENIN

(Handwritten October 15, 1921)

PAGE 282

451

TO L. K. MARTENS

COMRADE MARTENS!

If Hammer's plan to give one million poods to the Urals is serious (and from your letter I get the impression that your written confirmation of Reinstein's words enables one to consider this plan serious and not just hot air), then you must strive to give this the legal form of a concession agreement.

Let it be a concession even if it is not a genuine one (asbestos or other Ural valuables or what have you). It is important that we show and publicize (of course, only after the start of operations) that Americans have embarked on concessions. It is politically important. Reply.

With Communist greetings,
LENIN

(Handwritten October 19, 1921)

PAGE 290

464

(REMARKS ON THE WRITTEN REPORT
AND LETTER OF G. V. CICHERIN*)

It is exceedingly important for us to have concession agreements with Americans: with Hoover we have nothing. With Hammer we are close to an agreement. Amrruss is proceeding.

It is necessary to do all possible (you especially) to get rid of the friction (unfortunate and injurious) between Litvinov and Martens.

Yours,
LENIN

(Handwritten October 22, 1921)

*Minister of Foreign Affairs.

Appendixes

page 297

473

TO L. K. MARTENS

COPY TO COMRADE BOGDANOV*

27.X.1921

COMRADE MARTENS!

I received both contracts. I am returning them.

Why weren't the additional points put in which were shown to me (in draft form) by Reinstein and Hammer?

We must re-edit them and put them in the agreement.

We must give careful attention that we punctiliously and factually carry out our word.

Do not rely on giving orders! Unless we verify everything personally and supervise same, nothing will be done well.

We must name someone with ability to be personally responsible for carrying out everything.

We must give every consideration to the desires of concessionaires: This is economically and politically of great importance.

Keep me informed of the measures you or the Council of National Economy are taking.

> Chairman of the Soviet Council of Ministers
> V. ULIANOV (Lenin)

P.S.   It is important to clarify how we shall publicize this. There is much to be said to giving wide publicity to this concession and agreement.

(Handwritten October 27, 1921)

*President of the Council of National Economy.

PAGE 298

474

474

TO I. I. RADCHENKO*

27.X.1921

246

COMRADE RADCHENKO!

Comrade Martens sent me your signed copy of the agreement with the American company (Hammer and Mishel).

It appears to me that this agreement has tremendous significance as the beginning of trade.

It is absolutely necessary that you pay strict attention to the factual carrying out of our obligations.

I am sure that without intensive pressure and attention not a thing will be done. Take steps to carefully check and verify the execution of this agreement.

Keep me informed who you are appointing to be responsible for carrying this out; what kind of goods you are preparing, paying special attention that the goods are artistic and of good quality, etc.

2–3 times a month give me an accounting: what is being sent to the port.

> Chairman of the Soviet
> Council of Ministers
> V. ULIANOV (Lenin)

P.S. 25.XII.1921 Is the shipment due in Petrograd? Isn't that late?

(Handwritten October 27, 1921)

*Minister of Foreign Trade.

PAGE 303

482

TO ARMAND HAMMER

3.XI.1921

DEAR MR. HAMMER!

Comrade Reinstein informed me that you are leaving Moscow this evening. I am very sorry that I am busy with a meeting of the Central Committee of our party. I am extremely sorry that I cannot see you again and greet you.

Please be kind enough to give my regards to your father, to Jimmy Larkin, Rutenberg and Ferguson, all splendid comrades now in American prison. To all of them—my warmest sympathy and best wishes.

247

Once more, kind regards to you and your friends in connection with your concession. This beginning is extremely important. I hope it will be the beginning of great significance.

With all best wishes,
Sincerely yours,
LENIN

P.S.   Please excuse me for my extremely bad English.

(Handwritten November 3, 1921)
(This appeared first in the Russian press in English and Russian [facsimile] January 21, 1926, in the *Krasnoya Gazeta*, no. 17.)

PAGE 344

REQUESTS OF THE MINISTRIES IN CONNECTION WITH PREPARING THE REPORT ON THE ALL RUSSIA CENTRAL COMMITTEE AND THE COUNCIL OF MINISTRIES FOR THE 9TH ALL RUSSIA CONGRESS OF SOVIETS.

COMRADE BOGDANOV!
I request that you inform me for my report to the Congress of Soviets in very brief form (not more than ½–1 page), information regarding help to the Urals (the Hammer concession).

LENIN

December 17, 1921

PAGE 454

691

TO A. I. RYKOV*

COMRADE RYKOV

COPY TO COMRADE TSOUROPA*

COPIES TO THE MINISTRIES OF THE
COUNCIL OF THE PEOPLE'S COMMISSARS

I call your attention to the American concessionaire Hammer, now in Russia, about whom I have been advised personally by Reinstein.

According to Martens' words, we were embarrassed by the fact that the goods sent by the Ministry of Foreign Trade to America under the agreement with Hammer were of second quality. It is important to request information about this from the Ministry of Foreign Trade, also the Council of National Economy, as well as from Comrade Reinstein, who knows Hammer personally. It is necessary to exert all efforts to carry out our obligations under the concession fully and accurately and in general pay strict attention to the execution of these matters.

LENIN

(Dictated over the telephone April 5, 1922)

*Deputy chairmen of the Soviet Council of Ministers.

PAGE 473

723

TO ARMAND HAMMER

11.V.1922

Dear Comrade Hammer!

Excuse me please, I have been very sick, but now I am much better.

Thank you very much for your present—the kind letter from American comrades and friends now in prison. I enclose a letter for Comrade Zinoviev or other Petrograd comrades if Zinoviev has left Petrograd.

My very best wishes for the success of your first concession. This success will have tremendous significance for the development of trade between our republic and the United States.

I thank you once again and ask you to excuse my poor English. Please address letters and telegrams to my secretaries (Fotieva and Smolianinov). I shall inform them.

Sincerely yours,
LENIN

(Handwritten May 11, 1922)
(Translated from English)

Appendixes

PAGE 474

724

TO L. A. FOTIEVA AND V. A. SMOLIANINOV

FOTIEVA AND SMOLIANINOV:

Translate the above, read it and write down the name of Hammer and help him in every way in my name whenever he calls on you.

11/V LENIN

(Handwritten May 11, 1922)

PAGE 474

725

TO G. E. ZINOVIEV

1

11.V.1922

TO COMRADE ZINOVIEV OR HIS DEPUTY

PETROGRAD

(TO COMRADE ZINOVIEV OR HIS DEPUTY) (IN ENGLISH)

(In English)
I beg you to help the comrade Armand Hammer; it is extremely important for us that his first concession would be a full success.

Yours,
LENIN

(Handwritten May 11, 1922)
(The same written in Russian)

PAGE 475

725

2

11.V.1922

Today I wrote a letter of recommendation to you or your deputy for Comrade Armand Hammer. His father—millionaire, Communist (is in prison in America). He obtained from us the first concession which is very profitable for us. He is leaving for Petrograd to be present at the unloading of the first ship to arrive in Petrograd with wheat and arrange for the receiving of machines for his concession (an asbestos mine).

I ask that you immediately give instructions so that there will be no delay due to red tape and to see personally that the work is carried out quickly for this concession. It is extremely important. Armand Hammer is traveling with the director of his company, Mishel (Mr. Mishel).

LENIN

(Handwritten May 11, 1922)

PAGE 489

746

TO I. V. STALIN FOR MEMBERS OF THE POLITBURO
OF THE CENTRAL COMMITTEE OF THE RUSSIAN
COMMUNIST PARTY

URGENT.
SECRET.

Comrade Stalin, you are requested to circulate this to all members of the Central Committee (and especially include Comrade Zinoviev).

On the basis of information from Comrade Reinstein, I am giving Armand Hammer and B. Mishel special recommendations from me and I ask all members of the Central Committee to fully support these persons and their enterprise. This is a small road to the American "business" world and we must do everything possible to utilize this path. If you have any objections, I ask that you inform my secretary by telephone (Fotieva or Lepeshinsky) so that I can clear up any matters (and carry them through the Politburo in final form) before my departure, that is immediately.

24/V. (1922)   LENIN

P.S.   27/V. I have held this up until I received the reply from Comrade Zinoviev. I received his reply on 26/V.

                                                     LENIN

(Handwritten May 24 and May 27, 1922)

THE INSTITUTE OF MARX-LENIN OF THE
CENTRAL COMMITTEE OF THE COMMUNIST
PARTY OF THE SOVIET UNION

VOLUME 53

LETTERS

JUNE–NOVEMBER 1921

428

NOTE TO THE SECRETARIAT

Moscow, 1970
    Reinstein asks, was the agreement signed by Hammer's colleague and when will I receive the agreement and the draft of the additional decree from STO [Council of Labor and Defense].

                                                     (Lenin)

(Handwritten sometime between October 14 and 24, 1921)

483

TO V. V. KUYBISHEV

Comrade Kuybishev!

I send you a copy of a telephonogram from Comrade Reinstein to me.

Under par. 3 give me a memo please, how you finished with Rutgers.

Do you have the text of the agreement?

It is necessary to send it to me at once.

Under par. 1, the matter is extremely urgent. I request you show this to Bogdanov and give me his (and if necessary also your) view: what is the obstacle?

We must finish with Hammer and close the concession agreement.

With Communist regards,
LENIN

(Handwritten October 24, 1921)

THE INSTITUTE OF MARX-LENIN OF THE
CENTRAL COMMITTEE OF THE COMMUNIST
PARTY OF THE SOVIET UNION

VOLUME 54

LETTERS

NOVEMBER 1921–MARCH 1923

44

MOSCOW, 1965

TO L. K. MARTENS

To Comrade Martens   Urgent

Comrade Martens! Notify Petrograd and the Foreign Trade Department without fail. Without intensive follow-up not a damn thing will be ready and we'll find ourselves in a scandal.

Place the matter before STO [Council of Labor and Defense] and MCNX [Moscow Soviet of National Economy] regarding measures to be taken.

17/XI Lenin

(Handwritten November 17, 1921)

116

To N. P. Gorbunov*

Reinstein will give you a telephonogram about preparing a paper [of assistance] to Hammer's representative.

It is necessary to help him.

Write it up and if necessary put my signature on it.

6/XII Lenin

(Handwritten December 6, 1921)

*Assistant to Lenin.

TO G. E. ZINOVIEV

22.V.1922

Comrade Zinoviev!

Today Reinstein showed me a letter from Armand Hammer, about whom I wrote you (an American, son of a millionaire, among the first to take a concession from us—extremely profitable for us). He writes that in spite of my letter, his colleague Mishel (colleague of Hammer) bitterly complains about the rudeness and bureaucracy of Begge, who received him in Petrograd.

I will complain about Begge's conduct to the Central Committee. This is an outrage. In spite of my letter to you and your deputy, things were done just the opposite.

And nobody informed me about this, neither about disagreeing with me, or anything.

I ask you to verify this and give this matter special attention.

Was my letter (my telephonogram) to you or your deputy brought to the attention of Begge? If so, Begge is responsible. If not, your secretary or somebody is.

Who is responsible? It is necessary to find out. Can you bring pressure on Begge and clean up the matter?

LENIN

(Handwritten May 22, 1922)

THE INSTITUTE OF MARX-LENIN OF THE
CENTRAL COMMITTEE OF THE COMMUNIST
PARTY OF THE SOVIET UNION

VOLUME 37

MOSCOW, 1970   PAGE 365

RECOMMENDATION TO A. J. HAMMER
AND INSTRUCTIONS TO MY SECRETARY[1]

The bearer, Dr. Armand Julius *Hammer*, is the secretary of the Allied American Corporation—the first stock company to receive from us a concession, namely, the one for the asbestos mines in the Urals. This firm has also a contract for supplying to Russia a quantity of grain in exchange for Russian goods and it has also the exclusive agency for Russia for automobiles, trucks and tractors of the Ford Motor Company, as well as for the agricultural implements of the Moline Plow Company, etc.

The Allied American Company is to be distinguished from the usual capitalist companies in that it is well disposed toward the Soviet Union and we are very much interested to see that this company has every assistance for successfully carrying out its efforts.

I therefore urgently request all representatives in the Foreign Trade Department, the Railroad Administration and all other representatives of the Soviet Government in Russia and abroad to render the representatives of this company not only full consideration and complete attention and courtesies, but also every possible assistance, removing all unnecessary formalities, etc.

24/V (1922) LENIN

[1]The instructions to the secretary as drafts of recommendations for A. J. Hammer (the draft was put together with the help of B. I. Reinstein).

Armand Hammer—secretary of the American company, Allied Chemical and Drug Com-

Appendixes

[Note] Lydia Aleksandrovna [Fotieva]!
Type this exactly as written in duplicate.
Make two copies of this mandate.
Also in English and make 2–3 extra copies.
27/V 1922

---

pany, received in 1921 from the Soviet government a concession for the operation of an asbestos mine in the Urals.

A recommendation with similar contents was given to the representative of the company, the general manager for the American concession "Alamerico" in the Soviet Union, B. O. Mishel.

24 May 1922 V. I. Lenin, in a letter to I. V. Stalin, for the members of the Politburo of the Central Committee of the Russian Communist Party (b), wrote that he was giving A. J. Hammer and B. O. Mishel letters of recommendation and asked to be informed if there was any objections (see *V. I. Lenin, Letters and Documents*, Volume 54, page 272).

For other references to Hammer's concessions, see also *V. I. Lenin, Letters and Documents*, Volume 53, pages 267, 324; Volume 54, pages 61, 79, 252, 253–254, 270–271.

Letters of Governor Alfred E. Smith and Ambassador James Gerard Regarding Dr. Julius Hammer

APRIL 30TH 1943

BOARD OF REGENTS

ALBANY, NEW YORK

Gentlemen:

It has been called to my attention that Dr. Julius Hammer is applying to be reinstated in the practise of medicine. On November 12th 1924 as Governor of the State of New York, I granted a pardon to Dr. Hammer who had been convicted on a charge of manslaughter in the County of Bronx. The Pardon Board made a thorough investigation, at that time, of his case and all the facts brought up strongly suggested that he was entitled to a pardon for the purpose of restoring his citizenship, he having served the full period of his minimum sentence. His application for restoration to citizenship was backed by a large number of prominent people including a number of doctors. An examination quite clearly showed that he had no criminal intent. My recollection is that his application was opposed by the then District Attorney but investigation did not bear out any of their accusations regarding Dr. Hammer's character and previous reputation.

I feel perfectly free and safe in recommending that he be reinstated to the practice of medicine.

Very truly yours,
ALFRED E. SMITH

257

MARCH 19, 1943

THE HONOURABLE

THE BOARD OF REGENTS,

ALBANY,

NEW YORK.

Gentlemen:

I am retired from the practice of the law but in 1921 I was in partnership with the late Judge Francis M. Scott who had been for years a judge of the Appellate Division before resigning from the Bench in order to go into partnership with me.

Judge Scott argued the appeal in the case of The People against Julius Hammer which case had been tried in June, 1920.

When Judge Scott had been retained to argue this appeal, I happened to ask him why he had taken up this case which, as it was a criminal case, was not in our line of general practice. He told me that he had done so because after examining into the case he felt that there had been no guilty intent on the part of Dr. Hammer, the defendent, and that he felt that an innocent man had been convicted. He asked me to look over the papers, which I did, and came to the same conclusion.

I know Dr. Hammer's sons and know that they have a fine position in the business world of New York and I also believe that the restoration of Dr. Hammer to practice would be of great benefit at this time when there is such a need of skilled medical work.

Yours very sincerely,
JAMES W. GERARD

Armand personally appeared before the board and his eloquent plea was a deciding factor in the case. Julius Hammer was reinstated by the board in an unprecedented unanimous action. The doctor returned with a clean bill of health to the practice of medicine, which he pursued in an office on West 54th Street, Manhattan, as a general practioner, like an old country doctor until his death from a heart attack in 1948.

Statement by Dr. Armand Hammer for the Angus Cattle Dissolution Catalog

August 13th, 1953, was a day of great loss for Shadow Isle. Perhaps it would be more fitting to say it was a day of great loss for the entire Angus breed. On the morning of that day Prince Eric of Sunbeam was found dead in his paddock. The cause as determined by autopsy was an internal hemorrhage caused presumably by a sudden increase in blood pressure from undue excitement. There were some heifers in heat in the adjoining paddock and there was evidence that Prince Eric had tried to knock down his fence to get to them. He had been actively breeding until the day of his death. A veterinarian for Lloyds of London, who insured the bull's life even though he was almost eleven years of age, found in the autopsy that his organs contained an ample amount of live spermatozoa. Except for a short period when Prince Eric was not used because of an inflamed stifle joint, the "Bull of the Century" proved to be the most consistent breeder of all the bulls used at Shadow Isle. Fortunately at the time of his death, a large part of our brood cow herd was safe in calf to his service. All these calves are selling in this sale. Some have been weaned but most are at the side of their dams. How many future champions there are among these calves, only time will tell.

Forget, if you wish, his pedigree; forget his commendable show record, too, if you like; forget to recognize his excellent individual type and conformation, his top quality, his shortness of leg, his masculinity, but, DO NOT FORGET HIS CONSISTENTLY IMPRESSIVE BREEDING RECORD. In other words, judge Prince Eric solely upon his get in the show ring and in the breeding pen.

Sold as a calf at $40,000, Prince Eric of Sunbeam made money for Ralph L. Smith. He made money for L. L. O'Bryan. He paid for himself and made money for us, even though it required an investment of $100,000 to obtain him for Shadow Isle. His get in our 1951 sale averaged over $10,000. In our fall 1952 production sale 4 of Prince Eric's sons averaged $9,125 and 10 of his daughters averaged $7,330. In our All Prince Eric spring, 1952, cow and calf sale 100 lots carrying his service averaged $4,793. In our 1952 fall sale 170 lots averaged $4,705.58. In our spring 1953 sale 100 lots averaged $4,451. Two daughters of Prince Eric sold in this sale for $15,900 and $31,500 respectively. In our 1953 fall production sale 62 lots sold for an average of $4,150. These five sales totaled $2,454,800 and we attribute the major part of this huge income to the service of Prince Eric.

Due to the 1947 dispersion sale of the Ralph L. Smith herd, the get of Prince Eric was thrown to the four winds, so to state. Despite differences in handling, in care, and in fitting, these calves, those at side and those in dam, have made most commendable show records. His sons have made good breeding records. His daughters are proving excellent investments as producing cows. But, back to the show record of his get. We mention the international winnings, only. We do that because the international is more or less considered the "supreme court" in the show world. If we had the time or the space, we could likely compose quite a story on his record as a sire of champions at major shows. Starting with the 1949 International, Prince Eric of Sunbeam has been the sire to watch and with whom to reckon in anticipating the results of the great show. At the 1949 International his son, Prince Eric Esquire, a "Show Window" sale bull, came on from Adams Plantation in Virginia, after winning many awards in Eastern competition to cause some major excitement and wind up being named Reserve Grand Champion of the show. At the same show, the same year, Blackcap of R.L.S. 8th, also a consistent winner at major Eastern shows, was made International Reserve Senior Champion. At the 1950 event, two Prince Eric daughters, a Georgina and a Blackbird, stood one, two in class, for Senior Champion and for Grand Champion—and many were present who would state that either of the two would have been a most worthy champion. Well, they were, the Georgina, owned by Blackpost, was Grand Champion, and our heifer, the Blackbird, was

International Reserve Grand Champion. Certainly, Prince Eric of Sunbeam made history in 1950. Again, in 1951, and at the International, it was a daughter of Prince Eric that the judges selected for a class winner, a Senior Champion and the 1951 International Grand Champion. This heifer, Empress of Shadow Isle, was and is owned by General L. J. Sverdrup of Hillside Farm, Washington, Missouri. The heifer was purchased by the General in our 1951 sale at $21,000 and we exhibited her to the Grand Championship at Chicago. At the 1952 International our show string was made up principally of young calves by Prince Eric. They proved to be a sensation, winning three blue ribbons including the coveted Junior Get of Sire. In the bull class two junior Prince Eric calves won First and Second prizes. In the heifer classes two junior Prince Eric calves stood First and Third. A junior heifer calf sired by Prince Eric and exhibited by John Mecom was made First Prize winner and Reserve Grand Champion female at the 1953 Houston show, and again at the 1954 Denver show.

In 1953 another daughter of Prince Eric, Shadow Isle Black Jestress 2d, made a sensational record, being Grand Champion at every major show in the country where exhibited including the International. She had been purchased with her dam at our 1953 cow and calf sale for $31,500 by Ralph L. Smith, by whom she was shown. This investment paid off handsomely for Mr. Smith. The cow was rebred to Prince Eric and now has another heifer who George Cooper considers equally as good as her champion sister. This makes six International Champions sired by Prince Eric including the 1950, 1951 and 1953 International Grand Champion females.

A study of some of the comments regarding Prince Eric by breeders from all parts of the country reveals one thing only—that he is, unquestionably, the "Bull of the Century," the sire of profit-makers, show winners and great producers.

When we offered 100 cows mated to him in our 1952 Spring sale, we think the breeders themselves set their own appraisal on the service of Prince Eric when these 100 cows, 20 with calves at side, sold for $479,000 with no extreme top other than one sold for $27,100 with bull calf at side and one for $15,000 with heifer calf at side. We also think the fact that over two million dollars worth of cattle carrying the service of this bull were sold at auction and at private treaty in one year is proof of the breeders' stamp of approval of Prince Eric of Sunbeam. Prince Eric had that rare, and indeed, most valuable faculty of "nicking" with most any strain of breeding to produce better Aberdeen-Angus cattle. Prince Eric, more than any bull of any breed about which we have been able to learn, earned through the uniformity of his calves, the right to universal recognition as the incomparable sire. In our 1953 Fall production sale 18 daughters of Prince Eric averaged $5,050, 2 granddaughters averaged $6,500 and 4 sons averaged $7,228. Over 50 of his sons (counting calves) and over 100 of his daughters sell in this sale.

For the stated opinions of many others, read what many breeders have to say about Prince Eric. Their statements are to be found in this sale catalog.

And, may we state, with pride and confidence, pride that comes from confidence that your herd can be improved with the sons and daughters of Prince Eric of Sunbeam, that we believe the purchase of his get in this sale is the best investment anyone could make in the Angus business.

A Play-by-Play Account of the Oxy
Stock Action in July 1972

July 3, 5, 6	Stock at 10⅛. Normal for general Oxy stock action. Went up an eighth but back to 10⅛ July 11th.
July 12	Announced first oil discovery in joint venture with Nigerian government. Stock went up to 11⅝. Average volume from July 3 to 11 was about 33,000 shares a day. Volume of July 12 was 255,600. Stock stayed same price on July 13, volume was 123,700.
July 14	Up to 11⅞ on volume of 78,900.
July 17	Announced second discovery in Nigeria. Stock up to 12¾ on volume of 162,000.
July 18	Announced five-year scientific-technical agreement with the Soviet Union. Stock up to 15½ on volume of 1,118,900, one of the heaviest trading days in the history of the Exchange for a single stock.
July 19	Stock up to 18¼ on volume of 1,411,300. Trading suspended because of inability to keep up with demands.
July 20	Heaviest single day for any share in history of the New York Stock Exchange. Trading halted for hours. Volume was 2,330,100. Down to 16⅞ as details of Russian agreement were studied and realization came that balance sheet would not be affected for years. Peterson interview, also unfavorable article in Barron's.
July 24	Down to 14⅝ on volume of 502,000. Stayed in range for a month and then slowly declined.

The Doctor vs. Paul Richard

Excerpts from article by Paul Richard which appeared in March 28, 1970, edition of the Washington *Post.*

AN EXHIBITION OF LOSERS BY MAJOR MASTERS

The night the Armand Hammer Collection opened at the Smithsonian Institution, three women, all in evening gowns, stood between the Rubens portrait and the Rembrandt, scornfully condemning the pictures on display.

Their derisive comments, and those of other guests, sent hints of fraud and forgery drifting through the room.

Until then the evening had been glittering. Dinner had been served amid giant diamonds, sapphires and rubies in the Smithsonian's hall of gems, and then Dr. Armand Hammer—oilman and billionaire and omnivorous collector—had given every dinner guest a polished hunk of jade, but now the women sneered and snickered at the paintings on the walls.

"Never have I seen," said one, "a public exhibition with quite so many fakes."

She spoke with great assurance, but with no evidence at all. Though slick forgeries are daily sold to rich, naive collectors, these are not that sort of pictures and Dr. Armand Hammer is not that sort of man.

He had been buying expensive European paintings for almost half a century and the first collection he assembled, heavy with old masters, was accepted by the University of Southern California in 1965. He is a trustee of the Los Angeles County Museum of Art and five paintings that he bought for the museum, a Rubens, a Renoir, the Rembrandt, the Sargent and the Modigliani, are hanging in this show. His brother, Victor Hammer, operates a commercial gallery in New York.

Men with Dr. Hammer's money and connections do not often do their buying without the benefit of scholarly advice.

It is not surprising, therefore, that almost all the works on view are well documented paintings; the standard texts discuss them and their histories are known. The dark gossip that one hears is groundless. The authenticity of these paintings, in almost every case, has been established beyond doubt.

Yet the poisonous rumors will not fade. There is a reason for their persistence.

The Armand Hammer Collection may boast authentic pictures by the very biggest names but never have so many major masters been represented in this city by canvases so poor.

The Goya here is trivial, the van Gogh here is ugly, and the Cezanne landscape on display is a thoroughly botched up job. There are some handsome pictures in this show but they are heavily outnumbered by the losers on the walls. . . .

There are other equally off-hand pictures in this show. Neither "The Israelites Gathering Manna in the Desert" of Rubens, nor Goya's "El Pelele" were made for exhibition. Both are sketches for cartoons from which tapestries were made. . . .

First-rate artists, like other people, have some lousy days and produce some lousy work. When Dr. Hammer began assembling his 96-item collection (less than five years ago), masterpieces by the blue-chip painters he prefers were already hard to come by. Museums and collectors—with funds that were just about unlimited—had long been combing available supplies. Dr. Hammer bought works the best of them turned down.

Dr. Hammer, who has lots of money and is not afraid to spend it, bid —unsuccessfully—for the van Gogh "Cypresses" that was sold at auction earlier this year.

"Fortunately, I have a van Gogh of that period in the catalogue," he says.

His, however, is not fine as the one that got away. "Cypresses," an oil of 1889, went for $1.3 million. "The Sower," the 1888 picture that Dr. Hammer owns, was sold last May at Christie's for $1.1 million less than that. . . .

After it [the exhibition] closes here on April 30 it will travel to Kansas City, New Orleans, Little Rock and Columbus, Ohio. It will not be seen at the Los Angeles museum that Dr. Hammer serves as benefactor and trustee.

No major American museum—except, of course, the Smithsonian Institution—has agreed to take this show.

You would never know it from the catalogue. Rare indeed the small time exhibition that is accompanied by a book so lavish. Every painting is reproduced in color, one picture to a page.

That catalogue was extraordinarily expensive. Dr. Hammer paid for it himself. Those who feel he did so just to stroke his ego should realize he did not make a billion dollars by playing self-indulgent games. . . .

It begins with a statement by Dr. Hammer in which he lists the Freer Gallery of Art, the Joseph H. Hirshhorn Museum and Sculpture Garden, the National Gallery of Art, the Smithsonian Institution.

After thanking "the dedicated men who constitute The Establishment of this inspiring institution," Dr. Hammer enumerates the members of that largely honorary body. Their names appear besides his own in a list that begins as follows:

The Establishment
President of the U.S.
Vice President of the U.S.
Chief Justice of the U.S.
Secretary of State . . .

and so on and so on. The 27-name list ends with that of S. Dillon Ripley, Secretary of the Smithsonian Institution.

In his foreword, Ripley describes the Armand Hammer Collection as "superb" and adds that "it is a rare privilege" to see its artists "grouped as they are here."

When the exhibition opened, Dr. Hammer hinted broadly that the pictures on display might someday hang in a Washington museum. He has dropped similar hints in Memphis and Los Angeles.

"You get more pleasure from giving than receiving, isn't that right?" he asks.

Under the new tax law, a collector who holds a picture six months before he donates it to a museum may deduct its appreciated value up to an amount equal to 30 per cent of his adjusted gross income. The Smithsonian indicates that Dr. Hammer's is not small.

In 1957, a Smithsonian release relates, Dr. Hammer "took over the reins of a tiny, run-down oil company" with "a meager market value of $120,000." The Occidental Petroleum Company is today "a billion dollar concern."

Should Dr. Hammer eventually give his collection away, as he has often hinted, the Internal Revenue Service will have to make a determination of its value. The worth of this collection, in any case, has in no way been diminished by that grandiose catalogue, that imposing list of names, and the fact that S. Dillon Ripley regards it as "superb" and displayed it on the Mall.

REPLY BY ARMAND HAMMER

Many in the art world must have been surprised at the misinterpretations Mr. Paul Richard made in his review of my collection of paintings on exhibition at the Smithsonian Institution, published in the March 28 issue of The Washington Post.

Mr. Richard grudgingly admits, at the outset of the article, that there are some handsome works in the collection, but that they are heavily outweighed by the "losers." While he goes on to attack the "losers" by such intemperate remarks as "lousy work" by first-rate artists who have some "lousy days," he does not deign to mention the names of the "handsome works," much less to state why they are praiseworthy.

I am grateful, however, for his admission that the "dark gossip" about forgeries, which he attributes to some undisclosed source, is groundless and for his statement that the authenticity of the collection is established.

He attacks Mr. S. Dillon Ripley, secretary of the Smithsonian, for referring to the collection in the foreword as "superb," while he ignores Mr. Ripley's reference to the fact that particularly notable in the collection are the oil sketches by Goya, Rubens and Toulouse-Lautrec, "which allow us a glimpse of the artists' first thoughts."

If Mr. Richard were a competent art historian, he would understand that the uniqueness of the collection lies largely in the fact, as Mr. Ripley points out, that it shows the first thoughts of many of the great masters represented in the show, placing considerable emphasis on the artistic process in including oil studies and oil sketches for larger compositions, notebook sketches and drawings. The oil sketches—a predilection of only

267

the most sophisticated collectors—by Rubens, Fragonard, Goya and Toulouse-Lautrec, associates us with the artist in the first moment of creation
when he sets down his concept in the most personal, spontaneous manner.

The Gauguin sketchbook and additional drawings give us an insight
into the development of the artist during his most formative years. No
other private collection, for example, can boast of 268 sketches by Gauguin—landscapes, houses, animals and people, many of which were used
as the basis for Gauguin's masterpieces painted during his Brittany period.

Mr. John Rewald, the noted art historian, in the opening sentence of
his foreword to the book "Paul Gauguin, a Sketchbook," by Raymond
Cogniat, published by the Hammer Galleries, New York, 1962, states:
"With the exception of a somewhat larger sketchbook, filled primarily
with portrait studies and whose pages have been dispersed, and another
one, still unpublished, belonging to the Stockholm Museum, probably of
the years 1870–1880, this is the earliest of Gauguin's known sketch-
books."

Raymond Cogniat, discussing the importance of sketches by Gauguin,
states: "Thus we witness the origin, without any apparent order, of the
different elements which the painter synthesizes into final works. In many
cases we see the first outline, the first version and form of an idea. These
renderings are often done at random, but they reveal how the artist thinks
and works.

"Perhaps we experience the deepest emotion when we are confronted
by a rough draft, when a few strokes, at first illegible, suddenly become
comprehensible as they reappear in a finished painting. Poring over the
pages of this sketchbook, we have felt pleasure, the same joy that the
researcher experiences when he discovers the key to a problem."

Mr. Richard refers to the Goya oil sketch, "El Pelele," in the collection
as "trivial." I wonder if he has taken the trouble to read the explanatory
notes in the catalog before making this snap judgment. This oil sketch was
considered by experts as one of the gems in the collection of the late
Henry R. Luce, publisher of Fortune magazine and director of Time, Inc.,
and Ambassador Clare Boothe Luce, who acquired it from M. Knoedler
Co., Inc., one of the leading art dealers in the world. After Mr. Luce's
death I purchased practically their entire collection from Mrs. Luce at
close to $1 million, the price it was appraised at by Sotheby & Co., to
whom she was about to consign it for sale, presumably to settle the estate.
This oil sketch was painted by Goya in 1776 as one of a series of oil

paintings of Spanish life and was used as a cartoon for a tapestry executed in 1793, which hangs in the El Prado Museum in Madrid. Another version of this sketch for the Prado cartoon is in the collection of Mrs. R. H. Kress, the wife of the late illustrious art collector and patron. The Luce picture is considered by experts to be the artist's first concept of the subject.

This "trivial" oil sketch was exhibited in Madrid in May and June, 1949, by the Sociedad Española de Amigos del Arte and was included in the catalog prepared by the eminent Spanish art historian, F. J. Sanchez-Canton. It was also exhibited at the Yale University Art Gallery, May–June, 1956, and reproduced in the catalog. It is described in the book "Francisco de Goya" by the well-known authority on Spanish art, August L. Mayer, published in Munich in 1923.

Among other paintings from the Luce collection being shown in the Smithsonian exhibition is the "Madonna and Child Against a Rose Hedge," Italian 15th century. This is described by the greatest authority on the Italian Renaissance, Bernard Berenson, in his book "Italian Pictures of the Renaissance, Florentine School," London, 1963. Berenson selected this painting for Mrs. Luce in 1954 while she was United States Ambassador to Italy.

Another painting from the Luce collection in the show is the Fragonard "The Education of the Virgin," with a history and literature going back to 1806. It is reproduced as Plate No. 1 in the authoritative work "The Paintings of Fragonard," by the renowned art historian and dealer Georges Wildenstein, published in Paris, 1960.

Among other paintings from the Luce collection of the Smithsonian show is the Corot, "A Bend in the River with Houses and Poplars," reproduced in Alfred Robaut's "L'Oeuvre de Corot" (The Works of Corot) as No. 654, and purchased from the Knoedler firm.

Another Luce painting in the show is Renoir's "Roses," acquired from Knoedler's in 1952.

The Vuillard "At the Seashore" was acquired by the Luces from the highly regarded art dealer Sam Salz. This picture was exhibited at the Louvre in 1938 and in the New York Museum of Modern Art and the Cleveland Museum of Art in 1954. Also acquired by the Luces from Sam Salz is the Vuillard "Rue Lepic, Paris" which Mr. Richard belittles because it had 12 inches removed from the sky. This painting was one of a series of tall, narrow panels of streets of Paris designed by Vuillard for

269

the home of the French dramatist Henry Bernstein in 1908. Apparently neither Sam Salz nor the Luces thought the removal of the 12 inches of sky from the painting, which is 5 feet 5 inches tall and 18½ inches wide, destroyed its artistic value, because the artist's work is concentrated in the street scene below.

Two of the three Rouaults exhibited at the Smithsonian likewise come from the Luce collection—"Virgin and Child" and "Resurrection of Lazarus." They were originally from the collection of the renowned Paris collector Ambroise Vollard. The third painting, "Circus Girl," was originally in the collection of Ambroise Vollard, but later came from the Perls Gallery, the leading dealers in Rouault.

The Winston Churchill "Chartwell, Landscape with Sheep," was a gift to Henry R. Luce from Mr. Churchill and was exhibited in the Metropolitan Museum of Art in 1958. Churchill's paintings were never sold and are eagerly sought after by collectors. Presidents Eisenhower and Roosevelt treasured paintings given to them by Churchill.

Raoul Dufy's "Harbor at Deauville" was painted in 1929 and was acquired from Knoedler's by the Luces.

Marc Chagall's "Blue Angel" was acquired by the Luces from Frank Crowninshield and was exhibited in the Tokyo National Museum of Art in 1963 and the National Art Gallery of Kyoto in the same year. It is described and reproduced by Franz Meyer in his well-known book "Marc Chagall, Life and Work," published in 1964.

Assuming there may be among the 96 works of these great masters, one-half dozen or so of lesser importance, is that any reason to condemn the collection as Mr. Richard has attempted to do?

With regard to Mr. Richard's criticism of the van Gogh in the show as "ugly," I think van Gogh most likely would have taken this as a compliment, as he never tried to paint pretty pictures. Mr. Richard's expert opinion is undoubtedly colored by the fact that he took the trouble to look up the fact that I bought the painting at Christie's auction in London last May for $189,000, which he notes is $1,100,000 less than the van Gogh "Cypresses" was sold for recently and for which I was a bidder, up to $1 million. Every once in a while it is possible to get a "sleeper" at an auction. The van Gogh "The Sower" in my collection was just such a case. The picture was unknown until recently, having been purchased many years ago from the van Gogh family by the Rev. Theodore Pitcairn of Bryn Athyn, Pa., who had never exhibited it. Mr. Pitcairn is the same

·collector who, a few years ago, sold a Monet, "La Terrasse à Ste.-Adresse," at Parke-Bernet for $1,411,200 for the Metropolitan Museum for which he paid $28,000 in 1926. Because "The Sower" was unknown and was not published in any of the books of van Gogh's works, its authenticity was questioned by dealers and collectors, who therefore did not bid on it.

I took the trouble personally to investigate the background and history more thoroughly than just the brief statement that appeared in the catalog. I found out that Dr. Vincent van Gogh, the nephew of the artist, had written on February 10, 1969, to Christie's as follows: "In the notes of my mother there is a reference that, with other works, she sold in 1921 'Sower Against Purple Background' to the Montross Gallery, and she added that this was for Mr. Pitcairn, Bryn Athyn, Penn."

I obtained a photographic copy of this letter. This information was not published in the catalog. After I purchased the picture I was offered twice what I had paid for it by a dealer. I quote from the May 27, 1969, letter from one of the leading art dealers in Europe, Galerie Beyeler, Basel, Switzerland: "As you certainly heard in the meantime we were the underbidder on the van Gogh 'Sower' and I congratulate you for the purchase of this very outstanding work. I heard a lot of your selected collection and I am sure this van Gogh will fit well."

Recently I received a letter from Dr. A. M. Hammacher, of the Netherlands Institute for Art History, The Hague, dated January 5, 1970, as follows: "It took some time before I could confirm [to] you that indeed 'The Sower' appears in the revised edition of De la Faille's catalogue with a comment of the editors and the number 575a. It is probable but not quite certain that the catalogue will be available late 1970."

I am sure if all of this information had been known at the time of the auction, I would never have been able to buy the painting for anything like the price I paid. At the recent Parke-Bernet sale, when the van Gogh "Cypresses" was sold for $1,300,000, there was a second van Gogh of the same period, "The Laborer," similar in composition to "The Sower" in many respects, showing a farmer ploughing, but slightly larger, which sold for $875,000. I was the underbidder at $850,000 for this picture. I wonder if Mr. Richard would also have referred to this painting as "ugly."

Mr. Richard criticized the Cezanne oil painting which is in the show and which I recently purchased from a private collector in Paris. It is true that it is not a major work of Cezanne, but as I did not have an oil by Cezanne in my collection, I decided to acquire this until a better one

271

comes on the market. It is true Cezanne painted the tree in the fore-ground after the purchaser suggested that the landscape around the house looked barren, but I doubt if a great painter such as Cezanne would have put his signature on a painting if he was ashamed of it, as Mr. Richard implies.

Mr. Richard says that the Toulouse-Lautrec drawing "Dance at the Moulin de la Galette (Au Bal de Moulin de la Galette)" is a "hack job" and was drawn crudely for a Paris newspaper in 1889. I took the trouble to get a photostatic copy of *Le Courrier Français* of May 19, 1889, from the Library of Congress. The reproduction of the above drawing covers over two-thirds of the page, and is signed in full and dated by Toulouse-Lautrec. I wonder where Mr. Richards gets his expertise to pass judgment on such a great artist as Toulouse-Lautrec, who was willing to put his signature to an original drawing of his for publication.

This drawing, for which I paid approximately $100,000 (which is al-most what it brought at auction) comes from the collection of Mrs. Edward Hutton, Westbury, Long Island, who purchased it from M. Knoedler & Co., Inc., New York. It was exhibited in Paris in 1923 at the Exposition de la Musique et de la Danse; at the Yale University Art Gallery in 1930; the Art Institute of Chicago in 1930–31; and the New York Museum of Modern Art in 1931. The original painting by Toulouse-Lautrec of the same subject is now in the Art Institute of Chicago. This drawing has been written up by Maurice Joyant in his "Henri de Tou-louse-Lautrec," Paris, 1926. Mme. M. G. Dortu, who has written the authoritative book on Toulouse-Lautrec, has praised the drawing and advised me in a letter that it will be included in her Catalogue Raisonné, which is in preparation. It is also reproduced in her book "Lautrec by Lautrec."

Mr. Richard makes no mention of the splendid oil sketch by Toulouse-Lautrec in the exhibition and reproduced on the page of the catalog opposite the above-mentioned drawing. It is a study for the large picture "Au Salon de la rue des Moulin" in the Albi Museum. It occupies a full page in color in the book "Lautrec by Lautrec" by Ph. Huisman and M. G. Dortu. It was exhibited in Paris in 1896 while Toulouse-Lautrec was living and in Brussels at the Exposition Toulouse-Lautrec in 1902, the year after his death. I paid $500,000 for this "oil sketch" several years ago and it is worth much more than that today.

Mr. Richard criticizes the Rubens oil sketch "The Israelites Gathering

Manna in the Desert" as an "off-hand picture" which was not made for exhibition but as a sketch for a cartoon from which tapestry was made.

I remember the delight of Mr. Kenneth Donahue, Director of the Los Angeles Art Museum, when he discovered this oil sketch and asked me to buy it out of the Frances and Armand Hammer Million Dollar Purchase Fund, which we donated to the museum.

Evidently Mr. Richard considers himself a greater expert than Mr. Donahue and, no doubt, classifies this painting also as a "lousy work" produced by Rubens on one of his "lousy days." Mr. Donahue was delighted at being able to trace this painting back all the way to the hand of Rubens himself, since so many paintings by Rubens are from his studio. This picture was exhibited in Rotterdam at the famous Boymans Museum in 1953–1954; in Bordeaux and the Exhibition "Flandres, Espagne, Portugal de XVe au XVIIe Siècle" in 1954; and in Brussels at the Musées Royaux des Beaux-Arts de Belgique, in October through December, 1965, and was reproduced in the catalog. The oil sketch was a model for a very large painting (cartoon) from which a tapestry was woven for the daughter of Philip II of Spain, which now hangs in a convent in Spain. A copy of the Smithsonian painting hangs in a museum in Tournai, Belgium, and a School of Rubens drawing of this composition is in the Louvre, where there is also a Rubens drawing relating to this painting. Other Rubens oil sketches of the same series, painted at the same time, are in the Prado Museum.

Mr. Richard states it is no longer possible to purchase good pictures by these great artists because museums with unlimited funds are combing the market. Museums, unfortunately, do not have unlimited funds. Mr. Carter Brown, the talented director of the National Gallery, sat next to me at a recent White House dinner, just before the van Gogh "Cypresses" was to come up for auction at Parke-Bernet. He said, wistfully, how he would love to have this painting for the National Gallery, but, regretfully, they did not have the money.

Mr. Richard slanderously writes in his review that I had bought "sweepings," as many museum directors seem to be aware.

Aside from the Luce collection, which I had the opportunity to buy privately through my friendship with Mrs. Luce before it became available on the market, I wonder if Mr. Richard characterizes as "sweepings" such paintings as the Sargent, for which the Brooklyn Museum was willing to pay a handsome profit after I had purchased this out of the funds donated to the Los Angeles County Museum of Art and which is considered by many to be Sargent's greatest work; or the Modigliani which brought the highest price ever paid at auction for a work by this artist and is regarded by experts as probably his finest work; or the Renoir "Two Girls Reading," for which I paid approximately $500,000 after the previous owner was forced to remove it from loan to the Metropolitan Museum of Art because of financial reasons. It hung in the museum for many years and had been one of the centers of attraction there.

Mr. Richard makes no mention of Rubens' "Young Woman with Curly Hair" which occupies a full page in color in the book "Great Private Collections," published in New York, 1963, when it was in the famous collection of Jean Davray of Paris, from whom I purchased it after it had been consigned to Knoedler's. Recently Michael Jaffe, the famous art historian, has written a feature article in the Apollo Magazine of October, 1969, in which he points out that there are many copies of this picture hanging in museums throughout the world, but that this picture is the only original. I wonder if Mr. Richard includes this in his "sweepings."

He does not mention the Rembrandt, which was also purchased by me out of the funds provided for the Los Angeles County Museum of Art and was requested by the Chicago Art Museum for inclusion in their Rembrandt exhibition, a major show last year. This show is now at the Detroit Institute of Fine Arts. I borrowed this Rembrandt from the show in order to have it at the opening at the Smithsonian. After the close of the Detroit show on April 4, this painting will be on exhibition at the Smithsonian until the end of the show, April 30.

Mr. Richard makes no mention of the 18 Corots in the show. Each one of these pictures is illustrated and described in Alfred Robaut's authoritative book "The Works of Corot," published in 1905. They cover the entire span of Corot's life, from 1829 when he was 33 years old to 1875, the year of his death at the age of 79. I wonder if these paintings were painted only on "lousy days" throughout Corot's lifetime.

Surely if these works were "lousy" they would not have been exhibited by famous galleries and reproduced in the works of art historians who are authorities on their respective subjects.

There are many more paintings in the show which have equally fine background, coming from well-known collections and appearing in prominent exhibitions throughout the world.

Surely, even as a journalist, Mr. Richard knows that the art world is like a jungle, particularly in view of the jealousies among dealers, museum directors, art historians, and so-called art critics. There are intrigues and infighting because of the large sums of money involved with the high prices being paid for art today. No private collection contains only master-pieces. Even the famous Barnes collection of Pennsylvania has some Renoirs which are below par. However, a private collection represents the taste of the collector.

Also, it should be remembered that the collection is in the process of formation, as stated by me in the catalog, and as great works become available by these masters, they will be added to the collection to replace those of lesser importance.

Mr. Donahue did not write the introduction to this catalog as he did for the Memphis catalog because the Los Angeles County Museum, of which I am a trustee, adopted a policy after the Memphis exhibition of not sponsoring any private collection lest they establish a precedent.

However, since Mr. Richard makes an issue of this, I would like to quote herewith a few excerpts from Mr. Donahue's introduction to the Memphis catalog:

"A collection is a work of art. The collector, like the artist, selects and rejects from a wide range of techniques, styles, concepts and philosophies. Like a painting or sculpture, a collection reveals its creator.

Even though this new collection of Dr. Armand Hammer is still being formed (he gave his earlier collection to the University of Southern California in 1965), it has distinctive characteristics. The artists chosen are those who have rejected the normative goals and abstract geometry of the recurrent classic styles in favor of direct observation of nature, the sensuous enjoyment of color or individual emotional expression. Their interest is not in reconstructing nature according to an intellectual idea but in revealing what already exists for the eye to see or interpreting man and nature in a very personal way. The collection places considerable emphasis on the artistic process in including notebook sketches, drawings, oil studies and oil sketches for larger compositions. The Gauguin notebook and additional drawings give us an insight into the development of the artist during his most formative years. The oil sketches—a predilection of only the most sophisticated collectors—by Rubens, Fragonard, Goya and Toulouse-Lautrec associate us with the artist in that first moment of creation when he sets down his concept in the most personal, spontaneous manner.

"There are works in which the artist is making his first tentative explorations of some new concept or means, like the Rembrandt portrait in which the artist is investigating the effects of loosening his brushstrokes, beginning to dissolve his light and form for greater vitality and expressiveness. There are others in which he is wrestling with problems which beset every artist of his time, like the Renoir "Grape Pickers" of the late 1880s, in which the artist tries to rationalize the conflict between the Impressionist all-over pattern of light and color and the demands of three-dimensional form.

"Many of the paintings are small in format, like the cabinet paintings of great collections of the past, to be savored in a very personal relation between viewer and the work of art."

Mr. Richard intimates that no major museum would take the exhibition except the Smithsonian.

Apparently, Mr. Richard ignored the fact that four of the good museums in the Mid-West and South, the William Rockhill Nelson Museum in Kansas City, the Columbus Museum in Ohio, the Delgado Museum in New Orleans, and the Little Rock, Arkansas, Art Institute have accepted the exhibition for showing this year after it leaves the Smithsonian.

A large segment of the American public in cities that do not have museums as great as the Metropolitan in New York and the National Gallery and Phillips Gallery in Washington will have the opportunity to see these paintings thanks to the enterprise and efforts of such dedicated people as Mr. Ripley and Mrs. Van Arsdale, who should be commended for their efforts instead of being unjustly criticized by journalists masquerading as art historians.

In this regard, I wish to quote from a telegram sent to me on March 2, 1970, by Mr. Robert McKnight, Director of the Brooks Memorial Art Gallery in Memphis:

"Now that the exhibition of your private collection that began October 2, 1969, and closed on the 18th of January is finally terminated, I am glad to be able to report that our museum in the 53 years of its existence has never before had an exhibition meet with such a warm reception by the public and critics alike.

"The attendance doubled any previous period. We sold more catalogs than at any previous event."

With regard to the elaborate catalog criticized by Mr. Richard, he conveniently fails to mention the fact that one purpose of the exhibition was to raise funds for the Smithsonian, the National Endowment for the

Arts, and the American Association of Museums by the sale of this catalog.

Since they are being sold at $5.00 each, I felt the catalog should be worth it and hence spared no expense to make the catalog more salable and my donation more worthwhile.

I am glad to report that the Smithsonian has advised me that the sale is very brisk. The attendance at the museum for the first ten days has been 123,864, even though there was a bomb scare at the beginning and the weather has not been ideal.

Judging from this attendance, it appears that the public has passed their own judgment on the merits of this exhibition.

Index

Index

Nelson, Donald, 94
Nelson, Gaylord, 237
Newman, Ed, 187
New York
  childhood and youth in, 2–13
  Greenwich Village home in, 142–143
  return to (1930), 77
New York Stock Exchange, 192
New York Times, 87, 175, 181, 205–206, 208, 210–214
Nicaragua, 133
Nixon, Richard M., 154, 157, 174, 220, 229
  campaign contribution, 241–242
  Soviet relations, 176, 180–182
Nizer, Louis, 120, 193–194, 197
  Allen and Co. case, 200–204
  Armour and Co. suit, 204
  on Hammer's personality, 144–146
Noël-Clarke, Rosemary, 237
Norrie, Dr. Van Horne, 12
North Sea oil, 218–219

Oasis consortium, 133–134, 139
O'Bryan, Leslie L., 102–103, 106–108, 110
Occidental (Oxy), 122–140, 146, 154
  administrative policy, 193–194
  Allen and Co. suit, 200–204
  Armour and Co. suit, 204
  Berry suit, 126–127
  bonanza strikes, 124, 134, 135
  California oil drilling prevented, 226–227
  diversification, 125–130, 137–138, 193
  fertilizer deal, Soviet, 176, 182–184, 187, 192, 211, 213–214, 228–234
  gas deal, El Paso, 185–186, 192, 213, 223–224
  Kern County Land-Tenneco suit, 129–130
  Libyan operations, 131–140, 190, 191, 201–204, 216
  Machiasport refinery turndown, 225–226
  metal-finishing equipment deal with U.S.S.R., 185, 192, 212
  Moscow world trade center, 186, 192, 212, 214
  municipal waste conversion, 192–193, 212

New York Times articles on Hammer control and Soviet deals, 210–215
  North Sea oil, 218–219
  office staff, 144
  Peruvian oil, 216–218, 224
  retirement issue, 193–196
  scientific and technical cooperation agreement with U.S.S.R., 184–187, 212
  Securities and Exchange Commission and, 129, 190, 204–207
  shale oil, 219–223
  Standard Oil (Indiana) merger bid, 235–240
  stock value, 122–123, 137, 143, 189, 191–193, 212, 263
  stockholders, 189–191
  Umm al-Qaywayn oil, 224–225
Ocean Victory floating rig, 218–219
Ogbi, Taher, 201–202
Oil Shale Corp., 222–223
Operation for kidney stones, 195
O'Toole, James Aloysius, 198–199
Oxy Today, 184–185, 217–218

Pacific Gas and Electric Co., 124–125
Page and Shaw, 6
Parker Pen, 43, 69
Patolichev, N. S., 229
Peale, Norman Vincent, 154
Pearson, Lester, 117, 154
Permian Corp., 137, 138
Personality as described by friends
  by Nizer, 144–146
  by Prellwitz, 144
  by Tigrett, 153–154
Peru, oil and, 216–218, 223
Peterson, Cal, 109
Peterson, Peter, 192
Petroperu, 216, 223
Pharmaceutical business, 2, 7–10
Philanthropies and gifts
  art collections, 121
  cancer research, 121
  Goya to Soviet Union, 171
  Lenin letters to U.S.S.R., 176–179
  Roosevelt Campobello International Park, 117–119
  St. Patrick shrine restoration, 226

284

Truman, Harry S., 141, 154
Tweedie, R. A., 117

U-2 incident, 157, 161–162
Udall, Secretary, 226
Ulianova, Maria, 50
Umm al-Qaywayn, Sheikdom of, 224–225
Unitarianism, 4
United Distillers of America, 96
United Press International, 239
Urquhart, Leslie, 34
U.S. News and World Report, 192
U.S.S.R. *See* Russia

Vadina, Olga, 76
Vanderlip, Washington, 34
van Wingen, Nick, 123
Vinogradov, V. M., 156–157

Wadley, J. K., 122
Walker, John, 89, 209–210
Walkup, Bill, 135
Wall Street Journal, 239
War Production Board, 94
Ward, Charlie, 147
Washington *News*, 87–88
Washington *Post*, 175, 208–209, 269–277
Watson, Gen. "Pa," 115
Watson, Jerrold W., 191

Weinfeld, Judge Edward, 202–203
Weinstein, Gregory, 20–21, 33
Weitzner, Julius, 150
Westbrook, Philip, 127, 204
whiskey
  barrel business, 91
  business, 92–99
  tax litigation, 197–199
Wilentz, David, 199
Williamson, George, 138
Winchell, Walter, 125
Winter Palace, 70
Wolff, 17, 18
World War I period, 7, 9
World War II period
  British aid programs, 114–116
  delivery of jeweled egg to Farouk I, 151
  Soviet Union, lend-lease to, 158–159, 161
  whisky business, 92–99
Wormser, Maurice, 11, 200

Yorty, Sam, 226–227
Young, Lewis, 184

Zetkin, Clara, Lenin letter to, 176–180
Zevely, Angela, 90
Zhukov, Yuri, 169
Zinsser, Hans, 12